The CONQUERING *Soul*

The Key to Understanding Spiritual Psychology

Miriam Bostwick

Robert D. Reed Publishers   San Francisco

Having spent 30 years in the field of mental health in San Francisco, I know there are many, including practitioners, who feel little or no sense of fulfillment about the quality of their life's journey. "Something" is missing. This book on spiritual psychology provides insights on how to fill that void by achieving spiritual growth and harmony.

–L. Warde Laidman, MSW

This timely book is a challenging combination of soul wisdom, spiritual philosophy, clear guidance, and teaching. A compelling look at the games our personality plays. Each chapter contains truth to be studied, reflected upon and hopefully practiced.

–Susan Berthiaume

This book is gratefully dedicated
to the many teachers on both sides of the veil
who have shared their spiritual understanding;
and to the mediums who channeled these spirit teachings.

"We are more than conquerors through him that loved us."
(Romans 8:37)

Contents

Preface, ix

Spiritual Psychology:
Its Implications for Attaining a
Higher State of Consciousness / 1

Game 1
The Veil of Illusion, Delusion, Deception/ 17

Game 2
Identity Imbalance/ 27

Game 3
Denying Personal Responsibility/ 39

Game 4
Playing Judge/ 53

Game 5
The Fear Trap/ 69

Game 6
Bucking the Tides of Life/79

Game 7
The Destiny of Denial/ 93

Game 8
Motive for Self-Gain/ 107

Game 9
The Selfless Service Deception/ 115

Game 10
Stealing Desires from The Divine/ 121

Game 11
Finding Security in Money and Sex/ 139

Game 12
**Making Our Attachments Our Adversities
and Our Adversities Our Attachments/ 155**

Game 13
**Confusing Giving with Lending
and Borrowing with Owning/ 165**

Game 14
Refusing to Clean the Slate/ 175

Game 15
The Procrastination Thief/ 185

Game 16
The Bellyaching Game/ 197

Game 17
Conscience Deafness/ 205

Game 18
The Sell-Out Tactic/ 213

Game 19
Universal Motherhood/ 221

Game 20
Playing with Spiritual Teachings/ 229

Game 21
Meditating Without Purity of Motive/ 251

Game 22
Questioning Life Eternal/ 263

Game 23
Redemption Without Effort/ 269

Game 24
The Soul Talent "Put-Down"/ 285

Game 25
Feeling Superior Over Animals/ 293

Epilogue/ 311

New Age Interpretation of the Lord's Prayer/ 315

Permissions/ 317

General Index/ 319
Index of Affirmations/ 335
Index of Spirit Sayings/ 336

Preface

For many years I have been blessed and privileged to study spiritual truths from sources on high. This has enabled me to view and experience life in a richer and more loving way. As _"blessings are to be shared, not sheltered,"_ what follows is an attempt to share the understanding I have been so privileged to receive. It is an effort to guide one to his or her true inner self, for that is where freedom, truth, and everything worthwhile truly exists. If this book helps just one person to move closer to the Light, it has accomplished its purpose.

Spiritual truths are ageless and unchanging, for truth just is. However, it has only been with the advent of the New Age, which is a higher stage of spiritual consciousness, that a widespread openness in searching and finding answers has come about. No longer need one be defensive about contacts with guides, teachers, friends, and relatives who communicate with us from the spirit world. As we gain a deeper understanding of the universal laws, we know that "miracles" and so-called supernatural happenings are simply the result of these laws in operation; that we are in truth a world governed by Universal Mind—a neutral Infinite Intelligence we call God, an ever-present energy or power that animates all things everywhere—not a fatherly figure with long flowing white hair sitting on a throne, personally judging each person and every event.

God is not just the things our eyes and senses experience, but a great powerful and peaceful energy that ever waits to serve.

The intelligent power that sustains our very being is a servant to us, the greatest servant of all. Choosing more wisely how we direct the power of this great serving God is the goal of this book.

The approach used to accomplish this goal is an exposure of twenty-five games the mind, expressing through the five senses, plays in its attempt to reign supreme over the soul. It is then shown how the soul is enabled to counterbalance these energies of the sense functions to become the **conquering soul**. Metaphysically speaking, a "conqueror" is one who attains mastery over the sense consciousness. *"We are more than conquerors through him that loved us."* (Romans 8:37) Rather than annihilate the senses that are the instruments by which we function on the physical plane, these lessons show how to wisely direct them to bring about a harmonious interaction between soul and personality.

The great Avatar Jesus understood this perfectly when he said, *"I speak not of myself, it is the father than dwelleth in me, he doeth the works."* Jesus gave no credit to his personality for he knew that his *Real Self* was his soul, the *Christ Spirit*, whom he called the *Father*. This same indwelling God is known also as the *Buddha Nature*, the *Great White Spirit*, *I AM*, *Jehovah*, *Allah*, or by any other name, according to the understanding of the other respective faiths. There is only one supreme power that holds the stars in space and causes the earth to rotate on its axis. Therefore, we are all united. Not only is it our spirit that unites us since we are all part of God, but also it is our mind that unites us. Because all peoples are united, the mental games played are universal in the sense that the personality of everyone is ever striving to suppress the expression of the soul, and will do so until effort is made to gain mastery over the sense consciousness.

Each of the twenty-five mental games described within these covers contains sufficient insights to stand on its own, yet each lends deeper understanding to all the others. In spiritual awareness studies, to isolate a particular soul faculty or sense function to concentrate solely upon it, is not entirely possible, for they operate in concert with each other. Therefore, it will become apparent as the reader pursues these pages, there is a certain amount of repetition and overlapping. This is partly because of the interconnected nature of these expressions and partly for emphasis, as it is through repetition that changes in consciousness come about. Also, if a lesson is not perceived in one way, compassion dictates that it be presented in another way.

You will quickly realize that mental games are spiritual disasters, and that with balance, you can awaken to a realm of consciousness where you are freed from them. *"When your hopes in life equal your despairs, you will go beyond survival, which is only for fools, and rest in truth and awaken to the joy of life."*

Truth is one, but it is individually perceived; therefore, there are many paths back home. Instead of a spiritual smogasbord, find the path in life that is comfortable for you and stay with it long enough to give the seed a chance to sprout and grow. Hopefully, the truth contained herein will provide some guidance. It is planned to bring about a metamorphosis of the personality through spiritual psychology. Truth needs no defense for truth is sufficient unto itself, but if a statement seems untrue to you at this time, leave it alone. In all situations in life, if it is not of God, it cannot live. A soul does not get discouraged by truth. If discouraged, it is only a con game of the personality.

Other than the compilation and organization of this material into a mental game format, I take no credit for its teachings. Besides the obvious quotes from published works, these lessons came in bits and pieces through several trance mediums from high teachers in the spirit world whose love and compassion for humankind prompted them to share generously their spiritual understanding to show us a better way, a way to become a **conquering soul.**

To preserve the integrity of the teachings, the actual words of the spirit teachers have been used as far as possible, instead of paraphrasing and possibly losing the true meaning they wished to convey. Included are what we may, in this day, call clichés. For example, "the light of reason" frequently appears in the text and is shown to have spiritual significance rather than to be a trite expression. The *very special* philosophical sayings for which authorship has not been acknowledged in the text itself are those from spirit teachers. These gems of wisdom have been italicized. They were received prior to our era of "political correctness;" therefore, any gender references should be broadly interpreted to include both sexes. This was the original intent of the teachers. The terms *personality, self, mind,* and *ego* are used interchangeably throughout. Also, the names of the various spiritual laws have been capitalized for emphasis.

When one receives the Light, one is duty bound to share its love. So hopefully, this book will help each reader to identify some of the mental games we play, examine the dynamics involved, and based on spiritual teachings, offer a way to consider redirecting and balancing negative energies with positive spiritual energies.

"God, this is your work.
Help me to be the instrument of humility
that it may be given to the world."

Miriam Bostwick

Spiritual Psychology:
Its Implications For Attaining
A Higher State of Consciousness

As we move into the New Age of Aquarius with its promise of a more advanced stage of spiritual consciousness, our desire to unlock the seeming mysteries of the higher energies will rapidly increase. As a part of this pursuit, a body of knowledge known as Spiritual Psychology will no doubt emerge to help us better understand how to tap into these higher energies to bring about a harmonious interaction between the soul and the personality. For lack of a more definitive understanding at this time, we may consider Spiritual Psychology as a *study concerning itself with the introducing to the personality the ageless, demonstrable spiritual laws of an Infinite Intelligence, which once accepted by the personality, will become the very instruments used by the personality to free itself from its own limitations. By freeing itself, the personality will thus be enabled to freely serve the soul in its eternal quest to journey back to the Allsoul.*

THE DIVINE PLAN FOR SOUL UNFOLDMENT

Something cannot come out of the nothingness. Therefore, the individualization of the human soul must come from something. It is by God's plan that our soul, which started out on the highest level of consciousness, has descended into materiality that it may gradually work its way back to God. For whatever we come from we are destined by the very law to return to. All things must return to the source that gave them birth. As Mother Earth has given birth to our physical bodies, so Mother Earth is destined to reclaim that which is hers. So it is with the attitudes of mind. They are formed of mental substance from a

1

mental world, and they are reclaimed by the mental world. Because we have all wandered, we are all in the process of returning to God, the light, the love, the life. It is the divine circle of return. *"Be still, my child, and view and you shall know beyond the shadow of any doubt you are returning. Be not weary of the journey. See not the obstructions which are shadows of the past, and your path shall be clear, straight, and beautiful. That is the law, the joy of life."*

We begin as whole, complete, and perfect in expression because we begin as little sparks of the divine flame and become souls. The soul was meant to go through many, many varied circumstances and obstacles over many lifetimes to complete its path so that it can eventually step off the wheel of reincarnation to live in the real world which is the spirit world. The earth plane is our temporary abode to attend the school of experience. In that school we have free will, the God-given freedom of choice to take the upward or downward path.

Friction is the law through which the soul must evolve. We cannot escape the path and journey of life through creation for the law is inevitable, but we can grow through it. For every positive thrust forward in evolution there is an equal pull backwards. And through that, we shall in time clearly see peace. This awakening of peace is beyond the understanding of mental substance. It is *"the peace which passeth all understanding."*

To unfold the soul's divine qualities, the soul takes on a physical body and a personality—vehicles—through which to perfect itself. The soul knows what it needs to unfold. For example, a soul may need patience with which to expand. Therefore, it will use a personality that will experience the necessary situations that demand patience, unfolding a more open expression of that quality as the personality becomes more disciplined. In truth, we have a limitless supply of patience, faith, humility, peace and all of the other soul faculties. It is simply a matter of becoming receptive to the level of consciousness where we can experience them. Therefore, *"Growth [of the soul] is revelation, not change, in truth."*

In the perfect scheme of things, we draw to us, through the Law of Magnetism, the opportunities or effects of the laws that we have set into motion, not for punishment, but to grow spiritually. If we show disrespect for another, we set a law into motion guaranteeing that disrespect in proportionate energy will be shown to us. If we cause another to suffer, we, in turn, will suffer in like degree, for Like Attracts Like and forms the Law of Attachment. Whatever happens to us is caused by us. Divine justice always triumphs in the long run. We are always given the opportunity to polish each and every facet of our soul, unfolding and expanding all of its abilities and qualities to attain the true purpose of our life—illumination.

Although we are a part of the Infinite Intelligence, God has given us free will to progress in our own time and our own way. We are not robots. The rate of our progression depends on our ability to align our personality with our soul and ultimately to become one with Him. As the great Avatar Jesus taught: "*Is it not so written in your law, I said, you are Gods?*" (John 10:34). We come down and we go back up; that is evolution.

CHARACTERIZING THE SOUL

Our soul, which expresses through our heart, is that eternal or imperishable part of us that is the *Real Us*, or the *Real Self*, the *I AM* or *Christ Spirit*. Emmet Fox describes soul as "*that aspect of God by virtue of which He is able to individualize Himself.*" Fox also has characterized the soul as:

> . . . an opening through which Infinite Energy is seeking a creative outlet. If that outlet be a clear, open channel, all is well. If, on the other hand, it should become obstructed by any means, then the Infinite Energy, the Life Force, is frustrated, dammed back—and all sorts of local stresses are set up in that soul; and these we see as sickness, poverty, fear, anger, sin, and every kind of difficulty.

Some teachers tell us the soul is a sheath or covering of the formless and free spirit, giving the spirit a body in which to express. With many, the terms soul and spirit are frequently used interchangeably. *"God is a spirit"* (John 4:24), therefore, spirit cannot be destroyed or damaged.

Another teacher makes the distinction between spirit and soul this way:

> "Infinite Intelligence or God does not sleep or wake; it is. The soul is the individualization or covering of the Divine Intelligence. It is the soul expressing through the grosser form (person ality) that awakens. The soul garners up greater and greater understanding through greater and greater expression through the form. The Divine Spirit is formless and free, whole and complete. Nothing can be added to it for nothing can be subtracted from it. The only god that changes is the god of creation and the god of creation is equal to our understanding in any given moment.

The soul has faculties or attributes with which all beings are born and strive to unfold. They are the very Light of The Divine. This divine inventory includes love, humility, duty, tolerance, gratitude, understanding, faith, poise, patience, courage, strength, surrender, loyalty, continuity, peace, serenity, organization, care, acceptance, reason, consideration, kindness, generosity, to name but a few, love having the highest vibration. We unfold or express these Godlike qualities in varying degrees, but the **potential** exists for perfect expression because we are a part of the All Soul. When there is the highest expression of these faculties, that spirit may be called the *"only begotten son (or daughter) of God,"* as Jesus demonstrated. If God is perfect, then to be an *"only begotten son (or daughter) of God,"* we, too, must some day in eternity reach that highest state of consciousness.

From the foregoing, it is evident that our true spiritual power results from the expression of the soul faculties. No soul is different from any other soul in its potential. The difference between people lies in their ability to control the personality so that the attributes of the soul may fully express.

THE PERSONALITY AND ITS EXPRESSIONS

"*The personality,*" which Gary Zukav describes in *The Seat of the Soul,* "*emerges as a natural force from the soul. It is an energy tool that the soul adapts to function within the physical world.*" The personality may be likened to a display window, outpicturing our current state of soul growth. Unlike our soul which draws its unlimited power from the indwelling Christ Spirit, our transient personality pursues power externally through the five senses of seeing, hearing, tasting, smelling, and feeling. Its so-called power is limited to the experiences, knowledge, attitudes, and emotions we have stored in our subconscious mind during this lifetime. It is the subconscious with its memory bank of experiences which influences all our thoughts, acts, and reactions to outside stimuli. It is the personality that expresses anger, fear, hatred, vengeance, sorrow, shame, regret, indifference, frustration, cynicism, loneliness, self-pity, jealousy, envy, greed, guilt, anxiety, rejection, resentment, retaliation, judgment, embarrassment, and other low frequency vibrations that drain our energy if not controlled.

In *A Vision of the Aquarian Age,* Sir George Trevelyan describes the five-sensory approach: "*Our senses are tuned to receive the vibrations of matter. They are thus the instruments by which we function in our earth-bodies. They may be conceived as filters which allow only a little of the life of the cosmos to penetrate the human consciousness.*" And the opening lines of Martin Armstrong's poem, "*The Cage*" capture this succiently:

> "*Man, afraid to be alive*
> *Shuts his soul in senses five*"

Our goal, then, should be to spiritualize or transmute these sense functions. View them not as master but as tools to be used, not abused, for all things in God are good in balance. It is the *conscious mind* which must exercise control over the thoughts and emotions to bring about this balance. There is nothing in the subconscious memory bank that has not first been expressed by the conscious mind. Therefore, in order for the soul to unfold, it is the duty and task of the *conscious mind* to ever control what is coming through it, thereby, continually raising us to a higher level of consciousness.

THE ROLE OF THE MIND IN DIRECTING ENERGY

The personality uses the conscious (electric) and the subconscious (magnetic) minds, whereas, our communication with the soul is via the superconscious mind. Actually, the superconscious mind is part of the soul. The superconscious is at the top of our three levels of mind, with the subconscious in second place, and the conscious in third place with respect to how we work down through the levels. For example, what the soul may express as love may be so "watered down" by the subconscious that it comes up to the consciousness as hatred. The conscious mind is then in a position to control the final expression. What direction it takes is dependent on what level we are on, what efforts we have made to "clean up our act," so-to-speak. As we gain control over what and how we express, we are at the same time controlling what goes back to be stored in the memory bank. Can you not see why it is so necessary to clean out the subconscious to become more spiritual beings? All souls want to express their attributes; however, because of the judgments locked in the subconscious, they are unable to do so without sincere and repetitive effort by the conscious mind to control all thoughts.

"Man is the power of God in action. The power to control his thinking is the highest gift given to man." (Charles Fillmore)

The personality in dysfunction is the effect of an imbalance in the consciousness, an imbalance of the energies. This imbalance is the result of the energy going to sustain the faculties of the soul not being equal to the energy flowing to sustain the sense functions of the personality. And as Zukav points out, *"dysfunctions of the personality cannot be understood without an understanding of the soul."*

"A thought strikes the mind and a fool reacts. A thought strikes the mind and a wise person pauses to gain control."

Saneness is a perfect balance of energy between the electric and magnetic fields of the human mind. Therefore, a student on the path wisely works to balance the conscious and subconscious minds. That student also knows that the more in tune the conscious mind is with the superconscious, the better balance will be achieved between the spiritual and the material. This perfect balance of energy is possible for all people when they recognize and accept there is a greater authority that governs all life and sustains it. We, in the course of our experiences, which are the direct effects of our own direction of God's energy, must surrender our thoughts, our emotions, and our disturbances to the power intelligently expressed in all the universes. Sadly, however, we have made for ourselves a barrier between the balance of our mind and the surrender of the divine energy. It is understood that all things are in truth energy. Our eternal soul is what is expressing through an energy field. When we insist upon entertaining a thought and refuse to surrender the thought to The Divine, we become the obstruction. We block the free flow and balance of the divine energy.

There is no lack of energy in the universe. The seeming lack is because we have chosen to be the obstruction to the flow of this energy. Many, many are simply not ready to take the necessary steps to balance these energies. Intention or motive reveals whether that energy is going through the sense functions, known as the Law of Creation, or is being directed through the Law of Light, the soul faculties. This can be further clarified by thinking in terms of an energy continuum, placing the high frequency vibrations of the soul faculties at one end and the low frequency vibrations of the sense functions at the opposite end.

As we spiritualize our thinking, a sense function is transmuted into a soul faculty. Hate, for instance, becomes love and greed becomes gratitude. The triune sense function of want, need, and desire becomes the triune soul faculty of care, kindness, and consideration through the effort of will to send the energy up through centers of consciousness to ethereal realms within our universe. On the other hand, a soul faculty limited by the thought process can revert to a sense function. For example, when the soul faculty of consideration is limited by a desire in the mind, a person can be blinded to the faculty of care which is inseparable from consideration, and thereby, become the victim of the desire form. Consideration is reduced to a low frequency for now its one and only consideration is satisfying the desire. No longer does it have total consideration of all the factors involved in fulfilling the desire.

We can very easily discern when we are expressing through the soul faculties or the sense functions. If we are expressing through the sense functions, there is an experience, a feeling, and a stimulation of the senses. If we are expressing through the soul faculties, there is patience and an inner peace. There is no worry. There is no thought. There is no concern. We have but to listen to our heart, for the heart expresses the faculties of the soul.

IDENTIFYING THE LESSONS WE MUST MASTER

To oversimplify, if the personality is not cooperative, aligning itself with the soul, then we flunk whatever lessons we came to master and have to repeat them in the next incarnation. If bad karma is incurred, the soul must use enough strength and courage to override the personality's wanting to go in a direction that is detrimental. When we experience good karma, it means we have passed those lessons. *What are the lessons that we as individualized souls have come to this earth realm to learn?* Life herself reveals what the lessons are. For each person it varies, because each person is different and has had different lessons in prior incarnations. You can readily tell what your lessons are by looking at life and identifying the most difficult things that you have had to do or to face. The things that are difficult are the lessons that you did not pass in prior expressions of life. For one, the main lessons may be organization, faith, and self-control. For another, they may be tolerance, humility, continuity, and acceptance. If we do not unfold tolerance in one incarnation, for example, then we will merit being born into a family where the opportunities exist for unfolding tolerance.

We do not have to look far to realize that men and women are not born free and equal. The Divine created us free and equal, but the conditions existing at the time of our present incarnation have been established by the outcome of our previous incarnations. Thus, our own special requirements for growth must be fulfilled through the merit system. For that reason, there is no justification for discouragement regarding our merit system for we can always change it. However, if we should become discouraged, it means that we have been discouraged before, and we will just repeat that vicious cycle again and again until we learn the lesson. We consistently and repeatedly slip into the level of consciousness to cast the blame outside ourselves, out onto circumstances because we have been doing it for a lifetime, or perhaps, many lifetimes.

If we continue to shy away from so-called difficulties because of our unwillingness to face the struggle that is going on within us, then the lessons will become more difficult, and like the great boomerang, will keep returning to us. There is a part of us—the spirit that flows through us—that knows what our difficulties and struggles are. There is something within us that **just knows**. It keeps whispering to us to have faith and to have patience and to make greater effort. That is the thing to listen to—our conscience.

FACTORS INFLUENCING THE PERSONALITY

We should keep in mind that the personality is influenced by many factors. We bring to this incarnation a predisposition toward certain weaknesses or strengths of character and physical make up. These are the result of lessons which we either flunked or successfully passed in prior incarnations. We are also influenced by certain vibrations connected with our zodiacal sign, our name, and those with whom we are closely associated.

The memory par excellence (the permanent heart seed atom located in the etheric body) has recorded our every thought and act throughout our many lifetimes. It recorded, before our present incarnation, what we chose to accomplish in this lifetime, what bad karma we will try to erase, and what good karma or soul talents we will strengthen. This heart seed atom (an eternal built-in personal akashic record) releases into the blood stream reminders of what we came to earth to do. In other words, it prompts the soul when it is time to pursue a given course of action. This affects the uniqueness of the personality as it reacts to this prompting. *"Help me, O God, to remember the motive I came for."*

Until we educate the personality, that is, until we shine the light of reason over it, we will not know peace within our being. There will be no self-control, specifically, the conscious control of what we choose to think and do, and therefore, experience. Rather, we will have a continuous struggle between the sense functions and the soul faculties. We become an integrated being when the personality is in full alignment with the soul.

MOTIVE SETS A LAW INTO MOTION

As every action, thought, and feeling is motivated by an intention, it is the intention or motive which sets a law into motion to bring to us our experiences in life. We cause something to happen and we then experience its effects. *"Experience is not life. Experience is the effect of one's view of the law of life."*

As students of spiritual law, we accept the truth that we are personally responsible for our every action, thought, and feeling. There are no accidents in the universe, and when we face that truth, we will begin to face the Law of Personal Responsibility—*everything that happens to us is caused by us.* Therefore, it behooves the wise person to become aware of his or her intentions and direct his or her energy to experience only the good. We get back what we send out. As we accept the age old wisdom contained in the sayings, *"The world is what we make it,"* and *"We take out of the world what we put into it,"* then, and only then, will we truly work to surrender our self-will to divine will.

Truly, the Universe is our teacher. In time, the personality will bow and serve the true purpose for which it was designed.

THOUGHTS ARE THINGS

We admonish a person to guard his or her thoughts. But, of course, we cannot guard something that we are not aware of. So the first step is awareness. You work with awareness. *What am I thinking about? From what level of consciousness is my thought prompted? Why this and why now?* Those thoughts are forms and they exist in a mental world.

A thought is an actual form. This is important to realize. Whatever thought you have creates a form in your aura. Zukav explains it this way:

> The Light that flows through your system is Universal energy. It is the Light of the Universe. You give that Light form. What you feel, what you think, how you behave, what you value and how you live your life reflects the way that you are shaping the Light that is flowing through you. They are the thought forms, the feeling forms and the action forms that you have given to Light. They reflect the configuration of your personality, your space-time being.

These forms are in your aura, in the atmosphere, and they go to work for you, doing the job you created them to do. They are forms created by your own mind. Whenever you choose to be free, to find eternal truth, to have joy and happiness and fulfillment, the **negative** thought forms go to work on your mind and your emotions and they justify to you and deceive you to keep you from the fullness and the truth of life itself.

We all know as students of life that the spoken word is life-giving energy, but we do not pause to think what we are building in these mental realms. We have a thought and we express it without consideration or interest in the form that we are thinking. So it is the negative forms that we are feeding through our vehicle of thought and through the power of our spoken word that rob us of the goodness and joy of living.

That thoughts are things, Henry Van Dyke summed it up in a few lines of poetry:

THOUGHTS ARE THINGS

I hold it true that thoughts are things;
　They're endowed with bodies and
　　breath and wings;
And that we send them forth to fill
　The world with good results, or ill.
That which we call our secret thought
　Speeds forth to earth's remotest spot,
Leaving its blessings or its woes
　Like tracks behind it as it goes.

We build our future, thought by thought,
　For good or ill, yet know it not.
Yet so the universe was wrought.
　Thought is another name for fate;
Choose then thy destiny and wait,
　For love brings love and hate brings hate.

HOW THE THOUGHT FORMS ARE EITHER FED OR STARVED

Now the question must arise in our mind: *Why and how do those little demons that control my mind cause me my lack and limitation, my suffering and all those things?* The reason they do that to you is that if your soul rises any further to the Light, to freedom, truth, and joy, they will die, for you—your eternal soul—will no longer feed them the necessary energy through your emotions for them to live. There are literally thousands in our universe because we have so many emotions, so many fears, and so much sorrow and grief. These forms of darkness, living in our universe are without soul. They are always hungry, seeking pleasure, pain, and satisfaction. Having no heart, they do not assist us in rising to heavenly heights. They are forever seeking our life force.

Someday you may see them. If you have not seen them already, it is God's eternal blessing that you have yet to see them, for they are not creatures of beauty. They are certainly not creatures of joy. They are forms of magnetic force, attracting their kind and returning to you as hungry orphans without number to be fed with your life force. If you fear them, you feed them. If you battle them, you feed them.

If you pray for peace, the dark forms slowly but surely starve to death. Peace has a role in creating angelic forms for God is peace. When you flood your consciousness with peace, angelic forms begin to take control in your consciousness and you begin to be freed from that which disturbs you, and, of course, that which disturbs you controls you. Remember, dark forms disturb you because they take from you your life-giving force. *Soul-less creatures drain your vitality; angelic forms totally rejuvenate you.* The reason celestial forms lift you up is because you gave them birth in heavenly realms. The life force sustains them.

Bear in mind that the greatest defense the forms have is our ignorance of them and denial of their existence. As long as they can keep the blinders on us, we will not believe they are what they are. Unfortunately, we cannot gain control over anything we do not believe in. When we believe the truth in our heart, we will gain control over the forms. It means we have to make some changes which is difficult for most of us to do. If you were feeding off someone, perhaps being handed a continuous supply of money or something you really desired, and all of a sudden were cut off, what would your reaction be? All hell breaks loose with the forms. It is interesting that civilization has so effectively covered up this knowledge for so long, except for the few.

If others around you are emotional, it is only their energy that feeds the level as long as you do not react. If you become emotionally involved with another person's situation, you open the door—put out the welcome mat, so-to-speak—to the armies of the other person to come feed at your table. The forms have already cleaned the plates of the person they live with. Being greedy, they are now licking their chops to clean your plate because you have come into their aura. So by coming into rapport with the other person, you have polluted your aura and your forms battle with the forms of that other person to see who gets to feed at your table. The result is that you are drained and the other person is energized for his or her forms are feeding on you and have given him or her momentary peace. Therefore, emotionalism must be stopped for the sake of survival.

BEING MASTER OVER THE THOUGHT FORMS

Take to heart the old adage that *"Fools rush in where angels fear to tread."* Our personality thinks it is so strong that it will not get trapped in the hell of someone else's entities, but by the Law of Like Attracts Like, you do get into rapport and can be trapped. Angels fear because they know better than to get into rapport in the first place. When another individual is emotional, you must make the effort to control your mind, then everything around you will be harmoniously arranged. Or, as it is stated in Taoism, "To the mind that is still, the world surrenders."

You are the master of the forms until you let them become your master. That is what happens with thoughts, which in truth, are forms. As the spirit teaching goes, *"When the tools no longer serve the worker, the worker (the soul) serves the tools (the thought forms)."* That is also why the teaching was given, *"Dreamer, dream a life of beauty before your dream starts dreaming you."* Create angelic forms that will sustain you, not grotesque forms that will drain you.

Angelic forms are of odic power, perfectly balanced electromagnetic energy, for they contain the Intelligence of

Infinity. They know what to do for they have soul. They are expressions of the soul faculties. They are little gods serving you joyously when you call on them. They never drain your energy. When you enter a state of peace, angelic forms are created. Flooding the consciousness with an affirmation as simply as *"Thank you, God, I am at peace"* creates forms of beauty. If you want the Light, you must be willing to pay the price—self-control.

How does a thought know what form to take? Our souls have merited the experience of expressing through a layer of consciousness called the primitive mind. We understand that the primitive cultures of centuries ago had these experiences. The primitive mind was born of fear and continues to be perpetuated by fear. A classic little volume entitled, *Thought Forms* by Annie Besant and C. W. Leadbeater not only explains the effects of thought forms and how the vibrations act, but gives colored illustrations of the forms.

NEVER ANNIHILATE THE SENSE FUNCTIONS

Let it be clear that it is taught never to annihilate the sense functions for they serve a good purpose, if wisely directed. *"As the spokes of the wheel are indispensable to the hub, so the functions of man are indispensable to the soul."* The personality is an avenue of expression. It is through your efforts to educate it, that is, to cast the light of reason upon it that it will serve you well, that it will serve you in the way that it has been designed to serve you. It is your duty to separate yourself from this vehicle and to remember ever that the true you, your soul, is in charge. The personality is a tool and it is by its very nature in a constant process of change. Accept the demonstrable law of evolution of form. When you truly accept this demonstrable Law of Change, this process of refinement, then you will no longer be troubled and plagued by it.

THE NEED FOR FREEDOM FROM
THE BONDAGE OF THE PERSONALITY

Saint Paul said, *"There is a natural body and there is a spiritual body."* (1 Cor. 15:44) At so-called death, the spirit body departs from the natural or physical body and we take up our abode in the realm of the spirit world that we have earned or grown to in consciousness. Therefore, if we think we are going to a realm of Light, let us ask ourselves the question, *How much Light do I have now?* The key is not how much spiritual knowledge we have. The key is how much have we applied.

You cannot be attached to things here, then find yourself out of a physical body and be free. The mind does not work that way. As it reads in Matthew 18:18: *"Whatsoever ye shall bind on earth shall be bound in heaven; and whatsoever ye shall free on earth shall be freed in heaven."* It is the self-related thoughts that not only ground one's universe, but it is the self-related thoughts that keep the soul bound in creation. All of our experiences in the physical dimension are simply effects of attitudes of mind or thoughts that we entertain. We experience so much discord and disharmony because our thoughts are so discordant. Our thoughts are battling each other. That is why philosophies teach that the only path to spiritual illumination is the path of selfless service, and any effort you make to release divine energy into selfless activities is freeing you from the bondage of your personality. It is a matter of redirecting the Divine Intelligent Neutral Energy that we may truly flow in an unobstructed stream of life known as heavenly consciousness.

And so, the purpose of spiritual education is to make us aware of what can and does go on in unseen dimensions. Although we may not see these thought forms that we have created—forms that want to control us and take our energy so that they can stay in form—remember, they have all the intelligence we have and they make themselves heard. But the comforting thing is, as we make the effort to control our mind and to direct our thoughts to love, beauty, peace, understanding, and the good things in life, these forms do lie down in time, and our personality scores a victory in moving our soul closer on its return path to God.

* * *

"I am spirit, formless and free.
Whatever I think, that will I be."

Game 1

The Veil of Illusion, Delusion, Deception

Key Players:

Sense Functions:
Belief, Deception, Delusion,
Identification, Illusion, Self-Preservation

Counterbalancing Soul Faculties:
Awareness, Continuity, Effort, Honesty,
Peace, Personal Responsibility,
Reason, Truth

How the Game is Played:

In playing _The Veil of Illusion, Delusion, Deception_ game, the personality separates in consciousness from God, forgetting that it is only an energy tool designed to serve the soul, and in its forgetting, believes that it is the thought forms created by the mind.

If our choice is to play mental games, we become the victim and get caught in the web of destiny. We are the "spiders" weaving those webs. As the spider can only traverse the web that it has woven, so the soul can only express on the patterns of thought that we have chosen to express upon. It is when, through error of thought, we give power to people, to places, and to things, that the web which we have woven is limited and binding. However, as we align our personality with our soul, we will find before our very eyes our own divinity.

The first of these "games" to shine the light over is that of *"The Veil of Illusion, Delusion and Deception."*

SEPARATING TRUTH FROM CREATION

We must make the effort to separate truth, the eternal part of us, from the creations of the mind. In other words, separate the soul from the mind and its created thought forms. Use creation; do not abuse it, for in your abuses you become the victim and are destined to bondage, the bondage of obsession. For that is what illusion, delusion, deception have to offer all souls until they awaken. Suffering, struggle, disaster, and strife are the payments of such ignorance. In time, through the suffering of the senses, the soul is freed. When we have had enough, we do change. As the wise teacher would say, *"One who loves God more than one loves creation does not deny creation but uses it wisely."*

In this regard, in *The Seat of the Soul*, Gary Zukav states very clearly:

> The illusion holds power over you when you are not able to remember that you are a powerful spirit that has taken on the physical experience for the purpose of learning. It has power over you when you are compelled by the wants and impulses and values of your personality. It holds power over you when you fear and hate and sorrow and fester in anger or strike out in rage. It has no power over you when you love, when compassion opens your heart to oth-

ers, when your creativity flows unimpeded joyously into the present moment. In other words, the illusion has no power over a personality that is fully aligned with its soul.

To spiritually evolve first requires understanding how the mind works so that you have the option to exercise control over it. The mind is the vehicle through which our personality and soul are expressing. The personality uses the conscious and subconscious minds, while the vehicle for the soul is the superconscious mind. Spiritual evolvement also requires understanding the faculties or attributes of the soul and the sense functions of the personality and how they express themselves.

When you permit the personality to rise supreme in consciousness over the eternal you, your soul, your spirit, this opens the door of illusion, delusion, and deception. When you are in delusion, you are unable to separate truth, the soul, the spirit, from the created thought forms of the mind. A constant process of identifying and creating is taking place within the mind. It is then that the thought forms control you to the point where you accept them as the real you. You cannot tell the difference. Without the effort to become aware, you believe that you are the form. As you believe in this illusion, you become the illusion; the belief is the attachment. When you believe you are a thought and not the cause of the thought, then you are limited and controlled by the thought. That is delusion.

Depending upon circumstances and stimuli, you can be consumed by your emotions. If you become angry, or hurt, or guilty, or sorrowful, for example, without control of your mind, you think the real you is the anger, the hurt, the guilt, or the sorrow. You have become the victim of the game you have allowed your mind to play.

Instead of standing beside the event or situation, looking at it objectively and not letting things persuade or disturb you, you actually feel the emotion so strongly that it physically affects you. This is the "game" the mind plays to deceive us. The only way you can remain trapped is to continue to believe the level is you. Some people develop health problems. Others express their belligerence and nasty attitudes onto others. The latter is known as being "in the forces." Belligerence is one of the early signs you are serving the thought forms.

Until you become aware of the origin of your emotions, you will continue to be the victim of your thought forms. It is your motive or intention that creates the reality that you experience, reality being the conscious awareness of passing events. Only the mind makes your reality, but it cannot make truth. Therefore, a wise person becomes aware, awake, and alert.

The role of perception, a soul faculty, is to cast the light of reason over the emotion; however, as long as you insist on believing you are the emotion, there is no way possible you can be aware. You must separate the truth you are from the illusion of your mind, making the effort to talk to yourself: *I am not the illusion. I am truth.* By accepting that, you can do with it as you choose, but you cannot change that which you have not first accepted. We live and breathe in a world of illusion, but it does not have to be a bad illusion—*"Dreamer, dream a life of beauty before your dream starts dreaming you."*

REPROGRAMMING THE SUBCONSCIOUS

It takes daily effort to reprogram the subconscious. One effective way some have found to do this is to frequently talk to their subconscious, explaining that in trying to change their attitudes, they are not fighting with the subconscious or relegating it to a less important position. In fact, by cooperating the subconscious is actually serving a more important function to them than ever before. Further, its cooperation is needed to help them with their spiritual evolvement and work. They solicit this cooperation every day. If you want anything worthwhile in life, it must be a daily effort.

The master spirit teacher recommended talking to the subconscious as you would talk to a four-year old child. Program it with feeling because it is the seat of feeling or emotion. Do not order it around. If the conscious and the subconscious minds are in harmony, the inspiration from one's own soul and the communications from the spirit will come through clearly.

It takes constant effort and much energy to reprogram the subconscious. To make a change, as much energy is required to make the change as went into creating the pattern. Time has nothing to do with it. It is not a matter of time but of energy needed to reprogram or play a new tape.

DEALING WITH THE THOUGHT FORMS

The thought forms are our children. We gave birth to them. We are their parents. They want to be fed. The more energy we direct to particular thoughts or patterns, the stronger these forms become and the more they demand to be fed. You feed them through the repetition of the same thoughts. The mind records on the first impression. Everything else is a repetition of it. Thought continuously moves and, like a magnet, pulls everything of like kind to it. When a thought repeats, it gets stronger and you begin to serve it. The thought then becomes the belief. And that is when you believe you are it. You bounce up and down with the thought and laws get established.

Yogananda told the story of one of his students asking for help in dealing with the forms he had created that he no longer wished to serve by giving them energy. Yogananda advised his disciple to study the pigeons. They hang around the produce sections of a city, or in a park, wherever people congregate with food. Or, perhaps some one brings them a bag of grain. They come regularly to be fed and become very bold over time. They make their little sounds, and if we ignore them, they flap their wings to get our attention.

Yogananda counseled to observe the thought forms, but not to feed them. For that which we ignore, we do not identify with. And, of course, when we do not identify with something, it has no power, no effect, and no control over us. By excerthe very principle of ignore, In short, become the "bystanding mind." *Be the observer and not the observed.* Let these things scream in your head until they lie down and go to sleep from lack of energy being fed them, knowing they are not the real you—the eternal part of you—but creations of your mind. Always be aware of what is talking to you. *Is it the voice of light, or is it the voice of darkness?*

You do not fight with those forms for that only establishes the continuity of them. When you fight, you use entities of emotion from the water center (the solar plexus chakra). If you fight the forms, they will fight back. For example, say you have a weight problem. Food is a necessity, but how much do you need is the question. These entities, these forms, fight you by telling you that you are hungry. You must talk to yourself and tell them instead you are full. Make them wait until you make a conscious decision to eat. Do not be a puppet, allowing the thought forms to pull your strings. The situation may be likened unto a soldier coming over a hill and being met by armies of "have been's." By "have been's" is meant all the thought forms or tapes created by past experiences connected with the issue at hand.

When you **pause** in consciousness, you can **shift** in consciousness and use the light of reason. *"Pause is the lion's strength,"* for in the lion's pause he can survey the situation before taking action. These forces, the "have been's," come up to your turf, so-to-speak, and they are blinded by the light of reason. Fighting defeats the purpose of being in the Light. Do not fight.

When you make the change from patterns of license to patterns of discipline, expect that the armies of the past will rise to have their way, to be fed so they can continue to exist. Food has been used in the above example because it is a common problem. When you try not to "stuff your face" constantly and try to be more disciplined, that is when the armies rise. Do not think they are not *armies*. They work in the realm of self-preservation. When you battle forms of the past, they are cunning and set you up with temptations because you are fighting them, and they are going to break through unless you stand guard at the portals of your thoughts. It is when you are not on guard that they break through to have their way. This is why the diet programs frequently fail.

GOING BEYOND THE MIND

A helpful affirmation for those struggling with a weight problem is, *"God, I surrender my concern to you, and know that my weight is being adjusted by The Divine, not by my brain."* Or, *"God knows my correct weight. I accept that this adjustment is taking place at this moment and every moment."* By accepting from The Divine, you go beyond the mind and this frees it from concern that blocks the flow. If you are in concern, then you are rejecting that The Divine is working, rejecting that The Divine is adjusting your weight, or whatever else you may be seeking help in balancing.

It is necessary to spend more time concerning oneself with one's thoughts because those are the things that are bringing us disturbance, misery, grief, and misunderstanding. We need to think more than just once or twice a day to bring the mind with all its power back to its true home that it may become familiar with itself. We over-identify with our physical forms, our bodies of clay, and forget we are spiritual beings encased in a physical form so that we might express in this physical dimension.

ACCEPTING PERSONAL RESPONSIBILITY FOR CHANGING

When something goes wrong, stop blaming outside. Accept personal responsibility for your thoughts that brought you the experience. The greatest cloud or delusion created by the human mind is the delusion that the cause of any experience is outside and, therefore, beyond the power or the control to change it by our own efforts. Because we entertain so frequently that delusion of blame outside, we become ever increasingly controlled by the fluctuating changes of creation itself. We must learn to direct our attention inside for change to free ourselves from the delusion that changes must be made by other people and places and not by ourselves.

"The key of wisdom to the door of freedom is the ability, the willingness, and the joy of change."

ADDICTION TO OUR THOUGHTS AND DESIRES

That which serves us without the lamp of honesty and the light of reason, we are destined by the divine law to serve in time. We become the victims of our own creations and we are so deluded we think that is the real us. It happens all the time and we wonder what happened.

We are addicted to our thoughts and addicts to our taped desires. Whenever a tape in our head to which we are addicted is revealed to us by another human being, the reaction is always traumatic. It is always emotional. It is always defensive. When something runs counter to our thoughts, our reaction reveals the degree of our belief that we are the thought. It cannot be overemphasized that to be free, we must separate our free spirit from the thoughts that are running through our mind. We are not the mind. We are that which activates the mind.

POSITIVE RESULTS OF REPROGRAMMING THE SUBCONSCIOUS

As you work on reprogramming the subconscious, the tendency to react emotionally to people and situations gradually lessens. If, for example, you feel a sense of rejection or jealousy, you are better able to stop in the moment and declare the truth: *these feelings of emotion affecting my body are not the real eternal me. They are just those thought forms that I created now rising up to be fed.* You then gain power over them. Again, the admonition: use your will power to catch them when they first start to rise. **Separate truth from creation.** It requires eternal vigilance so that you are not deluded by the negative forms. Because you created them, you have power over them and you can transmute the energy from "demons" to "angels" by consciously changing your thoughts. *"When one smiles, the angels sing. When one grins, deception is satisfied."*

EXERCISING RESPONSIBLE CHOICE

We are here on this plane to free ourselves. We are not here to please or serve those forms of creation, whether they are our forms or someone else's. When you feed another's entities, you deny your own and they become twice as demanding. *"Charity begins at home."* Home is the soul.

As the creators of the forms, we are greater than the creation. Therefore, when tempted, make the choice of what you will serve. Zukav says it so beautifully:

> Only through responsible choice
> can you choose consciously to cultivate
> and nourish the needs of your soul, and
> to challenge and release the wants of your
> personality.

Levels of consciousness are attitudes of mind, or rates of vibration, created by thought patterns. Any thought repeated in the mental world becomes an established pattern. It garners up like kind throughout the mental universe and becomes a level of consciousness. The final strength of a level of consciousness—the ruler of any level of consciousness—is the extent of judgment.

The same levels of consciousness that exist in one person exist in all persons. We differ in what levels we choose to express on and how we package that expression. When you entertain "bummer" levels, you open the door to multitudes of others on the same level and get tremendous help in staying down "there." Therefore, it behooves the wise person to nip it in the bud in the beginning, before being trapped. This piece of clay (the physical body) does insulate us somewhat. It is much more difficult to rise in consciousness when on the spirit side of life because the Law of Attraction draws us to the like-minded.

Why not open up your home, your soul, to where a multitude of angels are expressing? Forms of light are forms of balance and harmony—soul faculties. They are celestial forms of heaven. They will help you. They will help sustain your efforts. Remember, thought forms work for us. We created them to work for us. Why not create them to work for the progression of your soul?

Learn to discern the difference between emptiness and fullness. Emptiness refers to the soulless forms constantly calling for life force. They scream and will not let go until they have had enough life force to let you go. Do not feed soulless forms. Create forms of fullness, healthy forms with heart and soul that will lift you to that state of consciousness known as heavenly heights.

GIVING POWER TO PEACE, REASON, AND COMMON SENSE

Affirm peace in your life, for there is nothing the mind can create that the soul faculty of peace will not harmonize with. That is why some philosophies teach to meditate daily on peace so that it becomes a part of you and you can tap into the state of peace at will. We cannot take pills to get rid of our addictions—it takes peaceful thoughts.

When we raise our levels of consciousness to a realm of reason and common sense, we free ourselves from the illusion that we are the experience. We are experiencing many things in our life but we are not the experiences unless we permit our minds to delude us into the false belief that we are. We are no more the experience than we are the physical body through which we are presently expressing. The experience contains within it the lessons that are necessary for the evolution and the freedom of our eternal being. But we cannot see those lessons that are there for us if we do not accept the right of the experience to express.

Remember, *that that troubles us controls us.* The only thing that has power over us is that which we give power to. Watch the things that trouble you. Take a look around and see what irritates you, what makes you happy or sad. Those are the things that are habitual patterns that are controlling your soul. Those are the chains that bind your soul to creation. *"You can exist but you never truly live life until you have unfolded the soul within."*

COUNTERBALANCING THE FUNCTIONS OF ILLUSION, DELUSION, AND DECEPTION

Only in our mental illusion, delusion, and deception can we believe that we are separate from God. We shall all return in consciousness to that source. Through the awareness of truth, the acceptance of personal responsibility, and the continuity of effort in applying self-control, we shall separate the creations of our mind from the truth of our eternal being.

"Truth is like a river, it continuously flows."

Game 2

Identity Imbalance

Key Players:

Sense Functions:
Belief, Deception,
Identification, Self-Awareness

Counterbalancing Soul Faculties:
Balance, Consideration, Inspiration,
Personal Responsibility, Reason, Self-Control

How the Game is Played:

In playing the *Identity Imbalance* game, we over-identify with experiences and with objects that we observe, and by believing we are the objects or experiences, we then go out-of-balance and become bound to creation.

THOUGHT OF SELF IS THE LAW OF IDENTITY

This *Game of Identity Imbalance* expands *The Veil of Illusion, Delusion, and Deception* by going into a deeper understanding of the Law of Identity. By virtue of the fact that you have read to this point indicates you have awakened to areas of consciousness that the masses would not yet consider. Continue to think more deeply, for in that thinking is your awareness given birth, and in that awareness you will now view more clearly the Law of Identity.

We enter the veil of illusion and delusion which is created by the Law of Identity and sustained by belief. In other words, it is through the process of identification with the objects that we observe that we come to believe we are the object of our view. We are then bound by so-called limit or form or creation. This is the reason we experience the suffering and struggle as experiences are passing through our consciousness. We actually believe we are those experiences.

We can only be affected by that with which we **identify**. God does not exist while we are in illusion. Only the created god of judgment exists in illusion. What binds us to illusion? Judgment enters in and being magnetic, the magnetic attraction working through the emotions binds us. **Judgment** may be thought of as the cement that holds illusion together. It is a very potent force. It is the indispensable ingredient that binds the soul to the illusion of mental substance, for judgment is the servant of the thought of self and the denial of the right and the will of God. The price of judgment is lunacy because *"the thought of self is the throne of judgment that stands between the eternal soul and God."* To stay free, gain control of the emotions and be in the illusion but not part of it. Be consciously aware that it is only illusion; therefore, you will not be affected by it because we cannot be affected by anything we do not identify with.

Look at life and the experiences that you have already encountered. Look at the many times you have made decisions. Look at the many times you have lived in regret. So often when we face the seeming obstructions within ourselves, we face them with levels of emotionalism. We face them in levels of darkness, instead of facing them from levels of objectivity. We must honestly ask ourselves the questions, *Who am I? What am I? Am I the things with which I identify? And if I am, then I am constantly changing.* You are not the things with which you identify. The personality is the great deceiver over the eternal you, your soul. *The thought of self or personality is the Law of Identity.* In the Law of Identity is the limitation, the bondage, the attachment, and all of the things that cause the struggles of life. When you over-identify with anything, you go out of balance, you open the trap door to the lower forms. The truth is we are more than what we believe for we are the cause beyond the belief. We are more than what we see for we are that which causes the seeing.

OUR TRUE BEING IS A UNIVERSAL CONSCIOUSNESS

Because we have free choice we can use this Law of Identity to take us on the path of personality that deceives us into the false belief that we are a unique entity in consciousness. In truth, there is no unique entity in consciousness, except the illusion created by mental substance, for the true being is a universal consciousness, inseparable from the great whole. Your soul does not identify because it is a part of the universal whole. It is when we think of self or personality that we identify. Disregarding this truth, our personality fully believes it is a separate and unique entity, and in so believing, becomes it in its fullness. In becoming one thing, the Law of Self-Preservation annihilates anything outside its identity. As you strive through the process of the mind to preserve what you have identified with, that preservation process is known as fear.

We find that this eternal struggle between identity and universality goes on and on with the eternal being constantly moving back and forth in the realms of creation. When we entertain the thought of peace from levels of personality—levels which are governed by the dual Law of Creation— we guarantee its opposite, war. We have a few moments of mental peace and much time of emotional war. True peace is neutrality, a soul expression.

29

When in self-awareness, you are no longer in the realm of universal consciousness where all things are. You have a choice of the fulfillment of life by being where all things are, or to be in want and need where things are not. The lack of identification enables a person to walk on coals and perform other feats. The only life a level has is the life you give it through your identification with it. It has no other life because it has no soul.

How beautiful life truly is when you give up the thought of personality— me, me, me!!! Your limited, restricted universe opens and expands and encompasses the totality and the allness. This wisdom was expressed around 200 B.C. by Patanjali, the codifier of Raja Yoga, who warned to be aware of the "Reality" at all times—the "Reality" in his terminology being the omnipotent and omnipresent—otherwise, you forget your essential nature and identify with the objects of the world. The moment you come to know your essential nature, you are freed from all fears. You can only express fear when you have self-awareness. So declare your right. Accept the broader horizons that are before you this moment, the moment of now.

IDENTITIES INCUR RESPONSIBILITY

Even before duty, the first soul faculty—duty to allow our soul to express—we must look and see responsibility, and before responsibility, we view identity. As previously stated, it is the thought of self or personality that is the Law of Identity. Our responsibilities in life, then, are ever in keeping with our identifications. Identities become attachments and you incur responsibility, or the ability to respond, to whatever you attach yourself to.

CONTROLLING YOUR IDENTITIES

You may ask, *How do I change my identity?* Your identity is in a constant process of change. The question should be, *How do I control my identity?* You control the process of identification by becoming aware of what you identity with for you can only control what you are aware of. When you feel good, become aware of what you are identifying with that makes you feel good.

When you feel the opposite, become aware of what you are identifying with that is not bringing you joy in your life, your divine birthright. We change our identity often. It is all a matter of choice, but choice is the effect of self-control.

To change your identities in life you must first accept total responsibility for them. That is why it is taught that the Law of Identity is interwoven with the Law of Personal Responsibility. Once you accept responsibility, you are in a position to choose your identities. The denial of responsibility deprives you of the power to change because you have given that power to whomever you blame for your experience. That person then has power over you. You become the victim. It is bondage. You will never be free as long as you deny personal responsibility. In the process of learning to identify with something better, we have to learn how to let go of the former identification. *"See the good in all things by choosing to identify with the good."*

One spirit teacher explained changing your identities this way:

> The soul enters into creation, identifies and is aware of self. Awareness of self can be likened unto a branch of a tree. The trunk is the tree of life. The branch is a consciousness that is aware of something else but it cannot move. As long as we permit ourselves to be the branch and not the trunk of the tree, we experience need. We judge need when we are incomplete. With need, we know something is missing. We refuse to make the move to the trunk and, therefore, we live in denial and dependence and our destiny is well established. The root cause of denial, dependence, and destiny is identity. We are out on a limb but only we put ourselves there.

When we are on the limb, we must look back to the trunk instead of looking out and seeing only the leaves fading and falling, and in the spring, green again. How do we make the move from being a branch on the tree to the trunk? How do we re-identify to get off the limb? Stop looking at falling leaves. Accept it is all inside where you are—accept personal responsibility. We must change our identity. We know what put us on the limb but we became satisfied—the sleep of satisfaction. There we can fascinate and be frustrated in the false glory of fear.

We re-identify by getting out of self to see what self is, otherwise, we cannot be objective. We must become the bystanding mind. The trunk is the tree of life. It is the soul. The soul is the covering of spiritual essence, but that which we are is the life blood (the spirit). When we are out on a limb there are many forms dependent on life blood—parasites living off us. When we go to step off the limb into the trunk, we have to pay the price of the parasites (thought forms). We built a house for them. What is the price? We either become frustrated or we fascinate, or we are filled with fear. To fear the forms is to give them more power. The load, however, is never greater that we are capable of bearing. We are whole, complete, and perfect when we return to the trunk and stop working so hard to be what we think we are and what we think others think we are. The game ceases only when we get off the limb.

**BECOME MORE AWARE OF WHAT YOU ARE
IDENTIFYING WITH**

When a person is poor or sick and has accepted that condition in mental consciousness, he or she has identified with it and, therefore, believes. If we insist upon identifying with poverty, then we will never experience wealth. If we insist upon identifying with poor health, then we will never experience good health. It is all in our hands. The Infinite Intelligence has given us charge over all creation, but the creation we must first work upon is the creation of our own being. You have charge over all thoughts and all things to bring peace and harmony over all creation.

Become more aware of what you are identifying with. Does it bring you the abundant good which is in truth your right? If it does not, then change the identity. Redirect the energy. Redirection is moving out of self-awareness. It is within your power to do so. Become more alert to what you expose yourself to. Be not so interested in being liked. Be interested in being free, for that which is free has no lack and no discord.

God helps those who help themselves by helping others because by helping others, you have less awareness of self and God can go to work. The more awareness you have of self, the greater the bondage to whatever you are trapped in. The danger of over-identification is that it offers self-importance. In Acceptance the Divine Will, we accept the right of a level of consciousness to express. By accepting that right from a soul awakened level of consciousness, we do not identify and, therefore, do not believe or establish "the law unto ourselves."

BE THE OBSERVER AND NOT THE OBSERVED

When we are no longer the *observers*, it reveals we have identified with what we are observing and have become the *observed* and have lost perspective. The teaching is to *"be the observer and not the observed,"* which means to be at peace with oneself and to have an acceptance of oneself and of the right of others to their expression. In other words, it is through our perception, a soul faculty which is not blinded by the observation or judgment view of the mind, that we accept the right of God to express through all levels of consciousness. Observing permits one to be unaffected by the variations in levels of expression in other people and experiences around us. For when we have acceptance of ourselves, we view ourselves in others, and although we are reminded by others of that level within us, we can choose not to identify with it. In our acceptance, we make the effort to understand the level that is being expressed, which frees us to live in peace and harmony.

Each time we allow ourselves to be trapped into experiencing the levels of another by identifying with them, we sell out our divine right to happiness, to peace, and to harmony in our life. Remember, we do have that free choice to *"be the observer and not the observed."* We must take hold of our thoughts, awaken ourselves consciously to what our beliefs really are. *"As you believeth in your heart, so shall you becometh."*

It is understood that creation is not something that is limited to our physical world. Creation is a form, and form is everywhere. When we rise in consciousness to the form of free spirit, which in truth we are, we will view forms objectively. We will then become the *observer*, not the *observed*. The *observer* is not affected by experiences known as creation. It is the *observed* that is affected. If as the observer we identify with what we are observing,we then become the observed and that is when we are affected.

RELEASE THE CHAINS OF FEAR AND OVER-IDENTIFICATION

We cannot hide thoughts and feelings. We feed them thrice the energy by our fear. They become even more blatant than before. All minds fear. Fear is the authority of the mind over the eternal soul, but its authority is only temporal and in a constant process of change. Throughout the universes we have journeyed already. The more we identify with the earth realm and its materiality, the more difficulties we will have in our journey onward. Learn the wisdom of not over-identifying with form, for the pain in our evolution is the direct effect of our over-identification. We are in truth the universality of consciousness. Wisdom teaches to broaden our horizons so that our passing from moment-to-moment shall not be so painful.

Through an acceptance of the death and birth cycle which is constant in creation, we will gradually but surely be released from the whole and the chains that over-identification have upon us. Because of lack of control of our minds, we experience the forces of our own emotions through over-identification. Let us identify with constant change. Accept the coming as graciously as the going—the loss, the gain. Only a fool tries to stop or stand rigid in the Law of Constant Change. Be flexible, and from the flexibility in consciousness, we will begin to identify with God's kingdom. Be prepared that when we make the slightest effort to change, our kingdom of thought forms will scream and our pain will become greater. Each time we do what we know we should be doing, the forms, in keeping with what we have done, build a wall of obstruction known as procrastination. We shall pass through it by giving to God our greatest gift, the gift of self-identification. By giving that, we give the kingdom that has made a slave of us.

INSPIRATION, REASON, AND CONSIDERATION

It may seem a simple thing to just say, *I shall shed my beliefs. I no longer believe in illness, I no longer believe in the struggles of life, poverty, and so forth.* However, we must awaken the triune soul faculty of inspiration, reason, and consideration to its fullness before the transformation can take place. It takes a balanced mind to express reason and to consider all things. When we are receptive to inspiration, we receive understanding from God, that highest state of consciousness. Then we will have qualified ourselves to flood our consciousness with the infinite demonstrable truth that we are spirit, formless, and free.

To believe in the goodness of life we must identify with the goodness of life—that means we must control the thoughts that pass through our mind. The greatest gift to God is the gift of self and that we can make only when we are in control of our thoughts. It is through the control of the mind that the soul faculty of reason—the light that transfigures us—shines and enables us to educate the desires that we entertain in consciousness.

ACHIEVING BALANCED IDENTIFICATION

When we over-identify with anything, we lose control and it gains control. Our thought is creation. It is something that we, by the powers of our mind, have created. When we over-identify with what our mind creates, we lose control and begin to experience the many functions of the mind. But we do not have to over-identify. There is a law in the universe called the Law of Balance. Instead of identifying with what we judge we are losing, stop in that moment and identify with what we are gaining. If we say we cannot see what we are gaining, it simply reveals that we have not made the effort to create it. All of our attention is upon the creation we judge we are losing. Without the loss, there is no gain, and without the gain there is no loss. That is evolution. Freedom from all creation is the acceptance of responsibility for it. Each moment thoughts arise within our mind. Ask if they are serving us, or are we serving them?

In rising from the lower realms of consciousness to realms of spiritual eternal substance, that humble and simple part of us is aware of our own Divinity, for our Divinity is an inseparable part of The Divinity. In rising to those levels of consciousness, we loosen the curtain of illusion of identity for we have gained in those moments the totality of Acceptance, the Will of God, and in that totality of acceptance are the horizons broadened to encompass the allness and goodness of The Divine. We then know beyond doubt that the harmonious path to the joyous expression of life is a balanced identification with our many levels of expression.

You can turn failure into success by the process of identification. You can use the energy of the "failure" experience and redirect it into positive energy, turning it into a good experience. Identify with that which will breed a harmonious manifestation in your life. The lion's strength, or the pause, is the moment to re-identify with the good. Never identify with the negative experience. For example, the moment you identify with a rate of confusion, the more confused you become. *"He who sees the obstruction never finds the way. He who sees personality never finds principle."* This is the Law of Identity. Redirect the energy to the positive. You must fully identify with what you want to manifest. If you do not identify with the spiritual, you cannot unfold spiritually.

TECHNIQUE TO IDENTIFY WITH ANOTHER BEING

The spirit teacher gave a technique, using the Law of Identity, to help one grow from level to level:

> If you will be loyal to its use and practice it daily, you will begin to see the changes within yourself, and your spirit will find a greater expression of freedom while yet in form. The mind has identified itself that you are John Doe, so-to-speak, or Mary Jane. If you will entertain in thought that you are someone else and you will choose as that someone else a person or persons, a place or circumstance that you find to be intolerable, you will come into rapport with that person or persons. You will in truth experience their feelings, their emotions, and in time their soul, their spirit, of which you are a part. Be honest with this technique and you will gain greater understanding.

CONCENTRATION

That which frees us is what we are, not what we think weare. We believe we are the form because through the Law of Identification, we become what we identify with. As the Law of Identification is the concentrated power of the Universe which we direct, we, therefore, become. Concentration is the key to all power because we identify with the experience totally. We become a part of it by being totally identified with it. People trapped in the emotional forces fully believe their thought is them. They are totally concentrated. Identify with the vibration of peace to still the activity of the mind. It is the same law applied. The only difference is what we choose to identify with. By concentrating on being the neutrality of Divinity rather than the duality of expression, we surrender the Law of Identity and separatism.

❋   ❋   ❋

*"What we **are** is God's gift to us.*
*What we **become** is our gift to God."*

Game 3

Denying Personal Responsibility

Key Players:

Sense Functions:
Blame, Deception, Denial, Discouragement,
Judgment, Justification, Lying, Pity

Counterbalancing Soul Faculties:
Acceptance, Honesty, Love,
Personal Responsibility, Reason, Truth

How the Game is Played:

By *Denying Personal Responsibility* for our experiences in life, we deprive ourselves of the power to change because the personality has given that power to whomever or whatever we blame for our experiences.

WE EXIST IN THREE DIMENSIONS

We are existing in three dimensions here and now—physical, mental, and spiritual. It is our duty and our responsibility to our soul, The Divine that is our only Light, to become awakened and aware of these dimensions. We must do this as a personal demonstration to ourselves, not only of this Eternal Light, but of our responsibility to it. Most of humanity is yet asleep in the cradle of creation. They are not aware as a personal demonstration to themselves of these three dimensions in which they are existing. At the moment of our soul's incarnation into form we were aware of these dimensions, but through education or over-identification with a mental and a mundane physical world, the awareness of entry into this life or of prior lives gradually, but surely, has been dimmed. Because the child is so often ridiculed for the seeming fantasies that he or she is experiencing, this Divine Light is clouded over. Therefore, it is our responsibility to reeducate the mind to the truth that is within us.

LAWS OF PERSONAL RESPONSIBILITY AND IDENTITY ARE INTERWOVEN

We are an infinite, eternal, intelligent energy called by many "soul." Beyond soul is a formless free spirit. As it expresses through the Law of Identification, it individualizes and gathers unto itself an untold multitude of experiences. Like Attracts Like and becomes the Law of Attachment, the Law of Personal Responsibility.

There is no god that punishes, and there is no god that brings pleasure, but there is an Infinite Intelligence that sustains whatever we choose to entertain in *our* thoughts. However, that does not exempt us from the law of the universe— personal responsibility. Whatever we think and whatever we do, it shall return to us, for that is the Law of the Universe.

Repeatedly, the teaching goes that all of life is the mirror, the mirror reflecting our own thoughts, our own attitudes. Because we are the fathers and mothers of our thoughts, we can change all experiences in our life, the experience being the effect of those thoughts.

We cannot change our identities in life without first accepting total responsibility for them. So the Law of Identity is interwoven with the Law of Personal Responsibility. Once we accept responsibility, we are in a position to chose our identities.

The philosophies of the world show us a way to go inside ourselves, for that is where our freedom, our truth, and everything that is worthwhile exists. The error occurs when we permit our mind to tell us that the cause of the experience is outside our mind—that the cause is another person, a circumstance, a place or thing. The moment we do that we have lost the power of our own freedom. God becomes our false god of creation in that moment.

PITY AND DISCOURAGEMENT

The person who deprives us of the goodness of life is none other than our own self. What do we derive from being unkind to ourselves? To the conservation minded, it is not practical to want to be frustrated—to use energy in such a fruitless way. What does pity offer us? It offers to the personality a temporary escape from accepting personal responsibility by justifying that we are not able or capable of assuming responsibility. There is no freedom when we are locked in the prison of pity.

Always encourage yourself because discouragement is nothing more than the "have been's," the experiences of the past, working to gain control. The pity of self comes from the "have been's" and the blaming outside.

*"Discouragement is the path to hell,
Encouragement is the path to heaven."*

THE PATH OF JUDGMENT AND DENIAL

Justifications protect judgments. They are nothing more than the denial of personal responsibility and the protection of our lies. *I can't do this because of so and so.* Lying to self, we become trapped in deception and go into frustration. When our misery demands company it seeks another person's support for its deception.

As long as we permit our minds to blame anything outside, we remain upon the path of judgment or denial. What a terrible deception to think it is **outside!** Sadly, our need reveals our denial of God.

Whenever you permit your mind to blame, to dictate to you that you do not have what you desire "because," the word "because" is the problem. For that is the first step that sends your mind into the delusion of the past and gives your precious freedom to a thought form. How often in the course of a day we do that!

"When you stop blaming outside, you will start growing inside."

The denial of responsibility for the experience deprives us of the power to change because we have given that power to whomever we blame for our experience. That person then has power over us—we become the "victim." It is bondage, and we will never be free as long as we deny personal responsibility. We cannot control what we do not accept personal responsibility for. Energy follows attention. When we spend our energies finding fault outside, there is nothing left to go into our own spiritual unfoldment.

HOW WE ARE AFFECTED BY REFUSING
TO ACCEPT RESPONSIBILITY

By refusing to accept personal responsibility for our own thoughts and actions, we are affecting our whole physical system. *"The constant denial of personal responsibility is indispensable to the aging process and poor health."* In closing ourselves in and pushing or projecting blame outwardly, there is no balance, no give and take, so-to-speak. In this tightening process, the heart is affected because love is not allowed to flow. Spiritual law requires that we love unconditionally by accepting personal responsibility or we will attract situations in this or another lifetime where we will have to accept responsibility. The lesson must be learned one way or another. Otherwise, the weakness will reflect on the physical, emotional, or mental level, or possibly on all three.

When we do not accept the Law of Personal Responsibility, all other laws are null and void in trying to apply them. When we do not accept the Law of Personality, we cannot be free from the personality—the self thought—which is dictating a repetition of experiences that we have already been living in— the shadows of yesterday.

How do we make the necessary effort to accept personal responsibility for all experiences in our life? By first accepting that we and we alone are the cause and the effect. To accept that simple truth is to make the first step in walking upon the path of Light and Freedom. If we feel a disturbance and are angry and upset because we have made a judgment which makes us feel miserable, we must first accept personal responsibility for the judgment. Step one, *"I accept this feeling."* Step two, *"I accept this feeling is a thought in my head."* Step three, *"I accept this is my thought that I have created."* Step four, *"I accept because it is my thought and mine alone I can change it."* Our soul only wants the lamp of honesty to shine. It is honesty that leads us through to accepting personal responsibility, but it takes determination and courage to express honesty.

The instant we accept personal responsibility we are free in consciousness from whatever is binding us to "hell." We have the world by the tail when we accept: *This is my thought. I put it there—and because it is my thought I can change it.* It is all inside. Truth is personal responsibility and that is what will save us. If we tell God *I am personally responsible*, in that moment we arm ourselves for the battle, for the war going on inside with our mind, our personality. If we have experiences we do not like, we should talk to ourselves and we will win the battle.

If you are not the first to accept personal responsibility, you cannot expect others around you to accept it. You soon find that everything you touch fizzles. In failure, self-pity expresses. When you are in self-pity, you kick out any or all responsibility that comes your way. You are so busy entertaining yourself with self-pity that you cannot cope. *It is the emotions, not reason, that kick out responsibility.* When the emotional garbage rises to protect the fragile personality, affirm, *"God, help me with personal responsibility and help me to see the childishness in my mind."*

The personality seeks perfection and has the need for an untarnished image, and uses cunningness in trying to achieve its goal. It is futile in the end to attempt to hide something, for without accepting personal responsibility and being honest, we only bind ourselves more tightly. The more energy directed to protect weakness reveals the degree of the weakness, whereas a weakness becomes strength when we face it. The soul does not need glory. It only seeks honesty which brings freedom, that good feeling inside in the area of the heart where the soul resides. The good feeling is God expressing.

THE WEIGHT OF RESPONSIBILITY
"The weight of responsibility must never exceed the love of God."

Whenever you make a decision, you establish a law and you incur responsibility for you have to respond to the law. So let your demonstration be of spiritual responsibility, not the "weight" of responsibility. When the weight of responsibility exceeds your love of God, concern rises over having to accept the responsibility. It becomes a terribly heavy weight when the personality is in charge. This heavy weight upon your shoulders is the weight of effects of the laws you alone established in your mental world.

> *"He who sees dimly finds responsibility a great burden, but he who has vision knows God's eternal joy."* There are no burdens in the spiritual consciousness. *"Cast thy burden on the Lord."* (Ps 55:22) and know that by so doing you make nothing of it, for God is not burdened with heavy cares and weary work. To cast your burden upon the Lord is as though it were dropped into the bottomless pit. When

you have thus thrown off this sense of
weighty responsibility see that you do
not take it again.

When the love of God is expressing, there is no weight of
responsibility, that is, no self-concern over responsibility. So it
behooves the wise person to stop thinking of self, self, self—"to
let go and let God," and then there will be no burden. We are
never given more than we can handle. By facing our responsibilities we know God's eternal joy.

Personal responsibility is a life line. It can be used to free
you, or in the denial of it, it can become a noose. Therefore,
when your love of God exceeds your love of self, you are free of
possession and obsession by the princes of darkness. In facing
your responsibilities, never forget that God alone—the neutral
principle of life itself—is at the helm and can bring a healing
balm over any and all disturbances in your life.

So it is that we must respond to the laws that we alone set
into motion. Often, however, we pray for many things and then
become discouraged, dissatisfied, and lose faith because we judge
that the divine law is not responding to our pleas and dictates.
What we fail to see is that the divine law is responding. In responding, the mountain of transgressions we have already created are being removed in keeping with the law established.
Not having the wisdom of patience, we are deceived by the slow
and sure process of the removal of the obstructions that we have
created. To the mind, removing dissension and discord is a painful process. To the mind, patience is painful because the mind
relies upon a mental world and it is a most unreliable dimension. It is unreliable because our thoughts change so frequently
for that is what the mental world has to offer.

OPENING THE FOOT LOCKER OF DESIRES

When you do something that you do not want to do, you
open the lid to your footlocker of desires, and those desire forms
look around and rise for energy. You will be in harmony with
duty as long as you are in control and do not allow the weight

45

of responsibility to exceed your love of God. There will be no frustration in doing what has to be done. If, however, you decide to procrastinate, you open the foot locker and the forms tell you to do the thing later, resulting in experiencing the forces of frustration. If you are honest, you will not have to suffer.

COMPLETING THE CIRCLE TO EXPERIENCE FULLNESS OF LIFE

We must consider what it is in our thinking that shies away from the ability to respond to the greatness, the goodness of life itself. In spite of ourselves, we are all growing up in consciousness where we find our home rising above and beyond. A straight line, which is the path of our spirit, is in truth a complete circle. So it is with our direction in life—that the path be straight and narrow, that we may complete the circle. For only in completing that circle, do we ever experience the fullness of life. That which we begin must by that eternal law have its ending or completion. The circle is not a half circle or a quarter circle. It returns unto itself, and so it is in our endeavors, we cannot leave them half done or just started, for the circle is not complete and the incompletion of it takes control of us. Though we see it not, someday we will.

When you have responsibilities, complete each one because you cannot be free until they are completed. When you leave your physical world, those incomplete endeavors in your life bind you to the realm upon which those forms are waiting to return to their source. Therefore, awaken within that you may be objective and no longer attached to the physical body in which you are presently expressing, for detachment from your physical body is not an automatic process by the law of nature.

When your soul has finished the work it has to do on the earth plane, if you are still attached emotionally and mentally to that physical form, you are held in those physical realms to view the natural decaying process of the physical body returning to the source from which it was composed. So it is with your creations. The law is universally applicable as a universal law. You create the thoughts and the feelings of an endeavor in your life. You begin it. If you do not finish it, you cannot be freed from it until it has gone through the circle to complete itself. Those are the things that bind and hold you. Those are the shadows that haunt you. Those are the obstructions that stand in your path. Life marches on. Those who remember that whatever goes out returns to the source from where it was created and formed, are aware of the circle of life. That awareness, of course, helps them to stand upon the rock of principle and face personal responsibility.

Because life is in truth a circle, our foundation is personal responsibility. Accept that simple truth that is ever with you, around you, about you. Your feelings, your thoughts, come from within you. They return unto you. So as you flood your consciousness with the divine right, your birthright, of harmonious, peaceful flow, you send that out into the universe. It ever returns to you, the source, for you are the creator. That which you have created, your children, know their home. Accept your responsibility for your life that you may respond in the light of reason, that you may be the living demonstration of the goodness of life. Then your whole world will brighten and you will see and know the way. There will be no question for there is nothing to question when you accept responsibility for all your thoughts, acts, and activities. From home we have wandered and to home we all are returning. We are doing that each moment, and we become aware of doing that each moment when we truly accept responsibility for all our experiences.

NO ESCAPE FROM FULFILLING THE PURPOSE OF OUR LIFE

We will not escape the purpose of our life. It behooves us to fulfill that purpose here and now rather than to be drawn back to this earth realm after transition. Once having made your choice in life, stick with it, whatever it is. It is a known truth that many spirit people, those who have once lived in this physical clay, are magnetically drawn back to this earth realm to complete the work that they were given to do, according to the Laws of Merit.

Besides those who cannot escape this realm, because they have not fulfilled the purpose for which their souls incarnated, there are many, many other reasons why spirits are drawn to the earth realm. Some are attracted to this realm through their emotional attachment to those still here in the physical body. Then there are those waiting in cemeteries for Gabriel to come blow his horn before they will rise beyond the grave. Others who were addicts on earth attach themselves to addicts here to vicariously savor drugs, alcohol, cigarettes, and so forth. And, very importantly, there are those highly evolved spirits who out of compassion come to teach, inspire, and guide us ever in keeping with the degree of effort we make for our own greater good. God has provided to all people, whatever religious affiliation or absence of it, spirit guides who are attracted by the Law of Like Attracts Like, who walk with us on our earthly journey.

WE ARE OUR BROTHER'S KEEPER

In truth, we are inseparably united through divine love to all things, at all times, and in all places—for the only thing that sustains us, known as Spirit, or God, is everywhere present and never absent or away. We are indeed our brother's keeper and are responsible for all creation.

We, through the Law of Responsibility, are directly linked to all intelligent life. Some people do not consider some life forms on this, the planet earth, as intelligent life. That only reveals that they have been so busy in the form in which they are presently expressing, they have yet to consider that intelligent life is everywhere around and about them. *"We are our brother's keeper"* is certainly a teaching of many ancient philosophies, and we can only keep what we are responsible for. Therefore, being our brother's and sister's keeper, we are indeed brothers. We are responsible for all form because, in truth, when we face who we really are, we will then realize beyond any doubt that we are an inseparable part of a great whole. Therefore, we are responsible to the whole to the degree of our spiritual elevation—always guided by the light of reason.

Even if we deny our inseparable part, this in no way frees us from our responsibility. Ignorance of the law is no escape from the law. Many things in life we do not wish to view. We do not wish to view them for we have judged what they offer. We have judged what they offer in keeping with what we have already experienced. How unfortunate that we live in the shadows of yesterday, for the mind cannot judge without past experience. *"And so the Bible teaches us to judge not that we be not judged, for he who judges lives in that which has been, and living in consciousness in that which has passed does not see the Light that frees him for he lives in the twilight zones of yesterday."*

DISCORD IN CONSCIOUSNESS HAS EFFECT UPON NATURE

Having been given charge of all creation, that is all of nature, in our ignorance and denial of the demonstrable truth of personal responsibility, we have disregarded our effect upon nature. Because of our ignorance, disregard, and disrespect for what we are responsible for—which means every thought in our consciousness—we experience catastrophes, disasters, discordant types of weather conditions, and so forth in nature. Pure and simple, these are the effects of discord in consciousness.

We see it in our personal lives. And because we deny it by blaming others for the discord, by blaming others for the transgression of the natural laws of abundant flow, by blaming outside for what is caused inside, we continue to live in the darkness of ignorance and despair. We seem to have no problem in our life in accepting responsibility for what we judge to be the good experiences in our life. We only seem to have difficulties in accepting responsibility for the disasters, the struggles, the pain, and the suffering that we have at times in our life.

"In all disasters, God's Light shines humbly, but bright, to one who pauses and accepts the wonderful, demonstrable truth of the ability to personally respond to all experiences and awaken in that response."

OVERCOMING "NEGATIVE SIGNALS"

As your current experiences constantly reveal your past ones in life, to overcome the "negative signal," you have to send out a potent new signal constantly until it overcomes the old signal of your mind. A constant affirmation of truth is needed: *"O God, let me never forget that the degree of my joy, goodness, peace, and happiness in life is ever dependent upon my acceptance of personal responsibility."* When your struggle is the greatest, that is the best possible opportunity to flood your consciousness because that is when the computer is wide open and at least partially receptive.

That which arrives in an instant, by the Law of Arrival can leave in an instant if we will only be honest with ourselves and wake up. Use the process of reason. *"Keep faith with reason. She will transfigure thee."* "She" is the mother, representative of creation. Who can best control creation but the creator, the feminine aspect?

ACCEPT A BETTER WAY THROUGH
PERSONAL RESPONSIBILITY

The mere fact that you are reading a book of this type is indicative that you have established laws which are lighting your path. Some of you may step aside if you over-identity with form, and, therefore, shall be trapped by form. But some of you will stay upon the lighted path and you will move ever onward and upward in consciousness.

We have been given the intelligence, in keeping with our own evolution, to be used ever at our bidding. Therefore, *"cast not thy pearls before the swine"* of the human mind in its multitudes of temptation, for that only builds our own prison. We cast this precious freedom constantly before the swine of the errors of thought. Each time we do that we go into bondage—fear becomes supreme. We then become the slave of this created master in our own head.

Become more thoughtful of your words, your acts, your deeds. Become more objective. *"He who does not accept the Law of Personal Responsibility is denying the great power that is waiting to serve him.*" Do not be so quick to judge. Do not be so quick to take the credit for everything you think is great, and you will begin to experience the greatness of the power that sustains you. It denies you nothing. It is your mind that denies you. It is not the Infinite Intelligence which is always present to serve you. You have a great responsibility to an Intelligent Energy that is so humble, which is so willing. Use it wisely that you may become what you are destined to become, not in some far distant future of time, but in the moment of now—in this moment. That, of course, is dependent upon your willingness to accept a better way, to expect the goodness and greatness that are yours, and to demonstrate the faculty of wisdom and to control the pain of patience.

We must accept our birthright to the goodness of life in order to receive the goodness of life. It is a grave responsibility to work daily on our thoughts because it is our thoughts that guarantee our experiences.

$$* \quad * \quad *$$

"With the blessings which come from on high,
come also its balance, responsibility."

* .* *

It is the way of the child
  And not the wild
That leads to heaven's bliss.
  The gentle kiss of a heavenly mist
Is more than the mind can know.
  Though talk is well and thought is good
The fire is naught without the wood.
  So open your hearts in a heavenly way
To all life's children who will lead the way.
  By this I mean
Though the mind is keen
  It is the soul that knows the goal.
Be ever a worm, so low in the dust
  And watch the world go by,
Doing ever your share in a humble way
  For God is love and truth the way.

—*The Wise One*

* * *

Game 4

Playing Judge

Key Players:

Sense Functions:
Belief, Delusion, Denial, Illusion,
Indentity, Intolerance, Judgment,
Justification, Need, Pride

Counterbalancing Soul Faculties:
Acceptance, Forgiveness,
Honesty, Personal Responsibility,
Tolerance, Understanding

How the Game is Played:

In *Playing Judge*, the personality is allowed to sit on the throne of judgment, dictating what others should or should not be doing and what the outcome should be, totally denying the right and will of Infinite Intelligence.

"I'm only a witness of time passing on,
A witness of things that have come and gone.
Never the jury or judge will I be,
For I am the witness, the life and the tree."

HOW AND WHAT WE JUDGE

"I'm only a witness." This is very important for it means *"I'm without judgment."* The illumined soul is expressing. In contrast, only that which is form can be a witness of time passing on, for awareness comes with form. How often are we without judgment? Because we are so quick to judge another, it is the revelation and the demonstration that we, in truth, are quickly judging ourselves. We judge who should be doing what and how they should be doing it. We judge the outcome of this and that and the other. We dictate to God how things shall be.

Our greatest struggle in life stems from our prejudices or judgments, and that is why the greatest lesson in spiritual awakening is the freedom from the error of judgment. We are prejudiced concerning politics, our material supply, our spiritual supply and on down the list. In fact, there is no area in life that we do not prejudge the outcome for ourselves. By so doing, we establish those laws and experience exactly what we have set into motion.

Who is so illumined to know what thoughts are right for you? Who is so illumined to tell others what thoughts are right for them? Right or wrong is ever relative to our understanding. God is not a judge and God does not bind or enslave our souls.

Most minds make 90% negative judgments. There is no tolerance or consideration in negative judgments. Each judgment that we pass is another prison that we place ourselves in and it is so easy to get in, so difficult to get out. Judgment is an unwillingness to change. It is very rigid because it does not have the light of reason or common sense. When judgments crack, we crumble with them. With judgment we have want and need. With judgment we have bondage, pity, self, and suffering. On the other hand, reason and decision free us.

Decision is the willingness to change, to consider all possibilities in the light of reason. Judgment is a bound decision, a vast difference from a free will or choice decision, for judgment demands and dictates what the effects of its bound decision or judgment shall be. Judgment is a chain that binds us to the laws of yesterday. Decision takes us on a path of peace and harmony while indecision points up a controversy. Indecision is really dual decision. It is a wasteful vibration to entertain for it drains much energy. A poor decision is almost better than none.

CHOOSING PATH OF LIGHT OR PATH OF DARKNESS

The moment that you **judge** you must have a basis or a foundation for your judgment. The basis or foundation is the **illusion** of the thought of self (personality) which separates you from the universal whole. You become in that moment an independent entity without recognition of the source that sustains you.

In binding us to illusion, our judgments also *blind* us for they are forms without light. The forms reveal to us they have no light to grant us. That is why they are blind. The forms of darkness rush in because they are hungry. The forms of darkness constantly are trying to steal the Light for energy. They cannot stand in the Light or they will be transformed. In other words, every thought has two paths–we face either the path of Light or the path of darkness. Thought of self keeps us in darkness. With each desire we face the path of either limit or limitlessness. If we choose the path of judgment, we limit ourselves. However, when we *pause*, the form is allowed to pass through and can be transmuted into Light. That is why *"to pause is the lion's strength."* It gives the soul time to rise.

The teaching is to *"keep faith with reason, she will transfigure thee."* Reason becomes a servant of the Light and brings good. Unlike the forms of darkness, the angels of Light—the forms of Light—only come when called.

FEAR RISES WHEN IN JUDGMENT

When we share rather than compare, we are freed from making judgments. The instant we compare we are in judgment. The special package of judgment, need, and denial, has the ribbon of comparison over it. The moment we compare we are controlled by what we are comparing. There is no fear unless we compare.

We experience fear only when we rely on our mind. When we go contrary to our judgment, we experience fear. Judgments control emotions and fear is an emotional experience. When we go against our judgments, they tell us we will loose out, then we believe the judgment is us. When we accept the judgment is us and we are unable to separate it from the true us, we establish laws to guarantee that we will lose out.

ENTERTAINING JUDGMENTS CREATES PRESSURE

In entertaining a judgment, you lose control of the mind because you open yourself, through the Law of Association, to all the judgments you have ever made. Then a person says, *I can't take it anymore!* The pressure is great because they are experiencing the flood of judgments. One of the forewarnings is when you think about how much you have to do and so little time to do it. The head wants to explode. It means you have opened the flood gates. When in time pressure, stop! Say, *God, look at what my judgments are doing to me.* Time pressure is a total division in consciousness. It is contrary to the Law of Harmony and guarantees serious problems. A so-called "nervous breakdown" can occur when one has totally lost control. The flood gates have completely taken over. You guarantee this as an escape mechanism.

RECALL AND HEARING AFFECTED BY LEVEL OF JUDGMENT

Is it not interesting that we sometimes do not remember what we say? It is when the level of consciousness known as judgment is in control that we deny because the level tries to preserve itself. Recall comes only after a change to another level of consciousness. Then when exposure of the level of judgment takes place, its last ditch effort is to nitpick by saying it did not say exactly what it is accused of.

When a judgment is made at the time we are asked to do something, we do not hear what the person says because we hear only the judgment of our mind. We are deaf to what someone else says if it is not in keeping with our judgments. It frequently takes great effort to get through the house of judgments.

MAKE DECISIONS AND PUT GOD FIRST

In making judgments, bear in mind that judgments are always dependent upon something outside. So often in life we look for the miracle and deny the law. Therefore, work each day to make decisions, not judgments. We can be free from pressure by reminding ourselves for whom we are really working. No matter who assigns us a job and hands us a paycheck, it is always for God first that we are working if we put goodness into what we are doing. *"Thank you, God, I had forgotten for whom I was working. With your help, all the work will get done."*

PRIDE MUST BOW

All of your feelings of rejection are caused by your judgments. Because you made a judgment, you can correct it and move on when you accept you are in error. It is taught that *"we enter hell on the steps of judgment, holding on to the handrail of pride."* The more pride, the greater the defense and support of your judgments. However, when you bow pride, there is no longer the defense of the judgment. But pride does not want to bow. Pride is the child of judgment and it wants to support its parent. Judgment cannot survive unless you have pride. Admit that your judgment is wrong and be free. Trauma is associated with admitting a judgment is wrong and changing it. That is why one's spiritual commitment must have a higher priority than pride.

EXERCISING PERSONAL RESPONSIBILITY

Remember that nothing you create is uncontrollable. If you are capable of putting a judgment in your head, you are capable of taking it out. No judgment is ever greater than its creator, and therein lies the hope. You have the power to direct it. It is your child and because of this you still have the authority over it in your house. You have dominion over your "house" (your soul) which means you have the power and authority to feed or annihilate any thought or judgment. You are never left without this choice; this is known as the fullness of personal responsibility. If you choose to follow the judgment, it will always take you from personal responsibility to losing control of your house, for you put the blame outside. Any judgment you make leads you outside the dominion of your house because it recognizes the fact that it exists within a house whose authority it does not have. It must carry you outside the dominion of your own house to gain its own authority.

NOTHING TO JUDGE WHEN WE UNDERSTAND

There is no such thing as neutral or impartial judgment. All judgment is based upon the understanding of the person who is doing the judging. This understanding may any time expand or broaden itself. The judgment of one day is not necessarily the judgment of another. The Divine Intelligence does not judge. We, and we alone, judge all our thoughts, acts, and deeds. We may say the immutable Law of Cause and Effect judges us because we receive punishment or reward as deserved. This judgment process goes on all the time. It is not a great trial to take place at the end of time. Even when we make our transition at so-called death, we, not God, judge ourselves during the review of our lifetime on earth.

We judge what we do not understand. The moment we **understand** a thing there is nothing to judge—there are no buttons to be pushed. *"He who **understands** the thing controls the* *thing.*" That is why the teaching, "*In all your getting, get under-standing, and in all your giving, give wisdom.*"

PUTTING YOUR ATTENTION ON BECOMING

Either the mind will rule and you will continue your dual creative experiences, or the soul and spirit will rise and all will be peaceful and harmonious. Laws are established by directed energy, and you are the "director." Therefore, it behooves you to *put your attention on what you want to become, not on what you want to overcome. This is how you give a thought or judgment to God.* Whatever you are thinking, become aware of what you are creating. Is it harmonious and beautiful?

A judgment is a form that gets its nourishment from your mental energy as long as you give it attention. It will die eventually when gradually its nourishment dwindles to the point where it is only a flitting thought across the mind. This is why *"Repetition is the Law of Change"*—repetition of putting your attention on becoming, of practicing the means of becoming, until the judgment (the obstruction) no longer receives "mental nourishment." The law that you follow is whatever you direct your attention to. "*If man is a law unto himself, then what are you doing with the law that you are?*"

WORK ON A LEVEL WHEN OUT OF IT

You must understand that death comes to a judgment by redirecting the thinking to something else, not by entertaining judgment or saying, *judgment, you bug me.* That only feeds energy to it. Direct your thought to something pleasing to your mind. Eventually, that judgment will disintegrate. Your soul moves up through the levels to what you have now placed your attention on; therefore, you no longer experience the levels of judgment. But you must concentrate, hold fast to the new level— the pleasing one. The key is learning the art of moving through the levels of consciousness.

The time to work on a level is when you are out of it (risen above it); to do otherwise, would be to feed energy to it. You get out of it by moving through it to another level. Then you must become aware of the things that trigger your response to experience the detrimental level. To "rise above it" means to take your attention, or energy, off a judgment and redirect it to something pleasing.

JUDGMENT DICTATES CHOICE

Judgment always rises when we do not make any effort. Often we have good intentions concerning the endeavors of our choice but we are controlled by the dictates of judgment when making a choice. This is unfortunate, though it need not be. *"One who chooses anything and respects with equal respect that which one has not chosen, is freed from the throne of judgment."* So we must ever look to the effect, or the result of any endeavor, and use the wisdom known as common sense to help guide us to do what is right because it is right to do right

JUDGING OTHERS GUARANTEES EXPERIENCE
FOR UNDERSTANDING TO BEFALL US

"Man takes pride in viewing what he has decided is weakness being expressed by another soul, for in viewing the weakness he builds the image of his own self-importance and superiority, guaranteeing the weakness he has viewed to befall him in order that he may learn the folly of judgment." Our soul, our Divinity, may have wandered from its home, from its source, but that which wanders from a thing in its very wandering is already on its way back home. Because one may be a little greater distance from his or her home than another may be, does not grant to anyone the right to judge the distance. It is the tendency of the mind to judge because of its own insecurity.

Intolerance or prejudice stems from judgment. We cannot be intolerant of anything until the mind has first judged it. The mind makes its judgment based upon the information and the experiences that it has accepted in its lifetime. Therefore, if it has accepted *this* is the right way to do something, or *that* is the wrong way, then it makes its judgment according to its acceptances. That which we cannot tolerate, we have judged, and having judged, we guarantee the experience to befall us some-time during our life that we may be granted understanding, not punishment. In this process, we gain greater awareness. We cannot understand what we cannot express tolerance toward. Remember, every time we are intolerant, we are building an-other obstruction to what we truly want to accomplish. The energy directed from that level of intolerance goes out like a great circle and it returns to us, and we have experiences we do not care to have. So it behooves us not to judge the acts and activities of another. *"Judge not that ye be not judged."* (Matt 7:1)

We cannot express to another what we cannot express to ourselves. Therefore, we must make a moment-by-moment ef-fort to recognize and realize that we are a part of the whole, and we are capable at any moment of expressing the levels we can-not tolerate in others.

BECOMING THE VICTIM OF OUR INTOLERANCE

"Hold not to form, for form (the form of thought) *will pass."* You cannot change another; you can only change yourself. Fight-ing on an emotional level will not change another; that is an attempt to play God. Only you can change your own thought; only the other person can change his or her own thought.

No matter where we go, and no matter what we do, how *we* think is the way our life will be, not the way someone else thinks. That is, unless we have judged that the way they think is intolerable to us. And if the way they think is intolerable to us, then they have control over us. The person we cannot tolerate is not suffering because of our thought. We are the ones that have the problem and have become the victim of our own in-tolerance. What we cannot tolerate in another is yet to be edu-cated within ourselves. When everything is wrong outside, it is simply directing us, our eternal being, to accept the divine truth that everything is wrong inside.

The soul faculty of tolerance, when expressed, frees us from the lack and limitations of our mind-computer. When we have tolerance, there is no judgment. The fewer the judgments, the more youthful and angelic one's countenance. It is worth it to forgive. Because our soul is truth and freedom, we experience the joy of our soul when we forgive. We rise in consciousness. There is a state of harmony and peace through which the soul can shine.

OUR PURPOSE IN LIFE IS THE DUTY AND RESPONSIBILITY TO REFINE THE FORM

Everyone has the need to accomplish something because we do not feel good unless we do, and not feeling good, we have no feelings of self-worth. Unfortunately for so many, accomplishment depends on the judgments of the mind and these fluctuate and are not in harmony.

When we over-identify with struggles in life, we forget our purpose for being here. Our purpose is the duty and responsibility to refine the form in which our spirit is passing through. We must change the form that it may evolve. We begin with our children—the thought forms, the judgments we serve. We can always tell which children are unruly and which judgments are constructive in this world of creation that we are serving. If they are no longer serving us, get rid of them. Forms are designed to serve a specific purpose at certain times. To hold onto judgments that are not serving us is to serve the past.

If you are not happy, make a list of why you are not happy. Study the list for a period of 72 hours, and then say to yourself, *This is too big a family to be feeding. Which of these kids can I do without?* Be honest! Then trim down the list to all the judgments that you honestly feel keeps you from being happy. When you do not work on the judgment forms, the judgments become stronger than the light of reason in your consciousness. The more you feed your mind with your judgments, the more you carve into your energy supply.

WHEN FACING IMPORTANT DECISIONS

Whenever we are facing an important decision in our life weigh it carefully, in prayer, in acceptance, for a minimum of 72 hours. To weigh something in consciousness for 72 hours is not to think about it now and then, it is a 72-hour process of facing objectively the various levels of consciousness. So often in making important decisions in our evolution, we make them in the errors of ignorance. We make them from levels of consciousness that dictate to us, which deceive us.

CENSORING HOW WE CAN FEEL GOOD

The good in life is always present but it depends on what we do with it. If the personality laps the good up, then no good is left in it. Feeling good is being in God, but our minds make the judgment about what makes us feel good. We do not have to censor how we can feel good. The judgment is the delusion, the payment. To feel good, many people depend on someone else because they have established that law in their own head — their mind depends on another mind. If we try to please people, we will always be frustrated because their judgments change so frequently. We become victim of the game. Remember, we cannot recognize another person's level if we do not know what level we are on.

Our "specialness" or uniqueness is contained in our particular brand of judgments. Why does one hold on to the judgments? We think that we lose self-importance when we no longer believe we are unique. So the more judgments we cherish, the more inclined we are to feel unique. It is quite evident then the way we allow ourselves to feel good is very expensive. If we make a judgment that we feel good by doing such and such, then each time we do what the judge tells us, then "he" lets us feel good. But "his" army grows and "he" tells us that we need to feel good more frequently. After awhile we may experience that it does not feel good because another judge got in and is furious. Do not limit yourself to only feeling good in certain ways for there is no freedom in that kind of thinking. Experience the joy in life by not allowing judgments to dictate how goodness will come into your life.

MUSIC AND HUMOR

Some day we must deal with our judgments moment-by-moment if we are to be free and experience the peace that is our divine right. Until that day, music helps to lift the conscious-ness. It drowns out the judgments playing in our head and helps us to deal with them selectively. The spirit teachers particularly recommend good classical music. Because of its variety and har-mony with the universe, one is less likely to become bored in listening to it. Humor is also very important, that is, when you laugh at yourself, not others. God gets in and the judgment goes.

USING JUDGMENT POSITIVELY

Thus far, in presenting this game of *Playing the Judge*, we have addressed judgment primarily from the falsity of the thought process. We now turn our attention briefly to its posi-tive side—the truth, or judging righteous judgments. We are in no way precluded from making a critical or discerning assess-ment of our relationships or the things we would or would not like to participate in, so that we might decide what is in the best interest of our soul's growth. We have a right to dislike the be-havior of the personality of another person without disliking the person. We love the soul of another in spite of what that person may be thinking or doing. Using that as our criterion, we decide whether an association or endeavor will be beneficial to us or to our dependent loved ones.

When we can honestly realize that each person is reacting to a plane or level of consciousness that he or she is on—be-cause that is what it all amounts to—then we are not being judg-mental. You are neither condoning or condemning another. You are accepting that person for where he or she is in conscious-ness. Socrates said, "If you would teach the people to act rightly, teach them to form correct judgments." Right judgment teaches to divide the true Self from the little self. The wisdom of God guides us to seek first the real Self or the Christ Spirit in every person, to hold that ever in mind. Then we are not surprised, or pained, or disappointed in the performance of the personal-ity. We neither criticize unjustly nor condemn. We see no per-sonality as wholly bad. *"Our judgment is just, and the false is un-*

covered but for the sole purpose of causing it to disappear under the healing influences of the Sun of Truth."

If we can be the instrument to help raise a person's level, fine. But, remember, *"unsolicited help is ever to no avail."* Jesus admonished us not to *"cast our pearls before the swine"* for in casting our pearls, we are feeding the glory of another person's personality and draining our own energy if that person is not ready to receive.

It would be a very sad world indeed if we could not say when things were wrong. We would simply shut our eyes and would never improve. So use spiritual discernment and understanding to see clearly and "judge righteous judgments."

SEPARATE TRUTH FROM CREATION

All we have to do is introduce a change into a person's mind after he or she has made a judgment, and we will quickly see how spiritually that person has grown. It is very difficult to accept change because of our need to possess. We make a judgment. We believe we are the judgment, or the judgment is us, and because we believe it is us, it controls us. We are trapped in the mental realms. This is why it is so important to separate truth from the creations of the mind.

By facing and separating truth from creation, we free ourselves. When the thought rises, put God there. *"O God, help me through this crazy creation. I am not creation. I am the mover of creation."* We have the power. Why take so long to declare our divine right to its use? Why do we want to continue believing our judgment when we know we are not it? It is because we are out of balance with the level of self-preservation. Delusion and preservation insist we are the judgment. It is in our belief that we suffer. Through belief self-preservation is triggered. It is a very hard step to withdraw from the crazy belief that we are the thing. The step to freedom is to talk to the mind. If we are unwilling to talk, it demonstrates we believe we are the judgments. We must remind ourselves how much we paid the last time around. We cannot afford to continue making payments. It is self-destructive. The forms bow when we stop believing we are them. *Just a minute, you are not me.* We must start talking to creation and stop believing we are creation. We get emotional because we have made a judgment and when it is exposed, a part of us dies —the delusion that we are the judgment.

BREAKING THE BACK OF JUDGMENT

One makes a judgment and the personality works overtime to support it and prove that it is right. The sadness is that one is not always aware of it and becomes the victim. You will go further spiritually with twenty minutes free from judgment on this side of life than with twenty years on the spirit side of life staying in the wrong level.

The most effective way to begin to break down judgments is to work first on the small ones and chip away at the mountain of obstruction. Work at the little ones. Do not try to tackle more than you are capable of doing at any moment, and do not judge how you are doing for that only builds another mountain before you. You can be free when you are ready to take the step. Therefore, when you have something to do, do it quickly. Every time you are granted the opportunity to change and you take the step in the spirit of spontaneity, you break the back of a judgment.

You do not have to wait until you are beaten down to give up the king of kings (judgments) and accept something greater. You cannot take another step spiritually or mentally until you bow your judgments. First become aware of the judgments you are making. Spontaneous or split second changes help you to evolve. Change is the Law of Evolution of consciousness, and if you do not make the changes harmoniously, then you have an uphill struggle.

REMOVING JUDGMENT THROUGH FORGIVENESS

"Accuser, you are the accused. Forgiver, you are the forgiven."

Another way of dealing with a judgment in order to receive from God is to forgive it. Once a judgment is made, it is solidified and cannot be changed in the memory par excellence where everything is permanently recorded, but you can change your thinking to balance it. To "remove" the emotion, pain, or feeling of unfairness of anything from the human mind it is necessary to give it forth, or to forgive it. To give forth or to forgive, you must accept something to whom you can give it. First, you must accept an authority greater than your mind or personality, to whom you may give these things of the mind. That authority must be so deeply registered within your consciousness that your faith guarantees that it shall not return unto you.

To free oneself, a person forgives a judgment he or she makes by communicating, discussing, exposing, and giving forth that part of self that has put the person into bondage. The forces of darkness know that without communication they can control. The forces of darkness prevent expression. What happens in exposure that frees the soul from judgment? Exposure brings about communication and confession.

If you choose not to forgive, you carry the emotional baggage. There is a saying, *"Put God in it or forget it."* It is better to forget it if God is not in it because of what judgment has to offer. The only thing judgment offers is suffering and a breakdown of health. The more judgments, the greater the discord in consciousness. *"It is human to forgive; divine to forget."*

Be constantly aware of where you are and how you feel. In praying outside, you are asking someone outside to free you. Instead, go within to pray. *"God, help me to bow in humility that I may see the truth revealed in my thoughts and acts. Amen, Amen, Amen."*

Let us no longer separate ourselves from the abundant good that is our home and our birthright. Let us broaden our acceptance and free ourselves from the errors of the past for this is a new moment, but it is only new to those who let the past go. We can do nothing about that which is past, but we can do everything about that which is in the present.

By way of summary: Judgment is based upon past experiences—not on that which is, nor on the possibility of what is to be. Being based only on that which is past is death itself. Judgment is a dead form. The only light it has is the Light we give to it by directing energy to it through the Law of Attention; otherwise, it is dead and gone.

> *"Judgment is entertaining the very thing*
> *that we fear and know it not."*

The only way suffering and struggle exist is by making judgments. It is not possible to be denied the abundant goodness of life except through judgment. With-out judgments, hell does not exist for hell is totally dependent upon judgment. A person who is already free is without judgment.

Are we becoming aware when we hold tenaciously to our different judgments? Are we making the effort to be aware, one, that it is a judgment; two, that it is our judgment; three, that we caused it; and four, that it is in our best interest to change it?

> *"When our love of God is greater than the love of our judgments, we will leave the glory train of self and enter the paradise of peace."*

Flood your consciousness with the *Tree Saying*: *"I'm only a witness of time passing on . . ."* If you are a witness, you cannot have judgments.

*　　*　　*

Affirm:

I am not the thought.
I am the mover of the thought.
I am not this feeling.
I am experiencing this thought **only** *because*
I believe I am the judgment in my mind.

68

Game 5

The Fear Trap

Key Players:

Sense Functions:
Concern, Fear, Doubt, Judgment,
Pride, Question, Stubbornness

Counterbalancing Soul Faculties:
Faith, Personal Responsibility,
Understanding

How the Game is Played:

The Fear Trap is played when the personality uses fear
as a way of exercising control over the soul. Faith is then
expressed negatively.

HOW FEAR EXPRESSES ITSELF

"Fear is the revelation of faith in the judgment of the human ego."

Fear is an expression we all have when we place the great power of faith in the judgment of our personality. Instead of moving freely in life, we are guided and controlled by fear because we have relied upon our thoughts, upon our mental zone and sphere of action. The prompting of the soul goes unheard since *"the ears of the personality hear not because the door is locked with the key of fear."* Fear is the ruler of hell. There is one Divine, Intelligent, Neutral Energy, an odic power, and through our choice we direct this energy either into a constructive way into faith, or into a destructive way into fear.

When we express fear, a multitude of experiences that are in our inner mind from very early childhood well up within us. As a child we did not have the conscious understanding of how to handle judgment and pride. Our past judgments and pride now take over. Every word or thought in the human mind is an image. When we identify with our personality, we are controlled by those images and we do everything we can to preserve those images no matter whether they serve us in the present or not.

Whoever has a great deal of either judgment or pride knows great fear. Fear is simply a device to defend and protect the judgments it has already made. When we fear, our judgments are in control. Fear causes prejudices and discrimination. Some one different is a threat. Fear drives them out. Fear is a part of our own defense not to look at things. Stubbornness is a defense mechanism of what we fear. Concern is born on the throne of fear for the King of Fear rules our mind. The degree of fear is dependent upon the degree of our reliance on our mind. The mind is a tool, not a master. The tool uses the weapon of fear which keeps us from freeing ourselves. That is why if God or goodness is in every thought, there is no fear and there is no reliance on mental substance, but that takes an act of faith. *"Fear protects but faith sustains." "Fear is the brain's control of the soul; faith is the beauty of the soul's expression."*

GIVING POWER TO FEAR

As Gary Zukav explains, "there is no power in fear, or in any of the activities that are generated by fear. There is no power in a thought form of fear," even if it is supported by armies of thought forms. God is the true and only source of our power, not the thought forms created by the mind.

Reason and common sense dictate that we be realistic and take precautions to avoid situations that expose us to known dangers and probable losses. At the same time, however, knowing the law that energy follows attention, do not dwell upon fear of something terrible happening to you. Whenever we express fear, we are giving our divine birthright to the thing that we fear. The more we entertain the thought, the greater is our experience of fear. We have in the very thought denied our divinity, and we have given our life-giving power to a thought form. We do it all the time. That is what fear does to us. That which troubles us, controls us. We are controlled by the thing that we fear, and in time, we bring that fear into manifestation.

What did Job mean when he said, *"The thing I fear the most has befallen me?"* Is that not the living demonstration that we have had in our lives so far? All we have to do is flood our mind with fear of anything and we can rest assured it will knock at our door. It will knock because it does know who its parent really is. The chicken comes home to roost. With this awareness, let us truly accept that everything takes place inside.

Superstition is the child of fear and ignorance. This is a magnetic force. It is what the practice of voodoo works on. When fear is triggered, that is what destroys us.

Fear is also a magnet, pulling in support for the lack and limitation levels within us. Expressing gratitude for what you have assures the continuity of your supply. Do not take for granted what you have and you will not fear the loss of it.

If you make the judgment that your desire will not be fulfilled, you experience fear. When you overcome the fear of losing, you will gain the goodness of life. *"If your priority for desire is never higher than your priority for God, your desire will always be fulfilled.*" Only the mind creates the obstruction to fulfillment of our desires—not someone else's mind, not someone else's circumstances. It is only our mind that is the obstruction. It does not have to be that way. When your mind is in full control and you are experiencing all that fear has to offer, you have in that moment the golden opportunity to exercise your divine right to choose what you will give your power to.

Whenever you start to experience the feelings you recognize as fear, at that moment, declare the truth, *"Whatever I give thought to, I give power to."* So often we allow fear to rob us of our peace and our joy. We give away our peace and joy until the day comes when we become so discouraged and fearful that we wonder if it is worth being here, or why make the effort?

As we are the creators of our fear, being the creators of a thing, we are greater than the thing. Of course, that deals with the Law of Personal Responsibility, the ability to respond to our creation instead of giving power to things outside ourselves. It is fear, the mind's control over the eternal you, that is the prison in which you live. Remove fear by giving each thought, each emotion, each experience to God.

By knowing ourselves, we can control our own thoughts by our will and keep ourselves from being the victim of our own self-triggered thought. This is why the Bible teaches *"O man know thyself,"* because then we are aware of all the things within us, and this is our self-protection. We cannot make daily effort to know ourselves without that effort returning to us someday. If we do not make the daily effort, it reveals there is no unity within. That means there is no communication between the levels of consciousness within.

THE FEAR DELUSION

Nothing in any universe is beyond our potential when we free ourselves from fear. The greatest delusion created by that force of fear is to convince us that we do not have fear in the very areas of life where the force of fear is the strongest. We know what happens when we feel smug and content about anything that our mind judges we have accomplished. We quickly find that it fizzles like Alka Seltzer.

QUESTION, DOUBT, AND FEAR SERVE THE REALMS OF DARKNESS

"Believe and receive. Doubt and do without." Believe in your right to the goodness of life. If you believe in judgment more than desire, it stands in the way of fulfilling desire. The person that is standing in the way is the one that you have created in your head and that is what brings the experience. The mind offers doubt and fear. To rely upon the mind is to live a life of deprivation.

If you question, you doubt. If you doubt, you fear. Question, doubt, and fear are a triune sense function. There is no way of serving the realms of darkness without this function operating. Does your mind say, *I accept something to work out a certain way,* or do you say, *I accept God's way?* Which is winning out, the functions of question, doubt, and fear, or Acceptance, the Will of God? The function of the mind is to gather and garner and to act upon what it knows. The human mind is not what you evolve through. Therefore, you must spend some time each day out of identification with the self in order to evolve through the soul. *Become a conquering soul!*

When you are inspired, make your decision in a matter of split seconds before the mind gets a hold of it and have the strength and determination to follow it through. That takes the faculty of character, and you will never do without. Be prepared, for taking a stand will go against a multitude of created forms, which only reveals where your reliance is. So, with each new thing or situation, you must immediately go to work to establish a spiritual law, otherwise, the mind instanteously goes to work to question, doubt, and fear in order to offer a repetition of the past.

You doubt and fear what is to be—the unknown—or of reliving the past which is limit or bondage, closing you off from power. However, when you review consciously what you fear, it will weaken it and it will disappear. The mind uses only what is programmed into it. So take the experience of fear, help it rise up to the conscious level and shine the light of reason over it. In reviewing the experience in the light of reason, the thought form loses control over the soul.

FEAR RETARDS OUR GROWTH

What is so valuable about fear? Fear keeps us where we are. Faith puts us where we want to be. It is really that simple. We say, *I don't want to give up what I have to gain something I'm not sure of.* That is when faith must rise in consciousness. It is the fear which is negative faith that keeps us where we are.

The world is filled with all kinds of diseases, financial problems, violence, disasters and so forth. The earth realm is polluted with fear. However, the spirit teachers assure us a great change is coming in this New Age of Aquarius; that out of the mud of fear will bloom the lotus of heaven. That will take place for the whole world. But at our present level, whatever the disaster may be—a fire, a flood, an earthquake, an accident—it excites the senses until through our own efforts we evolve, slowly but surely, into other types of thinking and higher vibrations.

THE PERSONALITY'S NEED TO CONTROL

You cannot experience fear without first establishing the thought of self, for in the thought of self you have separated yourself from the Universal Divine Consciousness and then you are filled with thoughts of fear. To give up fear, you have to give up the thought of self. When God is "there" (in your consciousness), there can be no fear. You lose God by the judgments of your personality that stand between your eternal soul and God. In the moment of fear, God does not exist for the authority of your personality blocks Him out.

We fear the future because the personality cannot control the future. Because it does not know all, it cannot control laws beyond its own realm. There is always something the mind cannot know, thus the saying *"When of thy **mind** thou seekest the truth, on the wheels of delusion thou shalt traverse."*

Fear not, for fear moves us outwardly on the mental path. In a mental world, we fear what we cannot control. If we are identified with the mental realm, our first need is to control. We fear only what we know and cannot control, or what we do not know. We know our weaknesses and fear them because we know them and cannot control them. It is the fear of what our levels will do to us. For example, we may suppress outrage at a particular action taken against a co-worker for fear we may not be able to control our emotions, and that speaking out so vociferously would place our job in jeopardy. *"Fear is the instrument of self-preservation, but an open heart fears no one."*

That which we know and do not control, controls us, and then we search for power. It is the weak who search for power for they know they are controlled. *"While strength is control, weakness seeks control because it searches for power."* Weakness goes out into creation and gets weaker, more degenerate, enjoying the lower centers of consciousness. That is why fear is such a destructive force. It uses the avenues of money, personality, and sex. It is not money, personality recognition, or sex per se that we seek, but the power we think they bring to us. Also, we take pride in viewing what we have decided is weakness being expressed by another soul, for in viewing another's weakness, we build the image of our own self-importance and superiority. In reveling in our glory, we guarantee the weakness we have viewed to befall us so that we may learn the folly of judgment.

FAITH AND UNDERSTANDING DISSIPATE FEAR

Fear is the foundation of the sense functions; **understanding** is the foundation of the soul faculties. **Faith** exists in the heart and fear in the mind. The force of fear is counterbalanced by the power of faith. *"Fools are the fathers of fear and courage the mothers of freedom."*

Fear is dependent upon the lack of understanding and that is why "in all your getting, get understanding." When understanding is gained, fear disappears. Therefore, we must make the effort to understand what it is that we fear. With understanding, which opens when we exercise self-control, the power of faith expresses. The teaching is, *"Faith as small as the grain of the mustard seed moves the mountain."* The only way we gain faith is through understanding. What understanding brings is an awareness of how The Divine truly works. When we see something work, we most certainly have faith in it. Emerson expressed it this way, *"All I have seen teaches me to trust the creator for all I have not seen."*

All your faith must be placed in God, and God alone. It will not do to have faith in the power of good, and at the same time, believe there is some power in so-called evil. *"Choose ye this day whom ye will serve." "Ye cannot serve two masters."*

If one says he or she has no faith, that person is mistaken. All have faith for faith is God. The only question, when seeking satisfaction, is *what have you put your faith in?* Our faith has been scattered and dissipated amongst a thousand false gods, and all that we have been putting into negativity and material things must be gathered and concentrated in the Infinite Intelligence.

If one's faith is in a power that is limited, then the life seems limited. Why place your faith in anything less than omnipotence? All that Truth teaches is to put your faith in the Supreme and not in anything or any power less. If you want to be free, you must enter truth. You cannot be free as long as you believe you are the form, for only the form fears. Only form seeks power. The formless are power and have no need to seek what they are, for their power just is.

How do we direct our energy so that we may experience greater faith? As explained in *"The Veil of Illusion, Delusion and Deception,"* we have to go to the subconscious mind and be objective with it for it is another part of ourselves. We must learn to talk to it as we would talk to a child, for this inner person that we all are, is very childlike. It has very sensitive, strong feelings and responds to love and consideration. It cannot be coerced into anything. It can only be guided through a feeling of indirection. Otherwise, this child inside us will retaliate and rebel or revolt against any suggestions that do not fit into its own programming. Work with it daily to gain self-control so that you may broaden your understanding and deepen your faith.

USING FEAR TO FREE SELF FROM FEAR

One way to free oneself from fear is by using fear. Fear puts you in the "fear trap" and fear can be used to take you out. *"That which begins in fear, dies in fear."* The fear of exposure helps one make changes. It is the fear that the image will be exposed. Two fears neutralize each other. An amount of energy equal to that poured into the first fear must be directed toward the new fear.

BE GUIDED BY THE LIGHT

When you have a decision to make, go in consciousness to perfect peace and the light of consideration will shine on the situation and reveal the truth. You can cross all bridges and stay in the light by never registering fear in your consciousness, no matter what the threat is.

"That that is yours only your fear will take away. And that that is not yours nothing you do can hold it."

Faith is the light that guides us to God because faith is the power of the soul over the force of the personality. When we choose not to allow fear to control us, our soul is expressing itself. We must then ask ourselves the question, *How often in my life is my soul expressing? How often am I truly free of fear?* Whatever is free is filled with the spirit of joy.

* * *

"Faith is the path that leads to God, fear the trap to hell."

*   *   *

Number 5 is the number of faith. The lesson to be learned on our planet is the lesson of faith. **Number 4** is foundation. **Number 1** is God. When our foundation is in God, we have faith. When we have faith in God 5 + 1, which is 6 and which is our heart, that is the only place where we can find God. If we want a foundation in God, we must have faith.

Number 9 is the number which man or humanity responds to. Those who will be "saved" include all of humanity—all of creation as God made us. We all have the right to make our spiritual progression as the doorway to reformation is never closed against any human soul here or hereafter.

*   *   *

Game 6

Bucking the Tides of Life

Key Players:

Sense Functions:
Blame, Deception, Delusion,
Discouragement, Excuses, Judgment,
Justification, Laziness, Need,
Ridicule, Self-Preservation

Counterbalancing Soul Faculties:
Acceptance, Application, Awareness,
Compassion, Continuity, Control, Courage,
Determination, Duty, Personal Responsibility,
Possibility, Reason, Repetition, Willingness

How the Game is Played:

In playing the game of *Bucking the Tides of Life*, the personality refuses to accept that change is an inevitable law of nature, and instead, clings to its patterns of yester-year to the extent that we are no longer consciously choosing our thoughts. We have become a prisoner of our personality.

As you study each of these games it will readily be apparent that the philosophy contained in each does not teach a passive attitude toward creation, rather, it teaches a harmonious understanding, and a movement through creation. Our difficulties begin when we forget that the mind that we have earned in evolution is in a continual process of change.

THOUGHT IS OUR VEHICLE OF EXPRESSION

Our **thought** in the earthly realm is the most important vehicle through which our eternal being is expressing. Our physical world is the effect of this mental vibration or thought. We would all like to believe that we are constantly *consciously* choosing our thoughts, but if we would pause and listen to them, we would quickly see *they are no longer what we are consciously choosing; they are what we have chosen in yesteryears.* We are controlled by the patterns of our mind, the ones that are the strongest. Those patterns of our mind have taken years to become firmly established within our consciousness. We cannot make a conscious choice as long as we believe the "have been's" are us. Thought was designed to serve a purpose, not sit in our universe and drain us.

BY DEFAULT WE SERVE THE SUBCONSCIOUS MIND

As we have stated elsewhere, *"When the tools no longer serve the worker, the worker begins to serve the tools."* When we no longer make the effort to choose what happens to us, we begin to serve the created tool known as the subconscious mind. With its compulsion, power, and control needs, the subconscious begins to dictate what our eternal soul must do. The mind is then deluded that it is making conscious choices, but if we are honest, we will clearly see the ever repeating patterns of yesterday. That is the revelation of how little effort is being made.

The sense functions of our being are expressed through our subconscious mind. Nothing gets into our subconscious until it has first gone through our conscious mind. Once having entered our subconscious mind and established itself firmly as a pattern or attitude, it is not easily nor readily changed if we do not make the effort each day to know ourselves; for we cannot change what we are not aware of. All changes that we experience without have first taken place within.

GROWTH, EXPANSION, AND EVOLUTION

We cannot have evolution or expansion of soul expression without discipline and growth of the personality. The soul is in a constant process of unfolding or revealing more and more of the beauty of its God-like qualities. However, the soul, in and of itself, is not where growth is taking place. *"Growth of the soul is revelation, not change in truth."* It is in the form or personality through which the soul is expressing that expansion and growth are really taking place. In reality, we cannot expand on Infinite Intelligence, but through self-discipline, we can expand the vehicle through which the Infinite Intelligence is expressing.

FREEDOM FROM JUDGMENT THROUGH ACCEPTANCE

Therefore, through **acceptance**, the immutable Law of Evolution—the continuity of change—which is the refining process of all form, we move with that law harmoniously, joyously, and experience the abundance and the good in our life that is truly our divine right. There is no intelligent power, God or otherwise, that dictates that what one shall have another shall not. Everything is possible to all people.

It is within our power to make whatever changes are necessary in this moment that we may be in the world of creation, that we may be with the things of creation, and never be a part of them. It behooves us to learn to separate truth from creation, to learn to awaken within ourselves to the infinite possibility of a greater life now and not sometime after we have left a physical body. Life does not become greater *then* unless we make it greater *now*. Do not look to so-called death as an open door to heaven, for heaven and hell are states of mind that we are in a constant process of growing toward. It is not some place that we are going to. We are in it now. When we lose a physical body there is no dramatic or drastic change that takes place automatically in our mind. Our mind takes us to a mental world, our spirit evolves us on to a spiritual world. We cannot experience spiritual worlds after we leave the physical body unless we make the effort to still our mind and experience those spiritual worlds in the here and the now—this moment. It all depends upon our willingness to accept the possibility of something greater despite what our judgments have dictated in the past.

"Be ever ready and willing to change." The reason we are not ready to change is because in our own mind we believe we are the judgment. We cannot make a change in a judgment until we stop believing we are the judgment, and we cannot stop believing that until we stop the love affair with self. The benefit of experience is that it teaches us to pause and think. *I've been through this before. Do I really want to repeat similar experiences?* Instead of continuing with old and worn patterns, pause in consciousness before you speak. It is the spoken word that establishes your law.

SUBSTITUTING THE TRUE FOR THE UNTRUE

What you consciously hold today sinks deep in the subconscious realm where lie false memories and habits of thinking; but persistent right believing will at last displace the old mind patterns and substitute the true for the untrue.

The renewing of our minds may be compared to the change which comes to those who have been journeying for months upon the sea, until their senses are charged with the motion of the ship. It may be that for days after stepping on terra firma the land will seem to rock and roll; however, if they continually remember the truth concerning their environment and themselves, at last their consciousness will be normal, and they will be at rest.

THE WILLINGNESS TO SURRENDER OLD PATTERNS

Everything takes place in consciousness where we have the wonderful opportunity to make changes. How do we change our patterns of thought? How do we then free ourselves from all of the dictates and all of the judgments of yesteryear? It is when we think of ourselves that we become the victims of past experience. It is when we think of self, the throne of judgment, with all of its negative effects, with all of its prejudices and discriminations, that the judgment rises and takes control. We cannot make changes until we first see what is happening in our own consciousness. We must be aware of how we perpetuate a pattern of an unpleasant experience. When we are so weary of an old pattern, a willingness arises to try something new. There is the caring enough to want to make the change, an acceptance of the possibility of something better, and also the commitment to make the necessary continuity of effort to cause a change in consciousness. *"The ability to make change in consciousness is dependent upon the willingness to surrender the magnetic field (or emotional body) to the light of reason which shines through the soul faculties and brings about transformation."*

USING IDENTIFICATION WITH SELF IN A POSITIVE WAY

If you set a new law into motion while in personality, you will only repeat old patterns in a new garment. If you truly want to be free from those chains that bind you to yesterday; if you want to be free so that you may have a more abundant, happier, and more joyful experience today, then free yourself from self, from your personality. The tenacity of the personality to hold on to its patterns, even when those patterns of mind are detrimental, is demonstrable. However, tenacity can serve a very good purpose when directed in a positive way.

What happens when you say, *God, I have had enough?* You then harbor and feed a new form, and, therefore, you have new experiences. Remember, the old forms scream for energy the minute you think of self. The identification with self helps the forms to garner and gather new substance. You have armies to battle the minute you think of self. The entities of darkness emphasize the weakness of the person who created them. They look like caricatures of the creator. Entities of light emphasize the strength of the creator.

THE PERSONALITY'S NEED FOR PERFECTION AND TO MANIPULATE

The greater our belief in our perfection, the greater our struggle to make changes because our perfection image is threatened when trying to make changes. Why do we need to believe we are perfect? We do not *consciously* believe we are perfect because the faculty of reason is available to the conscious mind. So what inside has the need to subconsciously believe we are perfect? Why do we need to pay such a price for judgments? It is delusion. We are not honest because we do not want to face the fact we just might not be perfect.

To have need we must first judge what perfection is. What does perfection offer us? Superiority. Whoever is perfect (without fault) has no need to change and, therefore, all the experiences in one's life are the fault of other people. There is no need to change if you have "arrived." We pay a heavy price for believing we are perfect. When we project outward, exclaiming that everybody outside ourselves is causing us misery for lack of fulfillment of our desire, that is the epitome of laziness. As long as we insist upon our great need to believe that we are perfect, the goodness cannot come to us. We can manipulate others by appealing to their perfection. We can only manipulate others while our perfection is in full bloom, then in time the petals fall. We pay a horrible price for manipulating others.

RIDICULE REVEALS FRUSTRATION AND FEAR

Frustration and fear may rise as we face the inevitable possibility of change. We resist by ignoring, ridiculing, and fighting it. And what is ridicule? *"Ridicule is an uncontrollable expression of the human mind trying to support the weak position it holds in its valued judgments, revealing to the world the depth of one's ignorance."*

DEMONSTRATING PERSONAL RESPONSIBILITY

The most important pattern to change is the blaming outside. Let us not give this great power of The Divine to things outside ourselves. Let us not look outside for the cause of our happiness, goodness, and abundance, for it does not exist outside of us until it first exists inside of us. Whatever we are seeking in life, if we have not yet found it inside, we cannot find it outside. How do we find what we are seeking inside? We find that by first accepting the demonstrable Law of Personal Responsibility—that we alone have the ability to respond to all things within our own being, within our own sphere of action. We must learn to direct our attention inside for change that we may free ourselves from the delusion that changes must be made outside by other people, places, and things.

Souls who have evolved in consciousness, and have steppped upon the path of spiritual freedom are, in truth, well aware of the need of change in the personality through which their eternal soul is expressing. They are aware of the need for change within themselves when they enter certain schools of spiritual thought and consideration. Unless they accept wholly and completely the divine, eternal truth that they alone are responsible for their acts and activities and that all experience is taking place within the consciousness, the personality will continue to make demands and dictates that changes be made outside. However, the soul knows the changes necessary are inside. When those changes are made inside, they will view a different world outside.

WHY DO WE BATTLE THE INEVITABLE LAW OF CHANGE?

The cry of John the Baptist was *"Repent ye! Repent ye!"* In other words, make changes in consciousness concerning the realities of life and seek the things of the spirit.

We change and die in many ways, sometimes slowly and painfully, sometimes quickly. We must ask why we battle the inevitable Law of Change, from which nothing in form escapes. Every moment changes are taking place in our mind and body. All of nature reveals that nothing stays the same. The only exception is truth. Unlike us, nature returns to the source what it has taken from the source. When we reject change we are holding on to "have been's," and because we have not surrendered them, we lose, and are in need, want, and unfulfilled desire.

'The tendency of the personality is to hold on because of the unwillingness to grow inside. Let us heed the demonstration of nature's laws and not attempt to hold to our thoughts, for in so doing, we are bucking the tides of life, so-to-speak. Bucking the tides of life is a deception to cover up that which is natural, that which belongs to The Divine. Often we oppose change when we are not ready. The law is working but we try to buck it because we are not ready to accept it. If the law hits us without our being ready, we can always turn to God. *God, help me to perceive the law. I'm not ready for the change but help me to perceive it and make the change.* Change is evolution. In spite of ourselves we grow, but we cannot experience freedom if we insist upon our attachment to our fruits of action.

TAKING CHARGE OF OUR MIND

Being in charge of our mind is a great responsibility for we must be on guard always, monitoring, directing, and talking to it. Our minds are not accustomed to being directed. We have spent lifetimes in the lap of license, doing as we pleased. Like a tape recorder, our minds have been playing on automatic reverse, taking us right down the river of past experience, rather than up the stream of life to new experiences of our conscious choice. When we begin to realize how little control we have over our thinking, and how much of our thinking is automatic, we will begin to make more effort to take over the controls, and exercise our divine birthright of being directors of our destiny by staying in the eternal moment of now. *"God, I declare the eternal truth. In this moment over which I have control, let me experience peace, joy, and freedom."*

If we want to get a new car, go on a journey, or fulfill another desire of our mind, and we are thinking of ourselves, then all of the limitations, judgments, prejudices, and denials rise and take control of our thought, our act, and our activity. To begin any endeavor in life with the thought of self is to guarantee the continuity of yesterday's experiences. So if we are in a business or profession and choose to make a change, we will only repeat past experiences if we are in personality when we make the decision. Oh, they will take a different form. We will meet different people. We will have what appears to be different experiences, but when we look with the light of reason and common sense, we will see, though the people are new, though the experiences appear to be new, it is the same old thing all over again.

We do not need to be psychic—all we need is to pause and think, and if we pause and think, we will observe. If we observe objectively, we will know what is going to happen for we will see the inevitable demonstrable laws of life working constantly. Energy follows attention. You cannot head toward San Jose and expect to wind up in Ukiah.

MAKING CHANGES THROUGH REPETITION, EFFORT, AND COURAGE

Repetition is not change, but it is the law or faculty through which change is made possible. By constant repetition, continuity of effort, and the courage to face the established thought forms, in time change does take place. It requires that the energy put into forming the new pattern be at least equal to or more than the old pattern so that the old one will no longer be in control. When we attempt change, justifications rise to encourage us to hold on to the old way. We are never left without the power or courage to make changes. However, if we are unable to exercise our right to express courage by moving on, discouragement will keep us from making the effort. *"Discouragement is a fool's paradise."*

It is not what we must put into the mind that awakens us; it is what we must change that is already there, and that is not easily done. Our subconscious mind is a cloud that lies in front of our conscious awareness and our true being. It takes effort and it is so difficult for us to break the patterns that we have placed ourselves in. So often in life we just do things without conscious thought. However, we must understand habit was a conscious cause. Never was it a subconscious cause. We set ourselves up to have many experiences in life. We often term those experiences as discordant or diseased, not in harmony, or not fulfilling. It is through constant repetition of the new pattern that eventually only a wisp of the old thought is left—only a flicker crosses the mind. When we make a change, all things around us change.

WHAT HAPPENS WHEN WE TRY TO CHANGE?

The expansion and contraction principle comes into play when we try to change. For example, as we direct more energy to a particular desire that we may be entertaining, the form of that desire grows ever larger. The other forms that we have created begin to shrink, so-to-speak. To introduce a new idea into the human mind takes a great deal of repetition to get it introduced in the first place, and secondly, to sustain it as a form that it may have life (though it cannot have life eternal for it is only created form).

When we make the effort to make changes in our life, it means that we are directing some energy to the new form of our choice, and in so doing, the forms of our mind already created and literally feeding off our energy become very upset. As we direct energy to this new form of our acceptance, that means less energy that we are directing to the old forms. This is why it is so very difficult for anyone who is overbalanced in self or personality to make any changes.

We are personally responsible for all the forms we have created. The awakening within to the light of reason will free us from reliance upon creation. But when we put our reliance in self-preservation, and not in the light of reason, the thought forms will scream in our head for attention. The discord resulting from their selfish, greedy desire to be fed stems from the control by the Law of Self-Preservation. We should not be discouraged for change is in process. Change is inevitable because change is the Law of Evolution and that law is superior to any other created law.

These forms will respond to the soul faculties of compassion, reason, and duty. Show compassion for their trauma, cast the light of reason over the forms to educate them, and put duty to the soul first, which balances self-preservation and places changes in the proper perspective.

THE "SPOILED BRAT LEVEL"

Whoever in the light of reason makes changes instantly is freed from the darkness of his or her own subconscious mind. Those who refuse to make changes are in those moments controlled by a child who must have his or her own way. It is the "spoiled brat level." Each thought is a form, so take control and cast the light of reason when you cannot have your own way. Do not blame others for the way you feel for those forms from realms below will take you out of the Light under the guise that the cause is outside. Make the changes inside. It is known as growing up.

Whenever we permit our mind to find security in form, to whatever degree, we experience trauma when we wake up to the change. Do we graciously make changes, or do we stubbornly resist change? Are we filled with trauma and resentment? It is in movement that we grow and expand. All things must move, whether they move ever onward and upward in a greater fullness of life experiences, or they move in the decaying processes of the return to their origin. All things return. As we willingly accept the new, the painful experience of returning to the original sources is no longer experienced by our mind. What is going from us is destined by the law to do so. Let it go graciously and freely. It is the uneducated ego that resents change and is the greatest stumbling block in our path to spiritual attainment.

Hold not to form, for form shall pass. Hold not to thought, for thought is passing, hold not to things, for things are passing. It means a control of identity that there may be a flexibility in our life, that we may enjoy life for life is intended by its very design to be enjoyed. And think, if we only held on to the things that we now have, surely we would soon be bored, and life would lose its spirit of joy. Our *joy* in life is dependent upon how *graciously* we accept change. The wise do not *sit* on top of the world, they *stand* so they can move as it turns.

"The key of wisdom to the door of freedom is the ability, the willingness, and the joy of change."

WE CHOOSE THE WAY WE MAKE OUR LIFE

If you are not pleased with what you experience, there is an intelligent energy that will sustain and support your right of choice. Once you make that choice to change your life for the better, remember, it is the same Intelligent Energy that supported the levels of consciousness you had before you made the change. It is up to us to choose in life how we wish our life to be. We cannot intelligently choose how we wish our life to be unless we know the laws that govern our life. The very simple law clearly demonstrated is, *"Life shall ever be the way you take it, for life is always the way we make it."* We can make our life whatever way we want it to be, for we have already made our life the way it is to this moment.

EXCUSE AND RESIGNATION

Unlike excuse, application is a soul faculty. Excuse, a sense function, is the brain's justification to guarantee the continuity of its pattern. Stop the excuses that only reveal change is not a priority. We only deceive ourselves to think otherwise. We must not throw personal responsibility down the drain. We are never left without choice. *"Resignation to circumstances"* is a banner the Queen of Justifications wears to signify the con game not to make any changes.

ONLY OUR IDENTITY CHANGES

Let the change be joyous, for no matter what we do we cannot stop evolution. We cannot stop changing. If you are weary of change, the Law of Evolution, then you must make the effort to go beyond it; for it is only the forms that change. The true being, the essence, the principle which you truly are, does not change; for it is above and beyond creation and, therefore, evolution. The Divine Spirit through which the soul expresses never changes. Your identity changes because identity is form. All things that are form, being all thoughts, change.

So the mind asks, *Who am I? What am I? Where am I? Where have I been, and where am I going?* You have been many, many things. Where are you going? You are going onward, and onward, and onward, awakening every step of the way that you may finally accept you are not the form, you are not the thought. You are that great essence that moves it all. When that is fully awakened, you will sail on a sea of harmony and peace. You will still be in the world, but no longer a part of it.

We must decide for ourselves—there is something better than what we have already experienced. Animals *are controlled* by established patterns. Mankind *has control* by establishing new patterns and, therefore, new experiences. Experiences tell us loud and clear what changes have to be made.

DIFFICULT LESSONS ARE BLESSINGS

It is the difficult lessons that offer us the greatest possibility for growth and freedom. *"O God, I am grateful for all life's experiences, especially the difficult ones, for I know in truth they are my greatest blessings."* The things we fight the hardest are our victories in life no matter how hard our minds fight against change. Bless the heartaches, hardships, pains, and inner emotion for the lessons they bring and let them pass. The path cannot always be easy. We grow only in struggles and challenges; then the dormant, latent power can rise and be expressed.

WHY THE SECOND TIME IS MORE DIFFICULT

If you have tried to change and have failed, it is more difficult to succeed the second time you try because you have weakened your control over the thought forms by giving-in to their demands on the first try. Though we stumble many times, there is something within us that always picks us up. All minds remember what they choose to remember, so why not remember the good in your life. To entertain your mind with thoughts of the bad is to create a continuous wheel of experiences so that your mind may prove that it is right. It calls for application of determination, hope, and especially, encouragement.

MOVING THOUGHT ON A VERTICAL LINE VIA THE HEART

It is the outward direction, the horizontal and parallel law that binds us to the wheel of experience. It is the *outward* Law of Continuity that keeps us upon the wheel. It is the *upward* Law of Continuity that helps us to view and to rise to the paradise that is our true home. When we entertain a thought, it moves on a horizontal line out into an atmosphere of vibratory waves. It is an energy and it calls forth all similar energies in the universes. When we take that thought and direct it upward into a vertical path, it returns to the divine source and there it is harmonized for our greater good by an intelligence that sustains all. In other words, we lift our thought by placing peace, God—the Intelligence of the Whole—in it. It then moves upon the vertical line from our energy field where it is harmonized and neutralized to uplift us. One is known as the Divine Will; the other, the horizontal path, the will of experience, self-will, or the will of our limited mind.

You cannot change the mind by working with the mind. The change takes place in your heart. It is your heart, the vehicle of your eternal soul, which lifts your soul above and beyond those mental and astral dimensions. It is through your heart that you are healed; it is through your heart that you are freed; it is never through your head.

PARTING THOUGHTS

See your true purpose in life. Remember that change is the eternal Law of Progression, but it is a change inside. Be ever ready and willing to change so that you will know the joy of change. Broaden your horizons. Come out of your tunnel vision and put things in proper prospective; then you can observe creation with all of its variety without being affected by it, and you will be free. You will become aware of the change even though another person may not have noticed it. Also in your observations, remember, you cannot change another; you can only change your attitude toward another.

"One who accepts the impossibility of change is governed and controlled by one's own mental law, but one who accepts the possibility of change is freed by the will of the Divine."

Game 7

The Destiny of Denial

Key Players:

Sense Functions:
Adversity, Blame, Denial, Fear,
Judgment, Need, Self-Will

Counterbalancing Soul Faculties:
Acceptance, Discipline, Faith, Honesty,
Personal Responsibility, Surrender,
Tolerance

How the Game is Played:

The game of *The Destiny of Denial* is played not only when we make judgments denying God or the goodness in life, but when we deny the rights of all things and all levels of consciousness, forgetting that God, a neutral power, sustains everything and rejects nothing. Our denials then become our destiny.

LIFE IS THE EFFECT OF THOUGHT

All of life is the effect of the release of energy on one of our many levels of consciousness. Therefore, experiences vary in keeping with our willingness to accept the goodness in life. This raises certain questions: *What is it that we accept and what is it that we reject or deny? How are our decisions reached?* We have free will. We have the right to accept a certain experience or thought and we also have the right to reject it. Whenever we reject a thought in our minds, what we are in truth doing is accepting an alternate thought. So, when experiencing a problem, a wise person looks at the struggle and asks himself or herself this question, *Am I accepting the right of this expression, and in so doing, moving on to something better? Or, am I denying this experience, the effect of my own thought?* We cannot deal with something that we deny. We have to face it, otherwise, we become the victim and the slave of it. It only comes back to the very foundation of personal responsibility.

"He who accepts with a joyous heart the lessons that life has to offer, is freed from chasing the shadows of creation."

When we accept that our life is an effect and we are the cause, then we accept the right of all experience. To accept requires honesty and willingness to say, *Okay, I and I alone set the law into motion to experience what I am now experiencing.* And once having accepted its return, we flood our consciousness with that which we have chosen to **become.** Place your attention, the door through which the intelligent energy flows, on what you have chosen and want to become. As energy follows attention, remove your attention from what you choose to overcome. Otherwise, you will continue to experience in keeping with your denials; for it is your denials that become your destiny. You will be destined to a constant repetition of certain experiences that you have judged are distasteful to you. Thus, you are personally responsible for how you choose to lose. In time the judgments must bow to divine right for it is the exclusive right of The Divine to sustain all the levels of consciousness within each of us. *"Man's judgments are denials of God's rights."*

Accept the demonstrable truth that it is our thoughts, and our thoughts alone, that bring to us the health, the wealth, and the happiness that are our divine right—divine right meaning the right God has granted us. We are the ones that create our thought. Our thoughts create our thought patterns. Our thought patterns become our attitude of mind. Our attitude of mind establishes the law that brings our experiences to us.

HOW DO OUR DENIALS BECOME OUR DESTINY?

When we deny God, we deny goodness, and, of course, it is our denials in life that become our destiny. It is not what we accept that binds us, but what we deny, for that creates another form. If we want to know where we are going, all we have to do is take stock of our denials and we will see the road map of where we are headed, for truly our denials are our destiny.

How do our denials become our destiny? To be adverse to anything means to reject. We reject but God sustains everything and rejects nothing. So when we reject, we become controlled by the mental world. And in so doing, we must follow the path of our rejection, the path of our denials, so that we may gain through that process, an understanding of something greater than the human mind. That something greater is the power which sustain us called Infinite Intelligence.

We look about from a very narrow view so often and suffer the consequences of our intolerances. *"God, I know there is something better. Help me to find it. Show me what is in my heart."*

It is a desire of all minds that are not secure, to have everyone do things and act in ways that they have accepted for themselves. When we experience people who do not do things and act the way we have accepted for ourselves, we find intolerance welling up in our emotions. We feel rejected but we must accept that we are the ones who have set the Law of Rejection and Denial into motion.

Remember, what we do not tolerate in life, tolerates us by controlling us. The person we cannot tolerate is not suffering because of our thought. We are the ones that have the problem and have become the victim of our own intolerance.

DIVINE WILL VERSUS HUMAN WILL

All of the goodness, all of the joy of life is already ours, waiting to come into manifestation. The power that brings it to us is simply called acceptance, known also as the Divine Will. Acceptance, the Divine Will, does not imply some authority or some divinity outside ourselves that has decided or is deciding what is in our best interests. It is a state of consciousness within ourselves—the highest state of consciousness possible—where Divine Will manifests itself and knows beyond any doubt what is best for our own soul. Divine Will is free of judgment.

"One who views for a truth what one cannot stop, stops making the effort to do so." That process is known as acceptance. In the moment that we accept, we become the clear channel of Divine Will and we are freed from self-will which is based on fear. *"Faith gives poise to keep the ego still to express humility so it can willingly accept."*

By contrast, self-will, human will, is the direct effect of the limited acceptances and rejections of our own personality. We are controlled and governed by the accepted experiences of our past when we are in self-will. Our energy then goes to activate shadows of the past, and we are exhausted. When we bring the personality into a perfect harmony with the soul, which is what stillness really is, then we will see and know that it is only ourselves "standing in our own light."

ACCEPTING THE RIGHT OF ALL EXPRESSION

Acceptance is theDivine Will because God does not reject anything. *"Acceptance is the miracle of transformation."* It frees us from our limited mind that expresses judgment and intolerance. The Will of God is the total acceptance in consciousness of God's eternal, infinite right to all expression.

Without acceptance there is no experience and without experience there is no growth, no progression, no evolution. It is the divine purpose, plan, and will, that the soul encased in form be in a constant state of unfolding and evolving. We already have accepted the patterns, and attitudes of mind that we have, because we are the ones experiencing through those patterns and attitudes.

We must free ourselves from the illusion that we—the eternal part of us—are the experience. The experience contains within it the lessons that are necessary for the evolution and the freedom of our eternal being. However, we cannot see those lessons that are there for us if we do not accept the right of the experience to express. In other words, we cannot set a law into motion and then reject the effect of it without being a house divided. It is evident then, if we wish to change our experiences, we must accept them so that we may gain control over them and not have them control us. In short, whatever we accept in life, we free from controlling our life. Take for example, our judgments concerning too much rain or not enough rain. Because we do not accept the right of the rain or the right of its lack, we are affected by it. Whenever we flood our consciousness with the right of expression of all things in all universes, we free ourselves from being controlled by those things. That does not mean that we should do all things, but it does mean that we should not rise in our superiority over divine law and judge what is to be and what is not to be. *"O God, help me to consider and accept the divine right of all your expressions. Let me not judge their worth but strive to understand their true cause."*

We must accept personal responsibility, the ability to respond personally to what we have established so that we can free ourselves from the payment of the experience. In the moment of acceptance, the will of God flows through the consciousness. *"As freedom is in the moment of our acceptance, bondage is in the moment of our rejection."*

"O God, help me to look in the mirror of life, which comprises all my experiences, and honestly face myself. I do not appreciate this level. Because I do not appreciate it, I have denied its right of expression in consciousness. Help me to trace this lack of appreciation for this level of consciousness deep within myself to see what walls I have built around me, and once seeing those walls and the cause for erecting them, I shall

free myself and move on the river of consciousness back home to para-dise, to peace—no longer in the chains of bondage created by the im-balance of my own mind."

If we do not accept the right of all things and all levels of consciousness, we are going to guarantee all the experiences necessary to understand them. This is why the teaching, *"What today I criticize, tomorrow I shall idolize."* Express your divine right to identify with those thoughts of your choice, using the light of reason and common sense.

BEING THE VICTIM OF NEED AND FEAR

When we say that we **need** anything, we deny that we have it because we cannot need what we already have. There-fore, we must first deny in order to need. And what do we deny? We deny the great intelligent power called God that has given us everything. In an error in our thought we deny that we have this power in our life.

What we already have, we have first accepted in our mind and then it has entered our material, physical world. So, to say that we need anything is to deny that we have it—to deny that it is waiting to come into physical manifestation—and by deny-ing that we have it, we keep it from us. This is why we hear the cry of the constant need of money. We can rest assured that if we are not experiencing money's effects, we are denying it in our life. *"When you are in need, you are the victim of the feeling. When you are in acceptance, you are the master of the feeling."*

This is such an important teaching and lesson for all of us—to take stock of our thought, to see how we keep from us the good that we seek. To deny God as the true source of our supply is to separate, to be out of the stream of consciousness, out of the wholeness and the unity that is everywhere in all universes. We cannot deny until we entertain the thought of self, because God does not deny anyone—ever.

FAITH IS A DIVINE PRINCIPLE

As long as we permit our mind to blame anything or anyone outside, we will remain upon that destiny path of denial, judgment, need, and fear, and will suffer the consequence of our own errors. *"Fear is a total denial of God. Fear is a total denial of faith. Acceptance is the key. The thought of personality is the only obstruction. There is no other."*

Many people throughout the ages have struggled with faith, not seeming to understand that we all have an abundance of faith, because faith is an inherent quality of the soul. It is the direction in which we place our faith that creates our struggles. All too often we direct it to the function of fear. We are taught to fear not, for fear is the personality's control over the soul, whereas faith is the power of the soul over the force of the mind. *"A problem is nothing more than a lack of faith in the power of God."*

Faith is a divine principle. It is a complete conviction not only of the conscious mind, but of the subconscious. When the subconscious and the conscious minds are in total rapport and in harmony on anything, The Divine, moving through the superconscious within us, brings it into manifestation. Faith is the Light that guides us to God. It takes faith to let go—faith in an Infinite Intelligence that holds all stars in the universes. We do demonstrate faith that we shall breathe, and so we breathe. We do demonstrate faith in many things in this mundane world, and we experience those things. It is a matter of getting our fears and denials under control to demonstrate the faith and acceptance of God's will so that our divine right to goodness will flow at all times.

"I have unshakable faith in the perfect outcome of every situation in my life, for I know that God is always at the helm."

ARE THE TERMS FAITH AND BELIEF SYNONYMOUS?

Faith and belief are not synonymous for we can believe a thing and have no faith in it at all. How many things have you believed in life that did not work out? How many things have you had true faith in that did not work out?

Faith is a power, a power that moves any and all obstructions. Belief is a function of the mind. You may believe in something and it will disappoint you. When you have true faith, there is no disappointment. Faith is one; belief is dual.

BALANCING DENIAL WITH ACCEPTANCE

In acceptance there is freedom from fear, freedom from judgment, and freedom from denial. Because we create our denials, we can change our destinies. We must accept a higher authority than our mind, an authority to which we give things of the mind; but it must be so indelibly registered within our consciousness that our faith guarantees it will not return to us. Place your attention upon what you accept and your acceptance will be broadened. *"Recognition of God is acceptance of God; acceptance of God is the expression of God."*

As we broaden our acceptance, we will be freed from reliance upon limitation and form. Remember, acceptance is the will of God, denial, therefore, is the will of humankind. We are alone only in our denials, never in our acceptances. So we see clearly that the will of humankind and the will of The Divine must be brought into harmonious relationship through the Law of Balance. Then, "destiny at my command" will become a reality for us.

It is our denials that limit our opportunities. Each time we deny our right to goodness, we remove a golden opportunity that is waiting to knock at our door. Our denials do become our destinies. We have a multitude of paths but each denial shuts off a path until finally it may be narrowed to only one.

If we ask from a level of consciousness of acceptance of God, then we shall receive from God. But if we ask with preconceived thought, then we shall receive from the realm of preconceived thought, for Like Attracts Like and becomes the Law of Attachment. So when we speak our word forth, we must be aware from which level the word is being spoken. *"The demonstration is the revelation."*

The obstructions, and the only obstructions, to the possibility of something greater than what we have yet experienced, are the judgments that we alone make. We establish the Law of Judgment, the Law of Denial, and that becomes our destiny in life. The moment that we judge how we shall gain anything, we establish a mental law, and all mental laws are dual laws. They are not only positive but they are also negative—the waxing and waning of duality. If we do not attach to the high, we will never experience the low. We can rise above those mental realms of consciousness by giving up the judgments. When we are seeking something, if we will apply the divine Law of Total Acceptance, then we will not have to travel along the mental laws of creation and experience the loss and the gain. There is no loss and there is no gain to divine neutrality. There is no loss and there is no gain to the spirit. There is no loss and there is no gain to truth for in truth, there is no duality.

When we truly accept, we flow in the divine will and all obstructions in our path are met by the light of reason. It is the light of reason that frees us through our own efforts. The light of reason is what will transfigure us into the heavenly state of consciousness that awaits the moment we broaden our horizons. It is the broadening of the horizons that is the freedom from the limits of judgment.

We may test ourselves, if upon awakening each day, we make conscious effort to perceive whether we have either limited ourselves or accepted an alternate path. We can do this by writing down what we truly want in life and how we expect it to manifest in our life. Then it will dawn in our consciousness what limitations we may have placed to create an obstruction to what we truly desire. It is a fact in creation that attainment comes from payment. Therefore, the effort must be made to always accept our right to goodness.

Have something to wake up for—awaken to the joy of life, the unexpected. Get rid of denials—they age you. You will look younger as God's angels enter in.

"When of thyself thou thinkest most,
thine heart is closed to angel host."

GAINING CONTROL THROUGH THE LAW OF ACCEPTANCE

Freedom from negative experiences is waiting patiently for your acceptance—of your right to an attitude that is beneficial to you. *"We have eyes to see and see not, ears to hear and hear not."* Become aware of the will of God which reveals the divine Law of Total Acceptance. If you accept the right of the thought, you place yourself in a position to control it, but you cannot control what you do not accept. Even if you have an aversion to something, by the Law of Acceptance you gain control over it, and by gaining control over it, it is then within your power to give it up. However, you cannot surrender what you do not have. Remember, that which you reject is that which binds you and controls you. Therefore, if you do not control the thought, you cannot give it to God. God moves in when our personality moves out. It takes acceptance for God to move in and the personality to move out. It behooves us to accept an attitude of divine right in order to experience our divine right.

CHANGING OUR THOUGHT

Whatever we want, or whatever we are experiencing that we do not want, we can change it by first accepting its right of existence. We, in that moment, have the power and the control over that form. When we reject an experience, that rejection is a form we have created. It is a form that we have created by a judgment that our mind has made. Accept the rights of all things and all levels of consciousness for they are all within us. That is the first step in freeing something from the mind. The next step is to identify with something better. If we truly accept something greater than what we already have, we will soon begin to experience something greater. When the rocks you turn over each have a scorpion, you will see they are all the same, and you will look for something greater.

Flood your consciousness with *"Acceptance, something good is happening!"* We must do our part by flooding our consciousness, then we move in consciousness to where something good is happening. Use this wonderful truth and never let go it. *Evolve into that kind of space!* The goodness of life is not subject to the dictates of the human mind.

All things to all people are possible when the acceptance of the possibility is freed from their mind and enters the depths of their heart. We know that our soul speaks through the vehicle of the heart. Because we know that truth, we bear the responsibility of making even greater effort that we may be the light of peace and joy which is in truth our true being.

The changes in our life will come ever in keeping with the effort that we are making. We cannot have a dictate in front of a request or it will stand as an obstruction to receiving what we are after in life. Accept that something will work out without dictating how it will work out. In so doing, remember the wisdom of patience. Many quit just before the victories in life, and they move on to something else and keep going on, and on,and on. Not only is there truth in the saying that *a rolling stone gathers no moss*, but also *only a fool quits before the victory.*

We have the divine right, and it is revealed over and over, again and again, to choose another level of consciousness by changing our thought, which changes our attitude, which, in turn, redirects the energy so that we experience something different. The moment in which we are aware is the only moment over which we have power.

Every time there is a step forward, the mind demands its payment, and to be free, we have to give up the thought of the personality. We have to work at it constantly. How do we remove the thought of the personality? By accepting the thought of All. If we are not accepting the thought of All, we are accepting the thought of personality. Become aware of what you are accepting. You will no longer be controlled by another when you accept the thought of All for that is total consideration which is divine love.

We all know the attitudes of mind that we alone must make an effort to change. How do we know which attitudes we must change? It is very simple—take a look at the experiences in life that you do not like.

TOLERANCE, ACCEPTANCE, UNDERSTANDING—
STEPS TO FREEDOM

Without the faculty of tolerance unfolded, we do not express acceptance, nor do we express true friendship. The wise, therefore, make friends with the undeveloped good within themselves. The process of making friends will lead to understanding. First, we must show total consideration (Divine Love) and secondly, acceptance (Divine Will) to understand. The moment we understand something, we are free. Therefore, in all your getting get understanding, because it frees you.

DENYING OUR RIGHT BY JUDGING ANOTHER'S RIGHT

We can always tell what a person desires for he or she judges the right of another to have it or not to have it. *"One who seeks that which is the right of another denies that which is his or her right to have."* Such a judgment of another's right shall deprive us of the greater good in our life, for in the judgment we establish a law for ourselves to be without. It is our self-important judgments that deprive us of a life of beauty and we are constantly in need.

ANOTHER PERSPECTIVE ON DENIAL

To add a few final thoughts on denial—another perspective—the following is taken from a little book of lessons published in 1904 by Annie Rix Militz who generously gave permission in her preface to use her lessons "without restraint":

Every religion has taught denial in some form. All fasting is but the symbol of the denying which is going on in the mind.

"If any man will come after me, let him deny himself." How is it that Jesus denied himself? By beginning in heart and mind to set aside the fleshly man. He says, *"If I honor myself, my honor is nothing."* ... *"I speak not of myself, it is the father that dwelleth in me, he doeth the*

works." Jesus denied his personality, for he knew that was not his real self. He knew himself to be spirit, not flesh. "*The flesh profiteth nothing,*" he said. He knew himself to be immortal, not mortal as he seemed to be. We, too, are spiritual, not material; divine immortals, not carnal and mortal. We deny the reality of the carnal mind and body under the name 'personality.' It is a good term to express all the collective errors that man has held about himself. The word 'person' (from the Latin *per* and *sona* , to sound through) was originally applied to a mask which ancient actors wore upon the stage. Most personalities seem to hide the real nature of the individual—beautiful natures obscured by ugly forms and features, great souls curtained by diminutive bodies. Denial of personality draws aside the curtain, dissolves the imperfect, and reveals the translucent body through which the spirit shines and works untrammeled.

The fleshly body is not yourself, and nothing done to it can hurt you. Mentally look at all personality as you would look through darkness to the light. Deny its actions, its foolishness, its sickness, its weakness, its meanness, its wickedness, and these will melt before your true word like mist before the sun. . . .

The mind that is determined to believe in God alone faithfully takes up the denial of all that is not God, and, as he walks along the way, he soon begins to see that truth proves itself true.

When the mind that dwells in the consciousness of God sends forth its word denying any place or power to sickness, pain, disease, then we see health spring forth as flowers spring up when a crushing weight has been removed.

The right denial of personality causes egotism to fall from one with its pride and vanity, its sensitiveness and stupidity, and the Universal Self to be revealed.

The denial of your personality does not destroy your individuality, but, to the contrary, establishes it. Fear not: *"He that loseth his life* (loses the limited personal conception of life) *for my sake* (the truth's sake) *shall find it* (the true individual life.)" (Matt. 10:39)

Game 8

Motive for Self-Gain

Key Players:

Sense Functions:
Deception, Greed,
Self-Glory, Selfishness

Counterbalancing Soul Faculties:
Awareness, Honesty, Purity,
Personal Responsibility

How the Game is Played:

The game of *Motive for Self-Gain* is played when our thoughts and deeds are motivated by the possibility of self-gain.

MOTIVE ESTABLISHES THE LAW

When we make the effort to find our **true motive**, we will understand all of our experiences, for motive or intention establishes the law that brings our experiences to us. At the very initiation of the law itself is where we stand to instantly choose the path of freedom or the path of bondage. It is in that moment in consciousness that we make that choice and there we face the Law known as Divine Flow, or we face a Law of Payment and Attainment.

*"He who hurts another shall live to see the day
when all his selfish motives pain shall take away."*

Motivation may be placed on a continuum. When our motives stem from a pure heart and a sound mind, they scale the upper end of that continuum. When our motives arise out of greed, selfishness, self-glory and the like, they must be placed at the opposite end of the pole. In other words, our motives or intentions determine whether our deeds, acts, and activities are spiritual ones, or whether they have been carried out for gain on the physical plane or personality levels.

If the motive is not pure, we will repeat the experience that we may gain insight. The end result of any experience is revealed in the true motive which began it. We are beginning and ending experiences each moment for each moment is, in truth, the eternity of consciousness.

OUR EVERY MOTIVE IS PERMANENTLY RECORDED

The Divine Intelligence knows our every motive, every thought, every act, and every deed. They are permanently recorded in the memory par excellence (heart seed atom) of the soul, and they provide the basis for all our experiences, including our state of health. The real meaning of the biblical scripture, *"As a man thinketh in his heart, so is he"* (Proverbs 23:7) is given by Earlyne Chaney in her book, *The Mystery of Death and Dying:*

> . . . The heart seed atom contains a
> complete electronic visual recording of
> everything that has ever happened to the

soul throughout its existence ... This is
the seed atom that records every emotion, every thought, every action, every
deed—everything you ever think, say or
do. It has created, and is creating, a motion picture record of the total YOU and
your present incarnation—so that, if you
could sit at the end of the day and view
it, you would see not only a complete
motion picture drama of all that you did
during the day, but all that you thought,
all that you felt, all that you expressed
mentally, physically and emotionally. All
is recorded there in its action, in its
karmic action ... The infinitesimal picture images flowing from the heart atom
into the bloodstream strike the endocrine
glands ... The choice [of how the glands
respond] depends upon the karma in the
images reeling out of the heart seed atom.
... Karma can be overcome, but it requires almost transcendental effort. You
must *constantly* guard your thoughts and
perform at the peak of your spiritual
awareness at all times.

OUR PLANES OF CONSCIOUSNESS ARE
IN HARMONY WITH OUR MOTIVES

It should be clear that our experiences are nothing more
than the mirror reflecting back to us our motives, thoughts,
acts, and deeds. We may deceive others but never the spirit or
God within. Nor can we fool our spirit guides and teachers.
Surely, we cannot expect to unfold spiritually, or to attract guides
and teachers from the higher realms of Light, if we do not make
the effort to purify our motives. Everyone has spirit guides

and teachers. As like attracts like, the levels of consciousness or awareness those guides and teachers are on will ever be in harmony with our true spiritual motives.

There have been many words written and many words spoken concerning the world of spirit and its various planes and spheres. These planes and spheres are not something outside us, they are something within us. They are states of consciousness or awareness. There are many levels of awareness or states of consciousness within us, with everyone having the potential for expressing the same levels. We experience ever outside ourselves whatever is inside ourselves according to the Law that Like Attracts Like and becomes the Law of Attachment. Before experiencing a particular sphere, or plane, or heaven, we would have had to gravitate in consciousness to that particular dimension, depending on where we are in thought and motive. Once having gravitated to the dimension within ourselves, we would experience its effect outside ourselves, as *"outward manifestations reveal inner attitudes of mind "* or motives. Again, we emphasize, we experience ever in harmony and in accord with the Law that Like Attracts Like.

OUR ACTIONS REVEAL OUR TRUE MOTIVE

It is the motive that is the germ. That is the seed that produces the tree and all the effects. A person may say, *I try to do good and all that comes to me is seeming grief and disaster.* Our actions reveal our true motive. It can only be said to that person, go within and find from what level of consciousness your motive has received its birth. Is your motive a seed from your faculties of being, your soul's expression, or is your motive given birth in the functions and sense world of creation? If we want to know the level on which we are expressing at any given time, we need only to ask ourselves what our true motive is in thinking, feeling, or acting in a particular way. Clearly, our motives can run the gamut of possibilities. It takes awareness to reveal our motive. *"Awareness is the soul of action."*

CHOOSING THE PATH OF DARKNESS OR LIGHT

How can you become aware of that moment in consciousness—for it is only a moment—in which you have choice to follow the path of darkness or the path of Light? The simplest way of seeing your motive is to become aware of how much you are interested in the effect of your effort. To the degree of your interest in the **effect** will it be revealed to you the degree your motive is guided and controlled by **desire**. If it is controlled by personal desires, it cannot possibly stem from reason and purity of thought. This is so important to understand because the cause of all our experiences and circumstances is to be found inside us.

MOTIVE AND DESIRE

The mind cannot desire anything that it has not first accepted. What then motivates us to either fulfill or not fulfill a desire? Desire goes through the computer of the subconscious mind and we are motivated by the patterns that we are addicted to in our mind. Our motives depend upon the values and the priorities we have placed on the fulfillment of our various desires. Suppressed desires may motivate us into action, and then through justification we defend the action we have taken.

FREEDOM THROUGH SERVICE

Motives expressed from the self or personality levels only ground us electromagnetically in our self vibrations. Freedom of the soul is gained through selfless service. If we are serving and yet not finding that peace and freedom that we seek from self-centeredness, we need to look at our true motivation for doing the work. Can we in all honesty say it is for the joy in the effort that we serve God? Or, must we admit that our motivation is to seek recognition or another gain that is self-related? *"Man's loss of God is dependent upon his purity of motive."*

When there is dedication to service, we must not be naive or emotional in looking at the principle involved. See if it is motivated by duty to the soul or if it emanates from a self-serving level. The latter is called a level of having what you want when you want it.

HELPING ANOTHER

"*If the motive is pure, the method is legal*" is a teaching that requires wisdom and discretion in its application, never to be used to control another or for self-gain. Its intent should only be to help another who is temporarily blinded or trapped in a particular level of consciousness. When the motive is pure, it has and expresses total consideration. Expressing total consideration, it is divine. And that which is divine is pure.

IDENTIFYING OUR TRUE MOTIVES

If you get yourself into a hole, so-to-speak, and try to get out of it, ask yourself, *Am I honest with myself? Am I accepting personal responsibility for my ignorance? Do I accept the possibility of something greater? And am I willing to put effort into making the necessary changes in consciousness?* Answers in the affirmative lay the foundation for pure motive, guaranteeing the effect to be beneficial; for all experience is the effect of what is taking place in the head. Let what has been cease to worry you. Worry takes away the chemicals needed for enthusiasm. Instead, use that energy to establish new laws. You cannot change what has been. Assuredly, you will see real changes when you let go of the past. How do you learn to let go of the past? Let the judgments go because each time you live in the past, you are supporting judgments. Be energy conscious. Budget your energy wisely. The effort being made to conserve energy outside reveals what effort is being made inside.

If we do not like what we are experiencing, let us try to understand our motives and express on higher levels of consciousness, for the law is clear that as we sow so shall we reap. That is why we do right, because it is right to do right, and we are not concerned with whether the world believes us or does not believe us. We do our job, whatever it may be, and in the doing, we have all of our pleasure, and all of our joy, and all of our happiness. But if we have to have constant feed back about how great we are and how much we did, and how much everyone appreciates us, then we must give more thought to what levels our motives are coming from so we can be free. When people get addicted to having everyone tell them how great they are, what happens when there is a change in that person's life and no longer does anyone tell them that? They suffer unbearably.

We must be honest with ourselves in identifying our **true** motives, not the **apparent** motives. We need to make the effort not only to find out what our motives are, but our attitudes and values as well. If we will look sincerely and honestly within, we will always find the cause of all things, for nothing can ever happen to us that is not caused by us. There is no power outside ourselves that gives us wealth or health, but it is the power that is within us. Therefore, it is our responsibility to awaken to that great neutral divine love and so express it in our lives.

No matter how widespread the help made possible through our gifts of a material or mental nature, in God's totally fool-proof plan, we do not garner up spiritual substance to express in the hereafter unless our motives spring from spiritual levels of consciousness in the here and now. (See *Game of Confusing Giving with Lending and Borrowing with Owning* for an expansion of this thought.) As we learn to give up a little of our selfish motivation, we shall receive divine inspiration.

In *Self-Unfoldment by Disciplines of Realization*, Manly P. Hall referred to a textbook on the art of Chinese poetry that explains the matter of motive very simply:

> Three manners of men attempt to write poetry. (In Taoism, poetry is an expression of harmonious or rhythmic living.) The first and lowest of these composes rhymes to sell, and his motive is profit. He can never become a true poet.

The second composes his lyrics to impress others with his superior abilities, or in the hope that they will advance him in reputation or preferment. His motives are egotism and ambition, and he can never be a poet.

The third class—and their number is comparatively small—are impelled only by the universal impulse of beauty. Poetry writes itself through them. Desiring neither profit nor fame, but moved by an irresistible impulse to express poetry, they alone are the poets. They have no personal motive, but a universal motive possesses them. It is the joy of beauty to reveal itself.

*   *   *

"God's hand is the poet's pen."

*   *   *

When the motive
Is pure,
The manifestation
Is pleasant.
However,
When the motive
Is right,
The manifestation
Is inevitable
For it
Is the law.

Game 9

The Selfless Service Deception

Key Players:

Sense Functions:
Concern, Convenience,
Selfishness

Counterbalancing Soul Faculties:
Duty, Humility, Illumination,
Love, Service, Selflessness

How the Game is Played:

The Selfless Service Deception game is played when we deceive ourselves into thinking our service is "selfless" when in truth our "service" is motivated by the thought of self, self-concern, self-gain, and convenience.

WHAT IS SELFLESS SERVICE?

Selfless service is service minus or less the thought of self. Selflessness means a freedom from the ever-changing gray matter of the mind-computer. It is a service to the Light within us—to the eternal Light, God, or goodness. It is only when we dedicate ourselves to goodness that we will be free. We must forget the self or personality and become totally absorbed in the service. God cannot get into the service until we forget the personality. When we work for God and goodness, who else is greater that we should let them disturb us?

Service to God directs God's energy back to the source from which it comes. In so doing, we become a free channel, free in the sense that we no longer depend upon mental, limited tapes of the mind for our freedom, or sustenance, or joy. When we choose to serve God, we have no thought, no dictate, no judgment of what the job may be that we will be called upon to do, how long it will take, how much it will cost, what we will or will not get out of it, how tired we are, where we will have to be, what we will have to do, or when we will have to do it.

We are here on the earth plane to serve God—that Light within—not our personality or the personality of another person. Our service to the Light must be unconditional. The moment we put conditions on how, and when we will serve the Light, we are in truth saying, *I will serve the Light subject to what my judgments demand.* That, of course, is not service at all.

When the personality decides what work it will do for God, the personality is being served; we are not working for the spirit. We are serving something every moment of every hour. Who is our master? Are we serving our own pride and ego? Are we serving the tapes of past experiences? It takes conscious self-control to wisely choose what we are going to serve.

When we do something and then view what was done with it, we are attached to the fruits of action. It shows we did it only with our mind. We did not put God in it. To brag about our achievements, to appear more accomplished or talented than we really are, is deceptive, and we will at some point be exposed. We deceive only ourselves and are simply giving lip service to God.

If we do things the way the personality dictates, it is known as "God at my convenience." We must face the honesty that will free us. The truth is: *Because I serve at the convenience of my mind, I serve my mind. I serve nothing else.* When service is rendered without the function of convenience, it is selfless. How do we rise above the function of convenience? We rise by exercising humility and accepting that we have a job to do for God. We have a duty to our own soul to serve. Service is a universal law of life.

Selfless service is an expression of love in a channeled and neutral way, releasing through our being divine power or energy. In selfless service we are at the apex of eternity. We are sitting at the *peace that passeth all understanding* and we are a clear and full channel. Therefore, the power known as love, or energy, or God is being expressed. In so doing, as the water that runs through the pipe leaves its multitude of mineral deposits, so the power that flows through us as a channel deposits its multitude of blessings in our life.

ASSESSING PURITY OF MOTIVE IN SERVING

If in our motive to serve the Light, we stop to think about the ways in which we are willing to serve, we are not serving God, we are serving our own personality. If we **think** we are doing selfless service, that is one of the first indications that we are doing **self** service because it takes the self to think that we are serving. That is contrary to the demonstrable truth of selfless service. Only being freed from all bondage of the personality, are we in the experience of selfless service.

If we find that we have difficulty in accepting all work as God's work— and all work is God's work if we put God or goodness into it—then we should truly examine our motives. Is it our personality that prompts us to serve for the glory we think we shall receive? Or, is it in gratitude to God that we accept the humblest of jobs as important ways in which to serve? To those who receive the Light, the responsibility is the greatest to, in return, spread the Light. The ways are numerous. Many behind-the-scene jobs are necessary in any organization; there are many mundane jobs in the home; and in everyday experiences there are always opportunities to lend a helping hand, a listening ear, and to upgrade the quality of a task. It could become very easy while doing mundane tasks to forget that it is God's work. Whenever we perform a quality service from the level of duty to our soul and not for the glory of our personality, then we are doing God's work, no matter how mundane.

It matters not whether we are helping a neighbor in need, a blind person crossing the street, a neglected animal, service in a hospital, serving on a planning commission, playing an organ in church, helping a child with homework, tending a garden, sweeping the side walk, or helping our friends in the world of spirit, as long as we are the unobstructed channel doing God's work selflessly. The same is also true on our paid jobs if we will but remember that we are merely the channels for a higher power. If we are willing to go that extra mile in doing more than just what is required, our own spirit will impress us in which way to serve. Our own spirit is willing to accept whatever job comes our way because no matter how humble the job, our soul knows it is God's work if we are godly when we are doing it. Service is an expression of our gratitude to the Divine Source of which we are a part.

Selfless service is emphasized as a way to free the soul from the bondage of the mind or personality. One might ask the question, is volunteerism the same thing as selfless service? That, of course, depends entirely upon the motive that prompted a certain deed, act, or activity. The motive will reveal our level of awareness or state of consciousness. If we assist in any manner for personal gain only, then we are expressing on a lower level of consciousness. Contrariwise, when we serve without thought of self, we are expressing on a high level of consciousness. There is a direct relationship between the level on which one is expressing and the good that will be accomplished. Also, if the personality takes the glory now, there will be no rewards to come after we leave this dimension.

The law that we set into motion to serve selflessly will attract to us, in keeping with that law, opportunity. And opportunity is like the hands of the clock—it meets every so often. If we are freed from the thought of self and our motive is pure when the hands of the clock meet, day in and day out, we will see the opportunity to do what our soul truly desires to do. But if we are blinded by the constant thought of self, then opportunity will knock at our door and we will not recognize it; for we cannot hear it, let alone see it; for we are so active with the thought of self. This constant identification with self places our soul in bondage to the personality instead of freeing us to experience the truth, love, and wisdom of illumination.

It is through selfless service that the energy that is flowing through our being is directed and expressed by the soul faculties. When we put selfless service into application, we begin to open our spiritual perception or vision and are inspired to do things of a higher nature. On the other hand, when the undisciplined personality acts as a cloud standing in the way of the Light, constantly thinking of self, we are destined to "the battle of the personality."

When the motive is pure, we are directing energy to build a spiritual body through which we can communicate with the spiritual realms. Without a vehicle through which to communicate, we limit ourselves to expression with lower realms. Concentration on mediumship or channeling per se does not guarantee unfoldment of the gifts of the spirit, but serving as we are truly needed, in whatever capacity, is in truth serving the spirit.

BEING GROUNDED IN CREATION

One reason why selfless service is so important in our soul's unfoldment is linked to our electromagnetic being. Our thoughts and deeds are sent forth into the atmosphere on an electrical vibration and, in like kind, are pulled to us magnetically. When our thoughts and deeds are related to self-concern and/or self-gain, we can literally become short-circuited or grounded "in self." These self-oriented thoughts rob us of *the peace that passeth all understanding* when we are grounded in creation. However, when we are not thinking of self, when our service is truly prompted by selflessness, when the soul is serving its own divinity, then we are freed from self or form to rise to higher states of consciousness within our being.

THE PATH TO ILLUMINATION

"Service is the path to freedom when selfless is the goal." Service in truth is the only path to illumination. There is no illumination possible outside the path of selfless service because illumination is truth, love, and wisdom. We have to keep our personality out of the way of the soul's expression to experience truth, love, and wisdom. Our soul knows what we gain from anything—our conscience will prompt us. We walk on the path of illumination and freedom through selfless service. The soul awakens when self is forgotten (goes to sleep). It takes selfless service because it takes total consideration and total acceptance for total expression and total understanding, known as God.

A person may say and set a law into motion, *I'm going to serve selflessly in this or that particular area. Consequently, I will become illumined.* Forget it! They have already set the law of self into motion. Selfless service is entertaining a thought or acting without concern for self. That is when the soul is serving its own divinity, the indwelling Christ Spirit, and is not concerned about form or thoughts about self. Therefore, anytime we entertain in thought that by selfless service we will become spiritually illumined, we have already set the law of self into motion, and the Law of Self is the Law of Limitation. Only when we put God first can we become illumined and experience that peace which passeth all understanding.

The wise see the wisdom of service—of giving—in order that they may receive what they desire. *"One who serves another in truth serves oneself."* When we neglect the opportunity for service, we obstruct the flow of spirit which is passing through us at all times. *"Wise ones live to serve. Fools serve to live."*

> *"To be master is the desire of the senses.*
> *To be a servant is the wise counsel of the soul."*

Game 10

Stealing Desires from The Divine

Key Players:

Sense Functions:
Depression, Greed, Judgment,
Intolerance, Satisfaction,
Stealing, Suppression

Counterbalancing Soul Faculties:
Acceptance, Attainment, Faith, Fulfillment,
Honesty, Humility, Personal Responsibility

How the Game is Played:

The personality plays the game of *Stealing Desires from The Divine* when it takes a desire and tells God how it shall be fulfilled, and then pays the price of its judgments, which only offer satisfaction and not fulfillment.

DESIRE, THE DIVINE EXPRESSION

We are never free of desire, which is the "divine expression." Without desire, there is no expression in form. There is nothing wrong with having desires. What is wrong is when the personality takes hold of the desire and will not let it go, telling God how it will be fulfilled. Then we have problems for we are stealing what rightfully is the prerogative of The Divine. The key to the problem is the judgment we make concerning the desire. Every time we dictate to The Divine how our desires will be fulfilled, we pay the price of the error of our own ignorance. Desire that has judgment in the package can never be fulfilled. We can satisfy it only for a time. Give your desire to God so that it may return to you, but be absolutely certain it is what you really want.

God is that which just *Is*. Truth is that which just *Is*. When we take God and truth and put it in that which has been (past experiences) there is nothing there. The Divinity no longer exists. You are then serving the shadows of the past. When we choose to direct energy to judgment and the shadows of the past, our desires cannot be fulfilled. That is taking that which *Is* and putting *It* with that which has been. It is like trying to mix oil with water.

The eternal soul is expressing through a created vehicle called the personality, self, or ego. Therefore, when the soul expresses, it must face and experience the duality of creation. In the moment the mind experiences desire, there is the thought of personality which is dual in nature. When the divine expression—desire—is flowing through the soul, it is called aspiration. As it enters the vehicle, it is called desire.

Desire is the most potent force of the universe because it is the expression of God. Our mind can only control the form of desire, not the principle of desire. It can only control the shell, so to speak. *"Thought is greater than man."* We can limit power but we cannot stop the power. So give your desire to God. Do not lend it. He makes loans to you. You do not make loans to Him. If you truly give it, the desire will not return ten minutes later.

Since we do not yet understand or accept the way energy passes through our mind, we create many forms to bring to us what we desire. That error of ignorance keeps us in a state of disappointment, confusion, and regret. We all know in truth that as the Infinite Intelligent Energy passes through the consciousness, it creates the very form of the thought and feeling that we entertain at the moment. Because it is an Infinite Intelligent Energy encased in the form of our thought, it is capable of accomplishing what we desire. These forms leave our so-called sphere of action and go out into the universe and do the work they have been sent to do. However, because we have other forms constantly being created, the forms of our desire often suffer from lack of sustenance. So, in working through the mental spheres of action, we soon learn to release our energy through higher planes of consciousness that we may free ourselves from the contradictions of the personality.

HOW WE STEAL DESIRES FROM THE DIVINE

In this game of *Stealing Desires from The Divine* we may ask, how does stealing take place? By not separating truth from creation, we delude ourselves that we are the desire. The truth, however, is that we are only that which experiences it. It is the delusion that we think we are the desire that makes us the thief, for desire is the divine expression—it belongs to The Divine! The great deception of human mental substance is in dictating how the divine expression will fulfill itself. We steal desire when we go to work to fulfill it. We put it in the mind to meet all the judgments. The soul, ever striving to rise in our consciousness, becomes again and again the victim of the deception of the mind as the mind strives to fulfill the desires that it has attached itself to. Then we pay for the theft of stealing that which belongs to God for its fulfillment.

Theft is bondage. We are bound to that which we steal. Fullness is total acceptance. However, if we steal desire, the mind limits with its judgments and there is no total acceptance from God, the true and only source of our supply. If God consciousness is in the desire, then you do not steal it.

It is in the thought of self that we abuse creation through the functions of attachment and adversity, because it is then that we steal from God and we pay the price. It takes humility to free us from our attachment to the judgment so desire can be fulfilled. Humility is as painful as our judgment for the pain is related to our belief that the judgment is us.

"The theft of desire is the birth of attachment and the guarantee of bondage."

HOW DESIRES ARE FULFILLED

When you cast the light of reason on a desire, judgments cannot survive in the Light. When this happens, the desire will be fulfilled in a divine way because you have put God in it, and you will no longer have the desire. It goes out into the universe when you do not hold it and comes back fulfilled. Accept the possibility of fulfillment which gives hope. Hope is a necessary ingredient for desire to be fulfilled. Where there is a will, there is a way. What good is will without a way?

To see fulfillment with the mind is a total waste of energy, for fulfillment is a faculty of the soul. If we feel a need to be satisfied, it is an indication that we still have need to live in the lesser light. When we *satisfy* a desire we have stolen a divine expression. We steal it from God when we direct it to a mental world of things. Satisfaction is limited to temporary sensation of the lesser light. *Fulfillment* has the full awakening of the Law of Personal Responsibility, for then all the soul faculties are in operation. When we have a desire, a divine expression, in that moment give it back to God.

Affirmation: *"O God, I give to you this desire, which in my ignorance I have stolen, accepting with a humble heart the fullness of your divine will."* Divine will is total acceptance. Desire released to God becomes divine right action. *"I have complete trust and faith that my word, through God, is in action now and cannot return unto me void."*

Anything of creation that has a higher priority than God in our consciousness, is destined to turn sour on us. If, however, our priority for God has a higher priority than our desire, our desire will always be fulfilled. God denies nothing, and so it is, if there is something that we do not have that we desire, that we feel is needed for us, recognize the great truth that it is right where we are. We just cannot dictate when, or through whom, or how it shall be fulfilled.

What determines how long it takes for a desire to be fulfilled is dependent upon our efforts not to identify with ourselves, for identification with the self activates the judgments. When we think of ourselves, we separate ourselves from the very things we desire. Once we know the law, we will perceive what is happening around us.

A helpful exercise is to write down what it is you truly want in life and how you expect it to manifest itself in your life. Then you will begin to think about why you have not already experienced it. You will see within your own mind how you have limited it. Because of prior experiences, you have created an obstacle or obstruction to what it is you truly desire.

When you speak out your idea to another person, you give it to another's universe and your chance of its being fulfilled becomes less and less. *Know* your word will not return to you void when you speak it forth. Do not merely hope, but know beyond the shadow of any doubt. *"That that is mine knows my face and is already on its way to my heart."*

THE PAYMENT FOR THE DESIRE JUDGMENT

To those who have been given much, much shall be demanded, not by some individual somewhere, but by the very law, for the law is the demand. And who establishes the law? We establish those mental laws through entertaining our desires and making the judgment that we, meaning our personality, and we alone, shall fulfill them. Each thing that we seemingly receive in life carries a price tag with it. The price tag is not often viewed in the moment we receive it, but the price is ever extracted from us. With the Law of Creation, there is always the payment before the attainment. Even our lungs pay for the air we breathe.

As long as we permit our mind to entertain the thought of how, or how difficult, it is to attain the fulfillment of our desires, we establish the law to pay a heavy price. We pay by facing every mental obstruction that we have created that is blinding us. The Attainment and Payment Balance Law is in keeping with our own acceptances and denials, for everything that we desire, some effort is extracted from us. It is a matter of our own willingness to make that effort. Desire and judgment are inseparable until we get out of personality. If we have a desire and say, *I can't afford this*, we will establish all the laws necessary to guarantee not being able to afford it. It is known as payment for the judgment. Get to the judgment. Changes are guaranteed if we stand firm. If we stick it out, the day will come when we see the attainment as equal to the payment.

It is in our own best interest that we bring a degree of balance into our desires and do not permit our minds to judge they are not being fulfilled. If we make the judgment that our desire is not going to get fulfilled, we experience fear. And the moment desire is fulfilled, we fear we will not get it fulfilled again. We can be freed from fear only by accepting personal responsibility, the ability to respond to our fear.

How much are you willing to pay for your desires? You pay to get them and you pay to get rid of them. You pay twice when the personality is in the driver's seat. The personality seizes any opportunity it can to control desire, and then, without light or awareness, it seeks its fulfillment *without concern* for anything else. Can you see why people are so inconsiderate at times?

Desire is truly the divine expression when consideration and the light of reason shine over it. Total consideration considers all factors in attaining the desire, including the payment. Should faith leave the guiding hand of total consideration and direct its great power to the human mind with its fluctuating desires, the desire no longer has total consideration over it. It has consideration limited to the fulfillment of its particular desire; therefore, it cannot see the price tag that comes with the fulfillment of that desire. It does not consider the payment. *"The uneducated ego hears only the echoes of its own unfulfilled desires."*

Our minds are constantly entertaining an endless variety of desires, many of which are not in our conscious thought. The effects of compulsive desire are emotional turmoil and discord as each desire vies with all the others waiting for fulfillment. There is a saying, *"Emotions, like ceaseless waves, eternally wash the thirsty shore,"* which means that desire is like a thirsty shore. Emotion washes the thirst of desire. Desire calms when emotion is expressed.

EDUCATING DESIRE

How do we educate desire? *"One gets out of something the same way one got into it."* And since fear is born out of the judgment made by the personality, use your personality's tool, the memory, to recall the payment you made in fulfilling the desire in the past. How does the memory serve to educate the desire? The memory offers all the feelings concerned with the desire and offers freedom from the compulsion to fulfill it. Memory serves to recall the payment for the fulfillment of a desire— fear. Fear is the mind's control over the eternal soul. Once the mind takes desire, fear is guaranteed. Fear over its lack of fulfillment takes over. This is the crawling stage we go through to get to the next stage of mustering the faith, acceptance, and patience to let the desire go and to let God in, by asking that we receive only what is for our greater good.

We can also approach it more directly by honestly shining the light of reason over the desire to consider carefully if it is what we really want and whether it is worth the payment. *Is this my desire or someone else's desire that I have come en rapport with?*

In reality, you cannot educate The Divine or the divine desire. You educate your mind when it takes control of the desire that it has stolen from The Divine. An educated desire becomes a fulfilled desire if you still so choose after educating it..

Any other way is a temporal satisfaction. *"When you educate the desires of your senses, you will find your true wealth."*

Talk to the desires you have been the victim of. If you do not stop and listen to them, you will never control them. So often people will listen to the radio or watch television as a distraction because they do not want to listen to their own broadcasts. You cannot control your desires unless you make conscious decisions regarding them. When the mind makes a judgment concerning them, that is when fear takes over.

GOD IS THE TRUE SOURCE OF OUR SUPPLY

We should be grateful when we do not have to pay the price called suffering and are motivated not to forever bask in the sleep of satisfaction, the sleep that descends our soul into darkness. When the mind is dreaming its dream of satisfaction, the soul is sold out. Until our faith rises supreme and receives all from the Divine Humble Light itself, we shall continue to pay the price of our judgments and dictates of the mind. It is through our recognition and acceptance that God is the true source of our supply. With peace flooding our consciousness, we do free ourselves in time. So, remember, each thought or desire your mind entertains, you pay for, and each thought you give to God, you are freed from.

RESPECTING GOD AS A PERSISTANT FLOW

"Distortion is the direct effect of an obstruction to a persistant flow." God is the persistant flow. Desire, being the expression of God, is, therefore, persistant flow. When we are unwilling to change one desire for another, insanity of the mind is the result. If we are exhausted, we can use another desire to get out of the insanity. Remember, the personality got in, so we use the personality to get us out by redirecting the energy to something we desire equally. Wisdom comes from the weariness of the struggle. Gradually we start making fewer judgments and simply go with the flow.

WHEN DESIRE GETS GREEDY

Until we demonstrate some control by becoming aware of and educating (shining the light of reason over) our desires, we will be caught in the web of blind desire or greed. The mind is never satisfied with what it has. No matter what it gets, in time it desires more and better. When the level starts getting greedy, it is time to stop satisfying the level.

A spirit teacher once said: *"Be not concerned with the fruits of action. Take all of the joy you are going to take in the doing because that is the only place that true joy exists. True joy does not exist in the effect. When we slip into the illusion that joy exists in the effect, we are on the path to what is known as greed because desire can never be fulfilled. One desire only guarantees a repetition and expansion of it. That is how the Law of Desire works."*

GIVING DESIRE BACK TO GOD THROUGH FAITH

When we educate the mind, the divine desire is allowed to flow through the mind. In other words, if we are at peace, and we accept that the desire will be fulfilled, the desire is allowed to flow from The Divine through our mind. That will free us from the payment and the attainment, free us from the fear, because it is back in God's hand. We are giving the gift of self. On the other hand, if we choose the thought of self, we deny God and establish the Law of Fear, separating us from the universal consciousness and fulfillment of our desire.

The sayings, *"As a man believeth in his heart, so he becometh,"* and *"We cannot receive anything in life that we do not first give"* are applicable here. For if we will first believe that we have what we desire, then we will come to a level of consciousness within ourselves where what we desire is expressing itself. And like the great magnet of the universe, where Like Attracts Like and becomes the Law of Attachment, we will experience what we truly believe. That takes more than a thought. It takes the sustaining power of The Divine. How do we become receptive to a greater degree to that sustaining power? They call it many words, and one of those is faith. *Faith is an absolute conviction in our own mind that we already have what we are seeking.* The power of faith can work miracles.

How do we express gratitude for that which we do not yet see, hear, or know? Through the principle or power of faith we express gratitude. That is how to release the pent-up energy of desire. The tenacity of the power of faith is almost unbelievable. When we truly desire something, we either sooner, or perhaps later, get it. But never let your desire of things supersede your love of God unless you want to stay wanting of things. *"Put God in it, or forget it."* If God is not in it, you will have all the experiences necessary to find God.

As long as we are in self, we will desire constantly and will constantly be censoring the desire, limiting it by the judgments we place on fulfilling it. So what happens to us when this divine expression wells up within our consciousness—the energy that gets locked in the subconscious mind when the desire is not fulfilled?

HOW WE SUPPRESS DESIRE AND ITS RESULTING DETRIMENTS

The average person suppresses desire with such frequency that it is important to understand more fully how it takes place. When we take a desire with our mind and if we keep it bottled up, we create desire entities. The moment the desire touches the consciousness, form is created and immediately screams for survival. The force that creates these forms has the intelligence of the creator. These forms become animated and express with a voice. Loud voices are those of suppressed desire and soft and humble voices are those of spirit. Desire forms have all of the force that the desire in our mind has; and they then start to become independent, just as independent as our own ego or personality. We then become the victim of the game. As we keep feeding energy to these forms, we attract spirits from the lower astral realms who are en rapport with our desires, compounding the bondage.

Do not underestimate the potency of a suppressed desire entity. If desire is suppressed, it will in time leap over reason and experience its self-created delusion. Suppressed desire is the first thing to rise at the slightest opportunity to take over our lives. It is dangerous and detrimental for it is Infinite, Intelligent, Neutral Energy that we have bound into a form of our desire. It is psychologically detrimental. It is an instrument of frustration and self-pity. What force in our mind suppresses desire? It is the judgment of how desire will be fulfilled. Day after day, and year after year, we suppress multitudes of desires until we begin to experience frustration. Stop and analyze your desire. Ask the question, *What is it behind the thing that makes me choose to deny its coming from God?* Get to the judgment. It is only the forms we are feeding that make us feel a certain way. The desire meets a wall of judgment and gets shoved down, creating frustration. As desire is the divine expression, you cannot stop it. The energy does not dissipate, and as each desire rises, frustration results. What do we get out of frustration? Nothing good. It is understood that fulfillment of desire is dependent upon the absence of judgment. So why do we go through life seeking fulfillment of desire while holding onto judgments?

Desires wanting to be fulfilled have to knock somewhere, so they knock on the door of judgment. The "judge" comes to the door. The desire form relates the message. The "judge" takes a look and says "no." So the desire entities knock at another door, the door of fascination, where they are let in by the "King of Judgment" for the king feeds on these forms. Therefore, the moral to the story is that you must educate (shine the light of reason over it) or fulfill the desire, otherwise, you will be drained in the realm of fascination. Be honest with yourself and you will see how clearly it works.

The more self-identified you are, the more difficulty you have in giving the desire back to God. When you suppress desire, you are trying to be greater than God. You will not be without desire, only without fulfillment. Entities of suppressed desire are different from disembodied spirits that have a soul.

Suppressed desire entities are mind-created forms without a soul and they can be very convincing. They can even persuade one into believing one is "possessed" by a disembodied spirit. St. Paul admonished us to **try** the spirits to see if they are of God.

Another danger of suppressing desire is that the thought forms will become so strong that, in keeping with the Law that Like Attracts Like, they will attract other entities of delusion. Soon you are ordered about by thousands of entities. This is why it is important to talk about and expose these areas of the mind, to release the energy that would be going to feed these forms. Otherwise, the suppressed desire leads to a person's becoming the victim of his or her own games. The suppression of desire leads to self-delusion. However, through communication, discussion, and exposure, you free yourself from the blinding control of desire. The teaching, therefore, is educate or fulfill desire, never suppress it. To suppress only guarantees the continuity of the experience in one's life. Also, it is one of the most detrimental levels of consciousness for it affects the physical body. It sends the desire body out to satisfy its desire, not in the physical realms where you have suppressed it, but while you are sleeping, or while you are doing something else. The desire pushes the desire body outside your aura or astral egg. It satisfies desire in another realm, draining your vital or etheric body. The desire will not plague you consciously so you are not aware that the desire body is out satisfying itself. A cyclic pattern of time pressure bombards the consciousness, but the conscious awareness of what the desire body is doing is not there.

Suppressed desire is, therefore, the cause of the illusion known as time pressure which is nothing more nor less than the temporary inability to gain control over one's desires. Desire priority determines the time we seem able to find to do a given thing. Those who have little or no control have great time pressure.

> *"Time pressure is a hailstone of petty desires*
> *demanding their own gratification."*

However, most people suppress their desires until they start to explode. Remember, we are dealing with energy that is pent-up. If we abruptly give up smoking, sex, or any other addiction, we become frustrated. We have to release our frustrations.

Another facet of suppressed desire to face is that of intolerance. When you are intolerant of another, take a deep look inside and you will find that desire in your consciousness—desire which you have suppressed. Tolerance for another's desire reveals you have educated the desire within yourself.

TAKE STOCK OF THOUGHTS BEFORE GOING TO SLEEP AND UPON AWAKENING

It is critically important to take stock of what kind of thoughts you have as you are losing conscious awareness in going off to sleep so that you can guide and gain control of your bodies. Take stock of all the unfulfilled desires that rise during the day so that they are not banging at you when your conscious mind is unconscious during sleep. If you wake up tired and irritable and with the "blahs," it is because you worked so hard with your different bodies out "doing their thing."

It is just as important to exercise control over your thoughts as you are waking up because those bodies are still active and still "doing their thing." If you want to gain control of them, then you must make the effort when you are going off to sleep, also when you are waking up. Again, that is why you must either fulfill the desire or educate it. Look at the desire, talk to it, expose it in discussion. Exposure means to bring it to the surface. Pit desire against desire and set priorities. Educate the desire by casting the light of reason over it—exposing and communicating with it. Then the energy in the suppressed desire (time bomb) will be released and the light of reason will transform it. It will not get rid of it, just transform it. Our soul basks in the sunshine of exposure. It is our senses that run wild because of their addictions to patterns of attitudes and judgments.

DO NOT RELY ON SOMEONE ELSE
TO FULFILL YOUR DESIRE

When we are in principle, we do not need glory or anything else. If the eye of eternity is open in consciousness, we can see what is going on and then can choose to have this or that desire. We make the decision and we do not let another make a decision for us. Be aware, for another person's desire can send a figure or thought to our mind and we can be controlled by their desires.

The greatest folly of the human mind to entertain is to think someone else is going to fulfill your desires for you. Someone else is going to bring you peace and harmony, someone else is going to take care of you, someone else is going to keep you feeling good. Someone else is not going to do it. Every time you depend on someone else for what you desire, you serve the form they have created by denying your right to your own form. You deny your God of goodness. Whenever you depend on something outside, you deny your right to it. You never know what the other person is going to do. When you depend, you make that person your god and by so doing, you deny your right of choice. Instead, be grateful for a little patience. All your desires can and will be fulfilled when you accept that they are truly yours. That means responsibility for their fulfillment and not depending or relying upon anyone else to do it for you. Rely on God. That is truly when one starts to grow.

CONTROLLING THE BOMBARDMENT OF DESIRE
BY FACING PERSONAL RESPONSIBILITY

The mind is constantly bombarded with choice, and we are torn between conflicting desires. Facing responsibility requires great effort to control the bombardment of desire that we have not gained control over—to keep the eye single that we may see clearly until the responsibility has been fulfilled. The single eye sees only God or goodness everywhere. As the scriptures state it, *"The lamp of the body is the eye; if therefore thine eye be single, thy whole body shall be full of light."* (Matt. 6:22)

Concentration is the key to all power. The effort must be made daily to gain control of your mind or you will be the victim of uncontrolled desires. One way to handle this is to make fulfilling desire, when it is so strong, wait for conscious control. For example, give the soul five minutes to pause. Go through the experience of climbing the walls, if necessary. Make desire the servant rather than being its slave. Put another way,*"Oft times no is God's direction."* When your desire is the greatest, that is the time to say "no" or to pause. Pausing gives you the opportunity to sort out without emotion what is right to do—listening to God's direction.

Then you are again in control. You must again have conscious control. When God is first, all things are good. Anything that is putting God second on the list will cause us to pay a terrible price until God is reestablished on the throne. We can know always what is ahead of God by being honest.

Creation was never designed to bind our free spirit, to descend our eternal soul into the depths of hell. That was not the design of the universe. We must gain control and face personal responsibility. Taking responsibility for fulfillment of desires brings our desires under the faculty of reason and patience. *"Keep faith with reason for the light of reason will transfigure thee."* Reason removes the blindness of judgment. Things come to us in God's time and God's way when we are patient. As *"wisdom lives in patience,"* the wisdom of the universe starts to guide our path and free us from the bondage of the mind. Wisdom guides us in the choice of our desires. In a fleeting moment of blind desire we may ask for something that we later do not want, or do not want the responsibility for taking care of. So let us, therefore, carefully consider what we truly desire. Do we want it to go home with us?

USE THE CREATIVE PROCESS TO BRING DESIRE INTO MANIFESTATION

When you are certain you can live with your desire, use the creative process. The mind, through evolution, has created an illusion that matter has form and is real: *"I speak my word forth into the universe knowing that it shall not come back to me void, but accomplish that which I send it to do."* How do you know it is going to do that? If the mind has no reference for it, you speak your word and nothing happens. Therefore, you must "image"— the creative process—the doorway out of the mind and into the truth to go beyond the mental realm. Until you have created in your world of illusion these things, they cannot be. The law that created the illusion you now have is the same law you use to create that of your own choosing. But you must put into the new illusion more potent energy than you put into the old illusion that you have your faith in. When you image, you have to put it in the **present,** so that it can be created. You can experience the effects of the creation in the building of the illusion. When you create these things, you have to give them form and substance through concentration, otherwise they dissipate. In this creative process, you must have the **fullness** of desire.

UNCONTROLLABLE DESIRES RESULT IN DEPRESSION

We may go along for a time feeling fine and everything is beautiful and then suddenly we get very depressed. That means that our consciousness has descended into to a level of self where darkness reigns supreme, or what is known as ignorance. We descend to those realms of darkness, to those realms of self, through uncontrollable desire. When this uncontrollable desire is expressing itself, there is no light. We do not know how we got there because the thing that sent us there has no light and we cannot see it

TRANSMUTATION OF DESIRE

Transmutation is one technique used by some to handle certain of their desires. This entails visualizing fulfillment of a desire, but in a way that is repugnant to you. If you crave a candy bar but wish to refrain from eating it for dietary reasons, then imagine it is spoiled. Rather than expressing itself as frustration, the energy is dissipated.

ACCOMPLISHMENT THROUGH MODERATION OF EFFORT

Never overdo in trying to accomplish something. Work a little while each day. It does not work to allow the emotions and desires to demand it all be done **now**. Desire then controls you. To set the law of whatever time you allot yourself into motion takes a degree of control of the mind. Desire only knows expression, not reason, and it wants its expression immediately.

THE VIBRATION OF THE ROBBER

If someone comes and robs us of what we have earned in life, we must ask ourselves the question, under what vibration is a person who robs or steals? Are they under the vibration of reason or personal responsibility? Certainly not. Nor are they under the vibration of consideration or regard for the law. It is evident they are under the vibration of blind desire and greed. They have total disregard and total lack of consideration for the laws that very clearly grant each soul its individual right to respect itself and be responsible for itself. Such disregard denies granting those rights to all those with whom they come in contact. For you cannot grant to another what you have not first granted to yourself.

WILL IT BE SATISFACTION OR JOY?

We turn to God to experience joy. We turn to creation to experience satisfaction. Do not ask creation for joy; it does not exist there. In fact, as long as we have the need to be satisfied, that is, satisfy the senses, we are not ready for joy. Satisfaction ever leaves us in need. We can only be satisfied for fleeting moments and then pay dearly. Is it not interesting that even when we know how to put God into something, we do not do so?

"When desire becomes your servant,
you are freed from being its slave."

TO REVIEW:

All desire passes through our soul and impinges on our consciousness. Due to lack of self-control of the mind, the moment we have a feeling of desire, the desire enters a world of

137

form. The trouble is with the over-identification with self. It would not be difficult in that second to give the desire to God if we were not so over-identified with self.

If we believe and accept our desire is already on its way to us, the form returns to God, and some day it manifests in the physical. Through the Law of Like Attracts Like and becomes the Law of Attachment, we will experience what we truly believe. To God all things are possible, but to the mind, it is not so, for the mind is form.

Suppressed desire is the power of God entering our consciousness, feeding the past unfulfilled and unsatisfied forms of yesterday; for remember, God sustains all things. A desire trapped in form becomes a demon. A demon is the power of God we have stolen and put into form. Because the power of God is in it, it drives us crazy because we have too many of them. We are never free of the divine expression known as desire. That is why the moment we have a feeling of desire, we should give it back to God. Otherwise, suppressed desire is bound in form unable to express. That is where our forces of frustration are.

We educate anything that we place the light of reason upon. We are not transformed by reason, but by the light of reason. *"Keep faith with the light of reason; she will transfigure thee."* The light of reason is wisdom.

We already have everything we desire, and even things we have not thought of desiring, but we deny our own Divinity. We judge how things will be through that state of mind known as self and, therefore, cannot see that we have these things. Every one lives in desire. Let your desire be for God. God's goodness is called growing up.

*   *   *

"Goodness shines in the smile of man. A smile is not a grin. A grin is what your mind does when it thinks it is about to get what it desires."

138

Game 11

Finding Security in Money and Sex

Key Players:

Sense Functions:
Fascination, Lack,
Limitation, Money, Sex

Counterbalancing Soul Faculties:
Acceptance, Enthusiasm,
Faith, Humility, Poise

How the Game is Played:

The game of *Finding Security in Money and Sex* is played when the personality usurps power from the soul and finds its security in controlling money and sex.

THE NATURE AND PURPOSE OF THE PERSONALITY

The personality or ego is that part of the soul that functions as an energy tool in the physical plane. Its purpose is to preserve the form for the expression of the evolving soul. The difference between the personality of the human mind and the animal mind is the difference between simplicity and complexity. The personality within the human mind becomes most complex from its own awareness, and the awareness in turn feeds the complexity of self-importance. In so doing, the personality becomes the supreme authority and the soul descends into bondage. This in essence describes original sin, for Adam in the Garden of Eden became self-aware and sought to usurp the sovereignty of God.

The human personality can, however, serve a beautiful and constructive purpose when under the control of the light of reason. Without the drive of the personality there would not be progress, change, and evolution in this world of creation. Therefore, because it was designed to serve constructively, is it not sad when through our errors, it serves the opposite?

The Tibetan Buddhist masters have deep understanding of how the personality or ego, as it is termed here, plots and deceives. In *The Tibetan Book of Living and Dying*, Sogal Rinpoche shares insights that are worth quoting:

> Two people have been living in you all your life. One is the ego, garrulous, demanding, hysterical, calculating; the other is the hidden spiritual being, whose still voice of wisdom you have only rarely heard or attended to. As you listen more and more to spiritual teachings, contemplate them, and integrate them into your life, your inner voice, your innate wisdom of discernment, discriminating awareness is awakened and

strengthened . . . as the voice of your discriminating awareness grows stronger and clearer, you will start to distinguish between its truth and the various deceptions of the ego, and you will be able to listen to it with discernment and confidence.

The more often you listen to this wise guide, the more easily you will be able to change your negative moods yourself, see through them, and even laugh at them for the absurd dramas and ridiculous illusions that they are. Gradually you will find yourself able to free yourself more and more quickly from the dark emotions that have ruled your life, and this ability to do so is the greatest miracle of all. Terton Sogyal, the Tibetan mystic, said that he was not really impressed by someone who could turn the floor into the ceiling or fire into water. A real miracle, he said, was if someone could liberate just one negative emotion.

We cannot overemphasize the power that the ego or personality has usurped from the soul. The ego plays brilliantly on our fundamental fear of losing control, and of the unknown. The way Sogyal Rinpoche puts it:

So long as we haven't unmasked the ego, it continues to hoodwink us, like a sleazy politician endlessly parading bogus promises, or a lawyer constantly inventing ingenious lies and defenses, or a talk show host going on and on talking, keeping up a stream of suave

but emptily convincing chatter, which
actually says nothing at all.

. . . Ignorance has brought us to
identify the whole of our being with ego.
Its greatest triumph is to inveigle us into
believing its best interests are our best
interests, and even into identifying our
very survival with its own. This is a sav-
age wrong, considering that ego and its
grasping are at the root of all our suffering. Yet ego is so convincing, and we
have been its dupe for so long, that the
thought that we might ever become
egoless terrifies us.

Now you understand the false guidance the personality or
ego has given you and that when it is not balanced, it becomes
destructive. The energy becomes grounded in the function and
does not serve its purpose to drive the soul in creation. It is the
uneducated personality that resents change and is the greatest
stumbling block in our path to spiritual attainment.

The older we get, the stronger we are bound by the patterns that have already been accepted and established. As the
family gardener once remarked, *"When ye gits old ye jus gits more
like ye self."* As we go on with that process, our spiritual perception becomes dimmer. The divine energy is going to the sense
functions at the sacrifice of our peace and harmony. The soul is
eternal, but the personality is the effect of accepted patterns of
a very short life span and must bow in humility and accept that
it is not the great God Himself. There is a difference between
saying we cannot accept authority and simply believing we are
the authority. *"The act reveals the thought."*

When our titanic personalities are in control, and we depend on someone else to fulfill our desire, they can never measure up to our expectations. To permit someone to measure up
is to admit a flaw in our perfection because of our love affair

with our perfection. If we cannot find a flaw, it means they are equal to us and the personality cannot tolerate that.

A STRONG PERSONALITY IS NECESSARY TO FREE ITSELF

Changes take place for survival. You pit desire against desire in your personality. It takes constant repetition to bring about change. That is why it is said *repetition is the law through which change is made possible.* If truth, freedom, and the abundant good of life mean enough, you will repeat a thousand times a day an affirmation to make the change. The bottom line is simply that your freedom is dependent upon your willingness to educate your personality.

Despite its many games and its tenacity in trying to control the soul, you must cultivate a strong personality to serve the purpose of your own good and freedom in life. Is this a contradiction? No, for it is your personality that takes you to the depths of hell, and it is your personality that brings you back up. In the depths, the personality is denying the truth and is taking you to hell to set you free. Hell is a freeing process, and for that reason the suffering is worth it. *"One is freed in hell and saved in heaven."* The personality will bring you back up once it stops denying The Source. Heaven, a state of consciousness, saves you after hell gets through with you. It is up to the personality to acknowledge that while it is a great vehicle, it is not The Source; it is sustained by The Source.

It is the personality that denies the truth. It blames outwardly—someone outside has us in their grip. The personality cannot stand the thought of someone else having advantage over it. Then it takes the first step of ceasing to blame outwardly and to accept responsibility for the feeling inside. This is the personality pulling the soul back up from hell. The personality is a very fine vehicle, if used constructively.

The personality is balanced by the soul faculty of poise. Poise is balance, an evidence of internal equilibrium. When we express poise, the personality comes into alignment with the soul and reason reveals itself.

MONEY AND SEX ARE SERVANTS OF THE PERSONALITY

Money and sex both represent security to the uneducated personality. Sexual frustration and money frustration go back and forth because of their total dependence on the personality or mind for security. Money and sex are opposite sides of the coin in a sense. The personality keeps them going, otherwise, they would not play. The uneducated personality, over which no light of reason shines, feels secure only in what it can control. Early in life it makes the judgment it can control money and sex. The personality also views time as security, therefore, the passing of time or growing older is viewed as a losing of its own security.

The desires in the subconscious are not only for money but for all material things—all the attitudes concerning physical things. A person who has just the desire for money, just the desire to have everything of this material world, is building a false personality. A personality true to the soul expresses the soul's attributes. When the personality is false, we manifest it as sex because all we are thinking of is gratification of the body.

Money and sex are the constant servants of the personality. However, it is not the use of money or sex, it is the blatant abuse of them that brings suffering. Money is directed energy. When the energy is directed to feed the thought forms, it cannot bring in money. The energy needed for flow of money is going to feed thought forms. Mental substance knows it is temporary, and because it has no security, it is constantly trying to prove itself. It is all taking place in our own consciousness.

HANDLING THE CREATIVE FORCE OF SEX

Sex serves the personality as the instrument through which you fulfill other things in the head. Ask honestly, *What are the original judgments I made about sex? Am I looking for attention or affection? Do I use sex to control another?*

People who need attention are literally starving for affection. That level plays all sorts of games to get affection. When we need affection, we judge where it should come from. We separate ourselves from the light of reason by dictating how we will experience love, the love of God, and by doing that we suffer. The judgment becomes our god and what a slave we become to it! Feeling good is feeling God, but we censor how we will let ourselves feel good. Face the judge! For example, say, *Just a moment! The only time I feel good is when someone does what I want them to do.* Think about this. We have built barriers to feeling good. Many people cannot be alone or still, or they are afraid they will become aware of what is in their heads.

We have limited affection to sex and touching, but we can get it from nature. It is not limited to physical contact. Broaden your acceptances of how you will experience God. When you think you need affection, look at the trees, the sunset, talk to the birds, your pets. Wonderful energy comes from this for we have let in God in all ways. The master teacher would say there has to be something in the consciousness greater than sex, or you will be frustrated until you stop over-identifying with that part of the anatomy. Having sex will not eliminate the sex thought. Only the personality will stop it when you make a change in consciousness.

The personality is the key to balancing money and sex. It is the personality that refuses to release energy in intelligent, constructive ways.

If the creative force released by the sex organs is not dissipated through copulation, it can be directed upward for its expression. In other words, when you transmute the energy from the root chakra to spiritual power expressed through the throat chakra, the personality engages in purified creativity. Use the will to direct some of that life force, the prana, to art, music, or other soul talents. Otherwise, you can drive the self crazy and frustration and dis-ease, disease, result from the lack of harmony. Take control of the mind and stop over-identifying with the need. Needs can never be satisfied. That is the nature of the mind. Balance, balance, balance in all things in life.

The energy that expresses through the soul faculty of humility is the same energy that goes through the function of sex or procreation. When this prana is directed through the soul faculty of humility, it has a great healing power. It is the power of life herself. We are dealing with a very potent thing in the kundalini, which is force to the mind and power to the soul. This energy flows up from the base of the spine and washes over the brain. If excesses are not released because of the limited judgments of how you will allow yourself to experience goodness, you will pay the price.

The "have been's," experiences of the past, of the sex act keep us from fulfillment. The physical body is there but the demonstration shows the consciousness is not there, or the next day or thereafter, there would not be the need for sexual fascination. Comparison goes on constantly. It goes on in the personality and has nothing to do with the partner. It is sad that people go crazy over one simple personality judgment.

In the Alice Bailey book, *Esoteric Psychology I*, dictated from spirit by The Tibetan, he forecasts that:

> In no department of life will the change toward brotherhood be more potently expressed than in the attitude of man toward sex, and in the readjustment of the marriage relationship. This new attitude will gradually come about as the slowly developing science of psychology comes into its own. As man comes to understand his own threefold nature, and as the nature of consciousness and the depth of his own subconscious life are more truly grasped, there will take place, gradually and automatically, a change in the attitude of men towards women and of women towards their destiny . . .
>
> As the creative urge is turned upwards from the sacral centre to the throat, man will live less potently in his

physical sexual urges, and more consistently in his creative expression. His physical plane life will proceed along normal lines, but it is necessary for men to realise that the manner in which man today satisfies his sexual nature is abnormal and unregulated, and that we are on our way to a wise normality. True marriage and right sexual relations should involve the marriage of all three aspects of man's nature: There should be a meeting on all three levels of consciousness at once, the physical, the emotional and the mental.

Bailey further writes that when people give expression to the Christ life and put this above the fulfillment of the sex urge, then when they have children, they will attract souls on higher levels. It will "make possible the more rapid incarnation of disciples and initiates . . . souls will be attracted to their parents by the urgency of those parents' desire, the purity of their motives and the power of their preparatory work."

The eager search of men and women for companions who will understand and appreciate their *true* nature is really the search for God. Satisfaction comes only as God is found. The earthly marriage can represent a heavenly union if the partners make of it a perpetual sacrament and a means of developing the hidden beauties of their nature through abiding gentleness, understanding, love-service, patience, and reverence towards the Christ Spirit in each.

Forced celibacy is not advised for the suppressed creative energies will manifest in some negative manner. A wise person abstains from excessive sexual activities and expends a portion of the creative energies through mental and physical activities.

The consciousness must move and not remain locked on the body or a dollar bill. Energy dissipated in fascination with either drains the vital body and the thought forms multiply.

HOW MONEY SERVES THE PERSONALITY

As we consider more deeply how money serves the personality, it is evident that we are emotional about money because we have made it our god. We have equated it with "security." We have never considered the source behind the object. The minute we get emotional about how little money we have, God will prove through our personality, working through the law we have established, that we are right. God works as the sustainer of the law we choose. The law we choose is what we direct our attention to. Stop! Become aware of what you are creating. Make a turn around in consciousness regarding money. When we release it freely, it comes freely. It does not mean a person should be a spendthrift. It does mean a person has to keep the emotions out of it. Emotions set up an obstruction. Fear is in the way of the natural flow from God. Be practical, but our practicality should not be guided by fear because then we place yourself under the Law of Limitation.

The money god starts as a child. It grows up. We keep feeding the entity and experience trauma. We can shut off the feeding and energy of the money god when we affirm: *"God is the true and only source of my supply."* Declare this truth each time you associate with material supply. Work on it every day in every way. Never let up.

If we say, *I'm a little short,* the false god will set us up to be shorter. We become obsessed by those entities. The false god is dictating, and in dictating, the entity drains us and gets stronger. If we have a financial problem, God will sustain we are absolutely right. If no money is coming in, then not enough energy is going to it. The energy is going to mental substance. When we feel as good with money going out as we do with money coming in, we will enter a neutral point where faith exists, for faith is the counterbalancing soul faculty to money. If, however, we put all our faith in ourselves, and not in God, then by the Law of Creation we guarantee the constant "feast and famine" cycle in our life. It is a "sin" against God to be poor for it is not God that keeps goodness away from us. It is the reliance on our minds. So control the mind moment-by-moment in order to experience the goodness. (Sin means making mistakes or being ignorant of spiritual law.)

The poverty tape may rise when we make a large expenditure that is not our usual pattern. The personality cannot accept blame for its own desires, so it goes through the priority list after the money is spent and fear rises. Then we blame things lowest on the priority list. Poverty is not spirituality, only delusion. Where is reason when God takes care of the blade of grass? Let no one be deceived into thinking poverty is a virtue. Could not he who increased loaves and fishes have increased money likewise?

THE PRINCIPLE OF FREEDOM FROM MONEY

In paying bills, send out your checks freely so that God can replenish the cup. We cannot rely on God until we stop relying on the brain. Fear holds onto money and faith frees it. Be joyous that you can pay any amount and it will freely return to you. Give grudgingly and it will return on the same vibration. As freely as we give shall we receive. If we receive freely, we know something in consciousness is giving freely. If not giving the gift of self freely, then what we desire is not returning freely. The cup must first be emptied in order for us to receive what we are seeking. When we do not empty the cup, it will continue to flow from God but into someone else's universe. Learn when the season is passed. What we hold onto here takes away from what is waiting in heaven.

The principle of the freedom from money is the continuity of giving. It takes humility to bow the personality and make small regular payments. The personality wants to wait and pay it all off at once. Waiting, without continuity of effort, no matter what size, is a transgression of the Law of Flow (supply). The result is that the debt only builds up and the mind sinks lower into the depths of despair because with supply shut off, there is less with which to pay. Continuity is essential. If one is depending only on his or her salary or other fixed income, then his or her mind is limiting the source of supply. They are relying on the job and other things and not on God. Remember, employers are only the channels for God's supply.

I am grateful to the spirit friends who suggested printing on checks above the signature, *"God is the source of my supply."* Most banks are very accommodating. Each time we write a check it is a wonderful reminder of whom the true source of our supply really is. As we let go freely, it returns freely. It also is understood that one should never write a check with red ink. If we have a desire and say we cannot afford it, we will establish all the laws necessary to guarantee not being able to afford it. That is the payment for our judgment. Judgment is a dictate which establishes a law. Our energy is going to the judgment instead of to gratitude that will make the crumb multiply.

Enthusiasm and flow are inseparable. If we are having money problems, it is an indication of a lack of enthusiasm. True enthusiasm is to be in God and good comes from it. When we do not show or express enthusiasm, we bottle up God, or goodness. The goodness does not get released from the aura and so it cannot go out and attract its kind and return. Enthusiasm is an important principle of divine abundance. It is easy to generate enthusiasm when we make the decision to get rid of the judgments. Put your attention on the feeling of abundance and it will emanate.

For every positive thought you have, you have a minimum of two negative thoughts. Rising from the subconscious is an automatic negative thought, plus a thought based on past experience in any way related to it, and those thoughts override the desire and enthusiasm. The admonition is to move quickly with your positive thought. The longer you play with the thought, the more the negative thoughts and obstructions arise and you are caught in the frustration of being unfulfilled.

ACCEPT THE RIGHT OF ABUNDANCE

We have to first accept there is a way, and secondly, the way is beyond what our mind has to offer. We set ourselves up. For example, we desire a new car. Immediately, the judgments rise and without self-control they will guarantee our experiences. The boundaries established by our mind create the limits of our realities.

"Accept the right for yourself and the way is provided." If you truly accept your right, you have no concern, for the way will be provided. Learn to shut off the "BBS" (Brain Broadcasting Station). The problem is we do not know when to flip the switch. The energy it takes to neutralize obstructions takes away from energy going into the flow.

The mind, a dual instrument, is in a constant process of broadcasting a message to you. It is constantly broadcasting past experiences. You must take hold of that broadcasting station and choose. Be firm in your choice of what you will permit it to broadcast into the eternal waves, for that is where you should stand guardian each and every moment. To one who broadcasts abundance and uses the soul faculty of patience and reason to sustain the broadcast, abundance shall manifest in his or her life. But when you permit the mind to broadcast the message of abundance—remember, abundance is a principle—put it in the hands of divine guidance that you may experience an abundance of what you desire to experience.

To have new experiences you must constantly rebroadcast a very potent signal to overcome the old signal. By the constant flowing, you will start to get little crumbs. Build on those crumbs. The most opportune time to reprogram the computer is when the struggle is the greatest. It is an opportunity to face fear and know God is your only supply. Supply is not limited to green paper. Think of your supply of being able to breathe, move your feet, the beauty of nature, and so forth.

You will know exactly what is coming into your life by what you are sending out into the universe. When you are caught in the middle of a predicament, let go. *Well, God, I've done all my mind can do.* Then let go. The mind is only letting go of its limited experiences.

You must be free of money temptation to stay on the spiritual path. You cannot do God's work and go hungry, if God is

151

truly in what you do. God works through the material world; you just do not sell out the spiritual to attain it. If you truly believe that something is going to work out, and you do not dictate the details of how it will work out, then it will work out. That is a demonstration of faith. You need to get in touch with the levels of consciousness inside yourself and declare the truth to the forces of darkness bombarding you:

"God is the true source of my supply. Everything is working out the way it should;, therefore, I am freed from all concern."

It is a daily process if you are to give up self thought. You may as well flood your consciousness with something good since it is already flooded with the negative. So permeate your consciousness with God as the true source of your supply. Everything else is a total delusion for the glory of the personality.

Whenever we have to face an expenditure, it is a golden opportunity to see how much the thought of self is driving us "bananas!" Instead of fascinating with green paper, saying we do not have enough so we can continue to play the game of the mind, affirm: *"God, I'm grateful for what I have and when I've earned it, I know more will come. Free me from this desire in my head, for you are the true and only source of my supply."* Then be willing to accept the crumb and it will turn into the loaf.

If you really **accept** the right to something for yourself, then you are not concerned with the way or how it will happen. If you are concerned about how it will happen, it never got out of your brain. In other words, how it will happen never got out of the realms of judgment. As God is the source of our supply, we cannot be concerned with how God will get it to us. When we accept from God, we are freed from paying creation. How it comes is none of our business because it comes from one source. Just open up and be receptive. When we "forget" about a thing, God goes to work. The question is, if you easily accept the limitations, why can you not accept the unlimited possibility of supply from a higher authority?

If you are **concerned** with "the way," it reveals that your mind insists on its control over that which is beyond the mind.

That which you accept, you experience. What you reject is your destiny. The negative faith in your mind has to go in order to experience your right to happiness. Negative faith or fear is faith in what the mind has to offer. Positive faith is faith in what the spirit has to offer. In all things, we are always faced with exercising choice and following one of the above. In everything we think and do, we have the choice of either mind or spirit.

Keep things moving in your life, then you cannot be controlled by them—such as the flow of money. That which you try to control, controls you. When you keep things moving, your mind never gets attached to them.

If we believe that God is the source of our supply, does it not behoove us to keep God close at hand in case we need a supply of something? Spiritual philosophy teaches the abundant good, the prosperity of life itself. We bear a great responsibility knowing that which is demonstrably true, and to demonstrate it by our thoughts, acts, and deeds. We cannot afford the luxury of the illusion of lack, of the delusion of denial, for then we become an instrument of darkness instead of an instrument of Light. We cannot say that God is the true and only source of our supply, and then demonstrate the direct opposite. That is the worst form of hypocrisy. The abundant good of life is ever dependent upon our vibration. Give up the fear. Demonstrate faith and flow with the endless, the ceaseless abundant good of life itself, never forgetting The Source. *"One who thinks one's gain is much and forgets the source guarantees the loss."*

PREPARATION TODAY TO TAKE CARE OF TOMORROW

Remember, at transition you take no physical substance into the spirit world because it does not exist in those dimensions. What are you going to take with you? What is going to comfort you on your journey? What is going to encourage you and keep you going? What do you have to take with you? The only thing you have is your mind. That is all. What kind of mind are you going to take? Are you going to be pleased with it? Think about that. Every moment is a death, and every moment is a birth, for it is a death and birth in consciousness.

So often we think, *In ten years or less I'll have this or that here in this physical world.* Is that sensible? We do not know how long we will be here. Is it reasonable to garner up all of the gold of this material world and put it all into a bank account? If we live in fear of losing our money, then when we leave our physical body, we will not be able to leave the bank doors because that is where our security is. Our astral body and our desire body will hover at those bank vaults, and that is all it can do— hover and go through its frustrations. We do not know what hour, what day, or what moment we are going to another dimension. Somehow we have merited the opportunity to recognize and consider that God is the owner and we are only the stewards. As stated elsewhere, we should be practical in dispensing our resources, but not fearful by selfishly hoarding riches. Take a lesson from the squirrel who, knowing its needs, puts away acorns sufficient for the winter.

> *"When our cry for God is as great as our cry for money, we will have the true gold of life, wisdom."*

The purpose of the personality is to use it, but to use it consciously— not to be the victim of its own addictions. We dictate with our own conscious mind where we get feelings of glory or pleasure. Make that conscious choice. Do not allow instead *"reward to tempt the personality while the soul waits to serve."* Remember that the personality is the key to balancing money and sex and that *"faith gives poise to keep the personality still to express humility so it can willingly accept."*

* * *

> *"Thank you, God, for granting me the opportunity to be your unobstructed vehicle for the divine flow."*

Game 12

Making Our Attachments Our Adversities and Our Adversities Our Attachments

Key Players:

Sense Functions:
Adversity, Attachment, Attraction,
Belief, Disrespect, Judgment,
Intolerance, Self-Will, Stealing

Counterbalancing Soul Faculties:
Acceptance, Dignity, Exposure, Forgiveness,
Graciousness, Honesty, Joy, Pause,
Personal Responsibility, Surrender, Tolerance,
Truth, Understanding, Willingness

How the Game is Played:

The game of *Making Our Attachments Our Adversities and Our Adversities Our Attachments* is played by becoming the victim of our attachments and of our adversities. Our need to control creates our attachments, and in that attachment is guaranteed adversity.

HOW THE LAW OF ATTACHMENT OPERATES

Like Attracts Like and becomes the Law of Attachment. It becomes it because we believe it. Our attachments then become our adversities. Our adversities become our attachments. *"Adversities are attachments awaiting recognition."* It is an immutable subtle law. How does that immutable law really work? Whatever we are attached to at any moment, we are in truth averse to. *"Adversity is caused by a dictate of superiority over that which we feel adverse to."* That is the law of creation, a just and beautiful, immutable law, for it is the divine right of God to free His children, our souls, from the bondage of our personalities.

Built into form or creation is the Law of Duality. *"When we feel the joy of attachment, in that feeling is the fear of adversity."* Take the simple example of being attracted to, and then attached to a lovely, fragile piece of porcelain. There exists the fear that it will be broken. That is the balance that the divine immutable laws have placed in nature, and from that balance, our soul is guaranteed in eternity to be free. This is why the teaching to *"Make friends with your adversities. They are in truth your own attachments."* That is the law that governs creation.

Another example of the law in operation is one from my experiences of some years ago. I vowed that when I got married I would never do any laundry, observing how my mother was burdened with washing for nine children. I insisted that any husband of mine would have to send out all of the family wash to a pickup and delivery laundry service. This adversity to doing the laundry myself became an attachment when I married and moved to a country home where such service was unavailable. The truth of the matter is, if the service had been available, the family income at that time would not have stretched far enough to include it. To add insult to injury, I had to use an old fashioned washing machine and an outdoors hand wringer, set up backwards for a left-handed person, which I am not. This is a demonstration of the greater the adversity, the greater the attachment which then becomes adversity again.

BE NEUTRAL ABOUT GAIN AND LOSS

When we attach to the gain, we guarantee the loss for we have denied our divinity. That being so, do we as wise people attach ourselves to creation, knowing that we are guaranteeing in the attachment a great adversity? We cannot be free when we are averse to anything. When you shift into neutral gear, you have no pain in the loss and you will have no pain in the gain.

When judgment takes control and you are thinking of you, you become aware of your attachment. The stronger your attachments, the greater your judgments, and the greater your blindness to the truth because of your attachments to your judgments. The sadness is that the mind thinks its attachment thought forms are perfect. You do not see them in truth because attachment is totally blind.

ATTACHMENT THOUGHT FORMS

Attachments start with a selfish motivation. Every attachment the mind has is a thought form created by our need to control and is supported by judgment. This need to attach is the denial of The Divine. Attachment is selfish because it is stealing from God. *"The thief of desire is the birth of attachment and the guarantee of bondage."* The moment the personality steals the desire, the form created may be inharmonious to other levels, and the battle goes on.

No one is ever attached to the formless and free, for it is in the magnetic field of creation that we are attached. The idols of "clay feet" as spoken about in the Bible are our attachments. Every attachment the mind has is a thought form. Our attachments become our false gods—our little gods that bind us to hell. These are the false gods we serve and suffer from. You can never move forward in life without letting go of what has served its purpose.

Just stop and think, our attachment is not really to a person or thing but to our thought form; and because it only exists in our consciousness, we can do something about it. These forms must be dethroned to be free. Put God where the thought form is, otherwise, you will pay the price of the attachment.

We and we alone create our own thought forms. But each time we refuse to accept the forms we have created, we direct energy through the Law of Adversity and become the victim of the forms. Again, the law of our adversity becoming our attachment comes into play. We are living with a multitude of forms. Freedom from the forms comes by separating truth from creation which takes place through the soul faculty of acceptance. Freedom is in the moment of our acceptance.

ALL ATTACHMENTS ARE PERSONALITY EXTENSIONS

"The more our ego extends, the less our soul evolves." All attachments are extensions of the personality and you believe you are the god of what you are attached to. And as long as it does what you want when you want it to, you feel good. It is only a delusion to think you are god of your attachment, for the very opposite is true. It is the attachment to things of creation, not the enjoyment of things, that creates bondage. That which sticks in your consciousness is that which destroys you. Let things go as joyously as you let them enter. It is demonstrable that you will never be without as long as you empty your cup. Wisdom reveals truth is like a river, it flows continuously, teaching you *that which you hold destroys you, that which you give unfolds you.* But wisdom dictates also that you use wisely what you have.

BE WILLING TO GIVE UP YOUR ATTACHMENTS

What you are not willing to give up, you will not only find that you have created gods of, but they will still control you on the other side of life in their astral or etheric counterpart. As the scriptures tell us: *"Whatever you bind on earth will be bound in heaven, and whatever you release on earth will be released in heaven."* (Matthew 18:18).

Because our attachments become our adversities, it is well that we consider another adage, *"Be ever ready and willing to change."* If we are given a job to do in life, it is in our best interest to do it with care, putting God into it without attachment to the job. If we are serving in any capacity in a selfless way, that is, if we are not doing a job for the honor and glory or personal gain of our personality, then we will have no attachment. Despite how much effort or time we have put into a particular assignment, we will have no emotion about a reassignment. If we have not built a little "empire" for ourselves, then we will graciously and harmoniously accept recommendations regarding changes.

ATTACHMENT TO THE "FRUITS OF ACTION"

It is the personality's attachment to the fruits of action that make us forget for whom we are working and, therefore, we are serving the forces of darkness within. *"When our love of God exceeds our love of self, we are freed from being the object of possession and obsession by the princes of darkness."* Emotional attachment is the delusion. You cannot work with the Light, that is, on a spiritual level, when you are attached to what the personality thinks it is capable of doing. There is no freedom in attachment because there is no Light in it.

What are the "fruits of action?" Usually we think of the things that we have garnered unto ourselves. We consider those things of creation our "fruits of action." Rarely do we consider the thoughts that we create in our mind as our "fruits of action." It is our attachment to these attitudes of mind. *"It is our attachment to the judgments and decisions we have made in our life that stand as great obstructions in our path to our eternal evolving being."* Attachment to the fruits of action begins when we become aware of what and how much we are doing. Then we begin to look around and compare our efforts with what others are doing. Especially, when you are given a job you do not like, you feel you are doing all the work. An immature person is very attached to the fruits of their labor. The degree of that attachment is equal to the degree of disappointment if it does not work out the way they want it to.

Avoid putting all of your eggs in one basket. Always have something going on in a variety of ways so that if energy expended in one area does not return as we would like it, it will return in another way. We cannot always know when and in what way something will return. Everything is pure energy directed by mind. If, however, the goodness is being eaten up by attachment, it cannot return.

When we do what we have to do in life and care less what the world does with it, we are freed from the bondage of attachment. We tend to be too concerned about what other people think. If we are not attached to our personality, we will not care what people think. We will do what is right because it is right to do and we will not be hurt, nor will we hurt others.

GRACIOUSLY ACCEPTING CHANGES AND CRITICISM

Your joy of life is dependent upon how graciously you accept changes. A person who is not attached to the fruits of action takes criticism in the spirit of graciousness and dignity. Graciousness and dignity go hand in hand with spiritual illumination. Graciousness is the rhythmic flow of The Divinity. When judgment dictates what graciousness is, it is no longer spiritual.

When judgment enters, do we hear only that criticism for which we have value? Criticism can be constructive if given from a level of care, kindness, and consideration, or it can be of no benefit if given from a level of intolerance. If it is from intolerance, we can rest assured it will befall us in order that we may be granted the understanding of it. If we find the need to repeatedly or constantly criticize anything outside of ourselves, then what we are in truth doing is expressing an intolerance of the level within, which in time will guarantee that level of consciousness to be attached to our life expression and experience.

A log that is jammed in a stream creates a stagnant pool, and in time, deteriorates; whereas, a log that flows unobstructed down a river, unattached, remains in perfect condition and arrives at its destination. Our spiritual growth may be likened unto the log that flows freely. Attachments only bind us to creation and serve to retard our spiritual growth. A wise person makes the effort to remain free of the control of anything and anyone so that he or she is free to rise to higher levels of consciousness. *"When the fear of attachment melts away in the light of reason, the fullness of attainment is realized."*

BEYOND CREATION TO SURRENDER

You must go beyond creation to total and complete surrender, surrender of all the attachments, surrender of all your known and unknown adversities, surrender of the things you cherish the most, not just physical objects, but your mental and emotional attachments, surrender to God of all those things in your mind. Surrender is the process of life herself. You are always surrendering every moment to something, whether it is to The Divine or to the dictates of your limited brain in order to preserve your ego or personality mechanisms. When you surrender all of them, you, your soul, will go beyond creation and there you will experience truth and freedom. If you can give the attachment to God, you will know God. If you are **willing** to give up your attachments, you may or may not actually have to give them up, and whatever way it goes, it will be the way to freedom for you.

ATTACHMENTS AFFECT OUR ACCOMPLISHMENTS

We drag out the completion of a job because of the glory of our attachments. The realm gets fed when we are asked how and when a job will be finished. We want to be constantly begged to get it done. If it is something that we compute takes too much of *our* time, the thought forms of self-pity complain that it is "endless." It can also work in another way, as when the longer the personality can take to accomplish a job, it can use that as a device not to do other things.

The defense mechanism of the level is to get emotional so it can have its own way. You cannot afford to react to it, or the kid inside of you will react, taking you into the emotional realm. You pick up the package and cannot rise out of the level. So follow the line of non-attachment and stand firm.

THE PAIN OF LETTING GO

If you were not attached to creation, you would not suffer. Become aware of your emotional attachments and the feeling of pain and pleasure; pause and declare, *God, I never knew I was attached. I, and I alone, am personally responsible for the way I feel.* Whatever controls you is your god. The strength of your soul is in the pause, and then you will see what you are serving.

The soul's movement in evolution is only possible by letting go of that which used to be and it is the pain of letting go that is our true suffering. *"The degree of suffering reveals the degree of attachment."* It is true suffering because we have entertained the thought that we are owner and possessor of the forms. Whatever you choose to hold to, you are bound by. It may be the freedom of another soul. For example, if we truly love, we do not bind or attach to the object of our love, for to attach is to limit. Rather, we respect the divine rights of another individual, recognizing that we are all God's children. To feel that we possess another soul and establish an unhealthy, dependent bond is to steal from God.

INTOLERANCE AND DISRESPECT ACT AS MAGNETS

If we have an adversity to people because we cannot tolerate the various levels they are expressing, we are channeling energy, and energy expressed from that level is magnetic. It will go out into the universe and pull all those people to us that we cannot tolerate. That is why it is known as *"Our adversities become our attachments."* When we become educated, that is, when we shine the light of reason over that level of consciousness, we will be free from attracting people that we cannot tolerate.

The disrespect you show another reveals the disrespect you show yourself. If you show no respect, you are shown no respect in life. Like attracts like. One who abuses is abused. If you have no respect for yourself, you are in the process of destroying yourself. *"When disrespect manifests, wisdom demands change and reason shows the way."*

The more you push away your lesson, the more it will come back to you. The moment you accept that you must make a change in your attitude, you have evolved and are ready to go on to the next lesson. It is our attitudes, our judgments, our intolerance that we must grow through. If we do not, the experiences will only repeat themselves. Our lessons get stronger as we evolve, so we must work harder on self-control.

It is when you accept all of the lessons, when you truly accept all of life, that you are freed from the destiny of the mind, for the destiny of the mind is a constant repetition of the things that you hold. It is only the things that you hold that hound you and bind you. So few people seem to realize that it is not the things of form outside that hold us in mental substance, but it is the forms of attachment and adversity that are inside.

FREEDOM THROUGH EXPOSURE

Willingness to expose our attachments or adversities is another important aspect to freeing ourselves. Whenever in life we have an experience that is traumatic, which is extremely emotionally disturbing to us, we tend to suppress the experience by forcing it down into our subconscious mind where we no longer are consciously aware of it. However, that energy directed to being averse to the experience must go somewhere. Thought forms are created which go out into the universe, gather like vibrations around and about them, and some day return to us, their creators. We are not consciously aware of this activity. Therefore, it behooves us to make greater effort to expose to ourselves the very things that cause us emotional disturbance. For without exposure, which frees the soul, we do not honestly and truthfully face ourselves, our levels of consciousness. When we do not face what we have in truth created, we become the slave to, rather than the master of, the mind.

No matter how strong your attachments are, you will be free if you declare, *I alone am personally responsible for this feeling of mine. I no longer give credit or power to my attachments.* In this way the personality serves as a vehicle for the soul as it was designed to do.

THE HIGHEST PRIORITY MUST BE TRUTH

Attachment cannot be a higher priority than truth. Nothing can mean more than truth to awaken to truth. Truth is not something you can acquire, because you already have it. Truth must be unfolded. It abides in fullness at the very core of our being. A philosophy is only a guideline to help you to awaken to what you already are. Ask yourself the question, *Am I serving where the Light of truth lives, or am I serving the forces of darkness where deception exists?*

It is through the soul faculties of tolerance, understanding, forgiveness, acceptance, personal responsibility, honesty, truth, and surrender that we can free ourselves from becoming the victim of our attachments and our adversities. Like can only be sustained by like. Unfoldment affects not only the individual soul, but everyone with whom we come in contact.

*   *   *

"Attachment is the weakness of familiarity
and the strength of license."

Game 13

Confusing Giving with Lending and Borrowing with Owning

Key Players:

Sense Functions:
Attachment, Concern, Generosity,
Greed, Selfishness,
Something-for-Nothing Attitude

Counterbalancing Soul Faculties:
Givingness, Personal Responsibility,
Surrender

How the Game is Played:

In playing the game of *Confusing Giving with Lending and Borrowing with Owning,* the personality, sitting on the throne of judgment, makes loans instead of gifts by refusing to allow the soul to give freely. The personality further ignores that God is the true owner of all by deluding us into believing we are the owner rather than being only a borrower.

GIVING THE GIFT OF SELF

"The joy of living is known as the Law of Giving," but giving is such a misunderstood word. When we think of giving, we usually think of things external that we have accumulated. It is very rare that we ever think of things internally in reference to the Law of Giving. The soul faculty of givingness has to do with what we give of ourselves. **The greatest gift that one can give is the gift of self, the giving up of the throne of judgment.** If we cannot give without the gift of self, then our gift goes in vain. For it is not a gift, it is a loan because our throne of judgment still has it under its control. It still thinks about it, and in so doing, is attached to it. When we have truly given, there is no thought of the gift after we have given it. It is when we give begrudgingly that we have not given at all, but have only lent. Loans become like a chain around our neck, ever pulling us to disturbance and grief.

DISTINCTION BETWEEN GIVING AND LENDING

Let us not confuse giving with lending. Loans incur debts; gifts come freely from the soul. A gift truly given comes from the Infinite Source and our soul is the instrument of that Infinite Source. A true gift is ever replenished and always replaced; for the law triples or may even multiply ten times, if our heart is in what we give. If our heart is not in it, the gift is not multiplied. We need not be in concern if we are truly giving. We are then the channels of the Infinite Divine Abundant Good that is everywhere.

"What of thy heart freely gives in God's love forever lives."

MOVING BEYOND GIVING FOR GAIN

One very strong delusion of the human mind is to defend the realm that absolutely refuses to give anything. Then, there are those who often in their so-called giving first make the judgment, *if I do this, I will gain that.* Time passes and they take a look. They do not see the gain. So they refine the judgment by deluding themselves further that they give, and give, and give, and gain nothing.

Remember, the moment that you **judge,** you must have a basis or a foundation for your judgment. The basis or foundation is the **illusion** of the thought of self (personality) which separates you from the universal whole. You become in that moment an independent entity without recognition of the source that sustains you.

Why do you not see the gain? You do not see the gain because all of your attention is upon what you have done. *"Be not concerned with what you do and you will be free from the doing."* In other words, do not be attached to the fruits of action. It is your concern that is your payment, for each concern that you have in life reveals the authority and priority of your mind over all of your experiences. Do what you know is right because you know it is right to do it. Move beyond giving for the purpose of manipulating and controlling another soul. Move beyond giving for the goal of having a memorial built in your honor. Ask yourself, *What is my motive in giving? Am I expecting something in return?*

A person may be generous for many, many varied motivations, but a person in givingness is in God. Let go joyously and then when yours that is truly yours comes, it will come joyously. It will be free, and you will be free of the fear that by giving you will not gain. You will be free of bondage to that kind of thinking.

EMPTY THE OVERFLOWING CUP

The scriptures teach that it is more blessed to give than to receive. Why hold on to what you have when something greater is waiting for you? To let go of things is a freer way of living. They enter your universe and serve a purpose for a time, then it is time to release them. When you find your cup is overflowing, it is time to empty it so it can be constantly replenished. If you do not empty it, then all the flow that is to come will merely run over. The Bible teaches, *"my cup runneth over."* Whatever cup overflows does not benefit the holder of the cup.

The law is clear that lack of use is abuse. What you are not using you are abusing and shall be deprived of. The law of abundant flow cannot work if your cup runneth over. That is what we have to understand. In what areas of our life does our cup runneth over? The fear that things will not work out the way our mind dictates is the crux of the problem.

The outward manifestation is the revelation of the inner thought. If you hold onto material objects that no longer serve a purpose, then it reveals you are holding onto thoughts and patterns of mind (behavior) that no longer serve a purpose—patterns that are detrimental. The Law of Abuse catches up with you if you do not let something go when it is not serving its purpose. It is abusing you with frustration and clutter when you do not use something for the purpose for which it was designed. The clutter of our abodes reveals the turmoil and upset of our personal emotions.

"As freely as I give, so shall I receive." Therefore, to gain, you must first give up—give up the superiority of the mind. Material things appear first in the mental realm. So, if you want to know if you are ready to receive what you are seeking, look and see if there is room and a place for it to get in.

If you give away what you have value for, then you empty your cup of value and receive even greater value. If you give away that which you have no value for, then in keeping with the Law of Like Attracts Like, you will receive only that which you will not have value for. To put it another way, to give to another what you want for yourself is a wise person. To give to another what you do not want for yourself is acting the fool, because you have set into motion the Law of Denial; and what you give out, returns.

"We do not want for another what we have denied for ourselves."

LEARN TO LET GO IN YOUR HEAD
You will see just how far you have come when someone asks you for a donation or to do a little work and you have judged you do not want to do it. You will then see how difficult it is to give up, and how much work still needs to be done on yourself.

The acid test perhaps is to let something go at the peak of its value. Learn to let go in your head.

"When you love your losses as you love your gains, you will have self-control."

"Be ever ready and willing to give that which you hold most dear and you shall know not of fear."

If you hold something to the day you pass over to the spirit side of life, then it will hold and bind you to the earth realm, "it" being your attachment. *"Truly I say to you, Whatever you bind on earth will be bound in heaven, and whatever you release on earth will be released in heaven."* (Matthew 18:18)

At first try letting go a little bit, then a little bit will enter your life. If you let go of much more, then much more comes into your life. When you let all go, then, yea, all will come back and in even greater amount. Why hold on to what you have when something greater is waiting for you? This is so beautifully expressed by Arthur William Beer:

GIVING

To get he had tried, yet his store was still meager.
 To a wise man he cried, in a voice keen and eager;
"Pray tell me how I may successfully live?"
 And the wise man replied, "To get you must give."

As to giving he said, "What have I to give?
 I've scarce enough bread, and of course one must live;
But I would partake of Life's bountiful store."
 Came the wise man's response; "Then you must give more."

The lesson he learned: to get was forgotten,
 Toward mankind he turned with a love new-begotten.
As he gave of himself in unselfish living,
 Then joy crowned his days, for he grew rich in giving.

"That which I hold destroys me and that which I free unfolds me." All those things we hold in the mental consciousness are those things that are destroying us (judgments). Our minds are constantly telling God how life shall be—how things shall come to us. We make the judgment, *I can't afford this because I haven't the money.* Yes, we have to be practical, but we pay a terrible price for telling God how it shall be. When something does not go as our mind thinks it should, reason dictates to give it to God. The mind wants to say, *Oh, just let it go,* to prove that the personality was right all along. God's work is never dependent on our judgment. We never know through whom God will work and how.

To give to *limit* and expect to receive from the *limitless* is not possible. To the givers all is given because they are in a vibratory wave of giving and the law states that Like Attracts Like and becomes the Law of Attachment. Continuity of effort in giving is essential to stay in the Law of Flow, free of the throne of judgment, thereby experiencing the joy of living. Life then has real meaning for us. Without the continuity of effort, the mind comes up with a multitude of justifications why we should not make that effort. When the thoughts of self bombard us, revealing to us that more effort is needed to control our own mind, we become despondent or discouraged.

It pays to let go, then you are not likely to be "stuck" in a holding pattern. Eventually, when one insists upon holding on, a pattern is established so one no longer knows how to let go. If we are in a "holding vibration" through lack of awareness, through ignorance and fear, then all shall be taken. The divine law is everywhere present. It is constantly demonstrating itself to us wherever we go. When the sun shines, it shines on all creation. It does not choose the apple tree and deny the oak, but it shines on both trees. So it is when we hold, through lack of understanding, that the only one we are holding from is ourselves. We are denying our own divinity. In other words, our faith is in lack and limitation. Our faith is not in the Divine Infinite Abundance. Look around this globe and see if you can find any spot where the Divine Intelligence has withheld the element of air? No, *"so to the giver all is given."*

ASKING THE GOD WITHIN

In the world of creation we must learn to receive as graciously as we give. We have to reap as well as sow. Many people have an obstruction to receiving because it is so difficult for them to ask. Therefore, it is easier for them to give than to receive. The failure to ask is the transgression of the Law of Receiving. By making a judgment that we, not God, are the source, we dictate the payment and instantly reject the channel. Receiving is then limited to all the obstructions of the mind. In other words, if we become confused and ask the personality of another, forgetting instead to ask The Divine flowing through the person asked, we become the victim of the mental realms.

"God works through man and not to man. You must ask the God flowing through man, not the man himself." Find the God inside you before asking and when you speak your word forth, you will be asking the God within. To receive freely, pride and judgments must bow. You can only receive freely when you accept from the true source. *"When you accept from God, you are freed from paying creation."* When you are no longer concerned about **what** you will receive, you are asking from the God within. The moment you are concerned, you are coming from the wrong level. Instead, affirm: *"I speak my word forth **knowing** it will accomplish that which I send it to do."* Only then, there is no concern, for then, it is in God's hands and what comes will come for your greater good.

Why do people have such a struggle in asking? How many times as a child have we asked and received "no" for an answer. The judgment is well established so we will not ask. Therefore, we avoid the repetition of the pain of those rejection experiences. Consequently, we cannot have the fullness of life if we are living in a graveyard of past experiences and events. We are the "living dead" when we allow vague memories of past experiences to cast a shadow on tomorrow's experiences. Put a light upon the shadows.

OPENING DOOR TO SELF-CONCERN

A practical way of living is not to waste opportunities for getting what you can, especially spiritual understanding. That does not mean that you hoard, for hoarding is greed. "*Abundance is the natural law; lack of using what you are receiving, the transgression* ." If you do not move things on to serve their purpose, you deny the abundant flow in your life and guarantee the day of need. If you hold things thinking you will use them someday, then you are in concern. "*The business of common sense is the lack of self-concern.*" When you rely on the personality to accomplish anything, you review past experiences and establish the Law of Fear and open the door to self-concern. God is not in it and no good returns.

GIVING UP ATTACHMENT

We are the greatest *borrowers* known in the universes. In truth, *we own nothing, borrow everything.* Everything, including the substance of our bodies, our thoughts, and so-called possessions, is on loan to us for a time. If we are wise users, never forgetting who the owner truly is—God—then the loan may be extended indefinitely. "*The guest will never quest.*" Because we forget the rightful owner, we go through much suffering in life by becoming attached to what we think is ours.

Let us pretend for a moment that everything we own materially is being removed from us. Which of our things would we find most difficult to part with? As we give some serious thought to this, we may find ourselves more than just a little bit emotional about the possibility of giving up our bank account, our computer, our car, our sound system, our favorite reclining chair, and other things. "*One who loses what one values and suffers is a fool. One who loses what one values and is free is a wise person.*"

The degree of attachment that we express simply reveals the degree to which we have enslaved ourselves to those particular things. We have made gods of them and we let them control us. Otherwise, we would not feel any emotion about their loss. This is not to be confused with denying that we must have shelter, food, and other essentials to live in a physical world. It is a question of priorities.

It is when we give up everything that we gain the whole. Now, by giving up everything, this is not to say that you just give up all your physical, material supply. No, you must give up your *attachment* to it. If you can give up your attachment to the things of creation without having them physically leave your universe, then they do not need physically to leave. It is different for each person on the path whether his or her material possessions must leave his or her physical world.

GIVING UP THOUGHT OF SELF

To put our faith in creations that come and go, is to put our security in the false gods created by the mind. We must dethrone these gods, otherwise, our satisfaction with them will increase our attachment to them. Let us instead find security through God, remembering the Divine Intelligence is the true and only source of our supply. But it is not so simple as saying that we will be free if we give up this or that, because that is just not how it works. It is the thought of self that possesses and builds the barrier between us and the infinite abundant supply that is everywhere present. By giving up the thought of self, the attachment not only to our material possessions but our judgments and ossified opinions, we gain the whole, we gain the abundant flow of life.

USE YOUR LOANS WISELY

Remember to use wisely whatever you have received on loan and it will remain with you until the purpose of the loan is fulfilled. If you fail to use it wisely, it shall be reclaimed by the very realm that lent it to you in the first place. Also remember, though something may come to you, if you have not earned it, you cannot keep it. One way or another, it will be taken away.

FREEDOM FROM BONDAGE OF FORM

Because of our possessive natures, our minds have forgotten, conveniently it seems, that we are indebted to the Universe, and being indebted, we are bound to the forms we have created. That we must remain bound is delusional thinking, for we can be freed by the soul faculty of surrender. Through the practice of disassociation, we can wrench ourselves free from the bondage of form, learning to be with a thing and never a part of the thing. That does not mean that we will not continue to express through form, but it does mean we can be free of its control.

BE A GIVER AND A RESPONSIBLE BORROWER

When we accept personal responsibility for all our thoughts, acts, and deeds, we will be a giver, not just a taker. We will be a borrower and not an owner. We are lazy because of our judgment patterns. All of us give to the limits of our judgments and each limit is a taker or an owner. We give or possess according to our judgments of whether it is convenient for us. To the givers, more shall be given. If a taker, more shall be taken away. It does not pay to be a taker. Be a giver. Be a responsible borrower, and leave to future generations what is rightfully theirs to partake of.

* * *

*"When our desire to possess is greater than
our reason to be free, life is miserable."*

Game 14

Refusing to Clean the Slate

Key Players:

Sense Functions:
Resentment, Self-Pity

Counterbalancing Soul Faculties:
Acceptance, Forgiveness,
Personal Responsibility,
Tolerance, Understanding

How the Game is Played:

The personality thinks someone has injured it in some manner and refuses to release its resentments by forgiving and forgetting.

Forgive

That slight misdeed of yesterday,
    Why should it mar today?
The thing he said, the thing you did,
    Have long since passed away;
For yesterday was but a trial;
    Today you will succeed,
And from mistakes of yesterday
    Will come some noble deed.

Forgive yourself for thoughtlessness,
    Do not condemn the past;
For it is gone with its mistakes;
    Their mem'ry cannot last;
Forget the failures and misdeeds,
    From such experience rise,
Why should you let your head be bowed?
    Lift up your heart and eyes!

—Anonymous

WE MUST NOT ONLY FORGIVE BUT FORGET

If we have not yet reached the summit of our spiritual climb, we still will make mistakes, and there will arise the need to be forgiven. As long as we have the need to be forgiven, we must forgive others. The Old Testament method of revenge, *"An eye for an eye and a tooth for a tooth"* expresses a total lack of compassion for the level of consciousness a person is on. Jesus taught a loving, rather than a vindictive way: *"If a man shall strike you on one cheek, turn the other,"* meaning do not quarrel or fight back. Do not get into rapport with that which is disturbing and of no benefit.

There is no greater release of energy then when energy is released with emotion, and there is no way of stopping a thought once it has left the human aura. We can, however, through forgiveness release a counterbalancing vibration from our aura and dissipate it. We are forgiving the level of consciousness inside ourselves, which through lack of self-control, we were unable to stop from leaving our universe.

What more generous an act of forgiveness than that displayed by Jesus, who nailed to the cross, looked down and said, *"Father, forgive them for they know not what they do."* He had been betrayed. Every single soul has to go through betrayal, a time when you feel you have been unjustly used or accused. How many times do you have to go through betrayal? Until you can totally forgive the individual who has betrayed you, forgetting totally. Some people can forgive, but cannot forget. With Jesus, it was total forgiveness. He so lovingly forgave because he knew those who were responsible for his crucifixion did not realize what they were doing to themselves. In their ignorance they were unaware of the enormity of their transgression. They were setting laws into motion that would hurt themselves more than he was suffering.

Forgiveness is the greatest blessing known to humankind, for when we forgive, we are freed from the bondage of our own minds. It is our need of the thought of self or personality that keeps us from the heaven of forgetting. That which we serve does not want to forgive or forget. *"To forgive is human and to forget is divine."* To forget something is to free yourself from the constant self-interest that is disturbing you. What you do not forgive, you hold in the bondage of your own consciousness. Until the effort is made to forgive or give forth, you cannot move to forgetting it and being free from it.

FORGIVENESS FREES US

The teaching of Jesus was always to forgive and not to seek revenge, for in seeking revenge you only hurt yourself and not the person who offended you. You have to let the past go. You cannot undo or change it. The only moment over which you have power is the moment of now. Forgive, bless, and release the one who has hurt you to the loving arms of The Father. In this way, you will both be free of any burden of hate or thoughts of revenge. *"I bless you (person's full name), and I bless you for the goodness of God within you."* Say it three times. Wonders can be performed by saying it, for as you give to others true, righteous thoughts and see them as good, spiritual, and lovable, you will make yourself receptive to the same thoughts that are ever radiating from The Father's presence.

Expressing peace and harmony is healing to the body and mind. Like attracts like. When healthy and positive ideas fill the mind, the body takes on a like condition. By contrast, to carry resentment is a heavy painful burden. Forgiveness frees you from that bondage that takes a toll on your health and happiness. You pay a dear price for not forgiving for it tears you down physically and mentally.

FIRST FORGIVE YOURSELF

Who or what is it that we should consider in forgiving first? Forgiveness first begins with the forgiveness of oneself. *"One who cannot forgive oneself is not capable of forgiving another."* Therefore, it is clear that we must learn not only to forgive others but to forgive ourselves as well, otherwise, it leads to self-condemnation which is a painful and destructive force. Jesus understood this and frequently said to those who came to him for a healing, *"Your sins* (mistakes) *are forgiven you."*

To forgive is to free and not to forgive is to bind. Forgiving does not mean condoning the action that injured. It simply means giving up the resentments we have toward others and releasing the energy that has bound us. In other words, we cannot forgive what another human soul is expressing until we can forgive that level inside ourselves, and we cannot forgive that level of consciousness in ourselves until we can awaken ourselves to it. It is understanding, spiritual understanding, which brings us to forgiveness. When we understand something, we can free it from our consciousness because we can forgive it. To forgive is to give forth. Once we forgive something, we free it. If we cannot give it forth, it places us in bondage to the thought and it becomes an obstruction to our freedom.

"Forgiveness is a true feeling and an inner humble request of the Divine Intelligence inside you to forgive you for the inability to control a level of consciousness."
We must forgive the sense functions for their transgressions. We cannot simply say those functions belong to someone else because we are part of the human race and we have all the functions that the human race has. Whatever thought is possible to one person is possible to all people. Learn to forgive yourself and pray for greater strength, acceptance, consideration, and understanding. For we cannot forgive what we cannot control, and we cannot control what we do not accept, nor can we can accept what we do not consider. It takes consideration and acceptance to understand. As we must forgive to forget, keep on forgetting until we become divine.

"God does not cease to forgive: it is wayward man that ceases to receive. We must be receptive to the Divine Presence, else it will not seem to exist for us." It is God in us—the good, the truth in us—that is the forgiving power.

There is a simple saying, *"Put God in it or forget it."* To forgive, we know is human, to forget is divine. If we feel that we are not yet strong enough to "put God in it," then pray to "forget it," for in so doing, we are freed from serving the untold complex realms of mental substance known as creation. We need no longer be concerned with the thought, for the thought will be dissipated by the counterbalance of forgiveness.

PLACE NO LIMIT ON FORGIVENESS
Without forgiveness, the mind continues to direct energy to the things it finds intolerable. It continues to repeat itself within the human mind like a broken record. It grows like a little child. It grows on and on, and one day becomes an adult thought form. And so it is necessary to express understanding and this giving forth, or forgiveness, that the soul faculty of tolerance may be expanded. The person who forgives is greater than the one forgiven. A person who harbors a grudge only feeds the thought forms and they multiply and multiply as we continue to hold on to the hurt.

There must be no limit to our forgiveness. "*Some errors seem so deeply rooted that it requires angelic patience and deific persistency in order to eradicate them.*" Therefore, when the Apostle Peter asked of Jesus: "*Lord, how often shall my brother sin against me, and I forgive him, until seven times?*" Jesus answered Peter by saying there is no limit to the number of times we should forgive one who offends us. God shows us how to forgive, for it is the God in us who is really forgiving. God does not limit. In forgiving, we are not simply indifferent to one who has injured us, nor do we have a spiteful or "that serves him right" attitude when something causes suffering to the offender. We are not only to forgive those who have offended us, but those who offend our friends and loved ones, and also those who are lovable and innocent anywhere upon the earth.

ACCEPT UNERRINGLY THE LAW OF DIVINE JUSTICE

If we believe another ought to be punished for sinning (making mistakes), that punishment is as likely to come to us as to the other, although we may not consider ourselves as deserving of punishment. So the only true attitude is to accept that divine justice unerringly brings retribution to those who violate the spiritual laws. This is what is meant by "*vengeance belongeth to the Lord,*" lord meaning law. Divine justice demands that those who suffer unjustly at the hands of others be compensated for their suffering, and that those who bring suffering upon another must similarly suffer. However, God in his infinite mercy does not always demand immediate justice, for it depends upon the spiritual elevation of a soul. A person on the kindergarten level of spiritual progression is not expected to accept the same responsibilities, or to be dealt with as harshly as one on the college level of spiritual unfoldment. But, rest assured, no one "gets away" with anything. It simply means retribution is worked off more gradually by the one on the lower level of consciousness. It will take more incarnations for the karmic debts to be paid, whereas for the more advanced soul, there is greater understanding and desire to balance the scales of justice. We are never given a heavier load than our soul can carry. The personality may take exception to this truth, however.

On occasions the apparent absence of justice on earth may lead one to doubt the existence of the Law of Divine Justice. We may show mercy on this plane of existence, but in the afterlife, mercy is not allowed to intercede, for that would be an injustice to the offended.

CLEAN THE SLATE WHILE STILL ON EARTH

It cannot be overstated that it is in our greater good for our "slate" to be cleansed of all transgressions toward others while still here on earth. The personality does not want to clean the slate, for it seeks solace for its self-pity. Its nature is to indulge in revenge or animosity toward the violator. Or, if it feels a sense of remorse or guilt, there may not be the strength of character to rise. For many, forgiveness is very difficult because they do not want those that they supposedly forgave to forget that they were forgiven. This is not forgiveness at all. It is an attempt by the personality to exercise power over another soul.

There is an adage, *"Let not the sun go down upon your wrath."* Make peace today for tomorrow may be too late. Sadly, many make their transition to the spirit world without having made their peace with those left on the earth plane. Unable to communicate, they cannot make retribution and evolve spiritually until they do so. They must wait for the offended ones to make their transition and then work it out on the other side.

WORKING BETWEEN DIMENSIONS

Those still encased in physical form who are aware of interdimensional communication and can arrange contact through a clear channel, will be privileged to either express their forgiveness or ask to be forgiven. Let us say that someone injured you when you were younger and that person passed to the spirit side of life, and you have not forgiven him or her; you feel you cannot forgive that individual. You wonder why that spirit does not communicate (assuming there is a clear channel through which to come), and tell you he or she is sorry for what was done to you. It is because you have to dump your "garbage" first. If you can get rid of this within yourself, if you can really come to gripes with it and truly accept what has happened and bless that individual and give him or her the power to go on, the right to go on, then that individual will possibly come back through a medium or channeler and say he or she is sorry. At that point it is over. However, one cannot be forgiven until one accepts that it is over, believes it, and goes with it. Those in the spirit world make their retribution after you are ready to accept and believe it. This process may be likened unto a bond or chain that must be loosen or broken, at least the first link, before the offending spirit can come to you and do the rest.

Therefore, to have forgiveness, you have to bless the spirit and put the past in the past. That breaks the bonds or chains, then the spirit can come and say he or she is sorry and make retribution. As long as there is resentment and not a total letting go, spirits usually do not come through and say they are remorseful. Sometimes, they may try but cannot get through a particular channel. All the while, if they are working on their progression, they are still watching over you and impinging helpful impressions on your mind. They cannot progress spiritually without trying to work it out.

If you are the offender and some one goes to spirit without your asking their forgiveness, remember, they are only a thought away. Send your thoughts to them, ask their forgiveness. At least get the process started. Rather than being consumed with guilt, work on right thought and right action now.

WE MUST PUT FORTH THE EFFORT

In *Jesus and Mastership*, it is simply stated:

> Remember, you must free yourself
> with forgiveness of others before you will
> be forgiven by others. Forgiveness opens
> the channel to your good, flowing from
> its Source, God. God love can only flow

to you through an open channel, so remove the blockage of hate, greed, envy,
criticism, resentment, fear and feelings
of lack, lust and discordant desires.
These negative emotions can only be
dissolved with God love.

The law is clear that it is only as we forgive those who
trespass against us that we shall be forgiven of our trespasses.
We must put forth the first effort. True forgiveness cleanses
and sanctifies those who are are receptive to it. And the
outpicturing of this divine process is in being cleansed of the
error in our thinking and in having purer, holier motives and
thoughts. There are no accidents. We are accountable for what
we experience and, therefore, must accept personal responsibility, that is, the ability to personally respond to whatever happens to us. We then gain power over the personality and become the *conquering soul.*

*   *   *

*"An apology is the acceptance and recognition
that the vehicle of the mind is not infallible or perfect."*

* * *

God is love. I am the child of love, and like my father, all loving and forgiving. I now lovingly forgive those who have offended me, and those who have offended my loved ones, and also those who commit unjust acts against the lovable and innocent anywhere upon the earth. I know there must be no limit to my forgiveness, and I thank my heavenly Father that I am now fully forgiven, and I go forth manifesting perfect life, strength, and health.

* * *

Game 15

The Procrastination Thief

Key Players:

Sense Functions:
Fascination, Justification,
Procrastination, Self-Will

Counterbalancing Soul Faculties:
Application, Care, Consideration, Cooperation,
Organization, Personal Responsibility,
Promptness, Respect, Unity

How the Game is Played:

The personality plays the game of *The Procrastination Thief* by allowing distractions to make you habitually tardy, or to cause you to put off indefinitely doing anything it thinks it can get away with.

PROCRASTINATION—THE THIEF OF TIME AND ENERGY

"Procrastination is the theft of all time, but it is greater than a thief. It is the device and devious ways and mechanisms of your own self-will, controlled by the fascinations of your own mind."

Procrastination is not only the thief of all time, it is the thief of precious energy. Letting this thief of the night lap up all the self-glory is why you have nothing to show for your efforts. Therefore, wisdom dictates to do things when you have the thought, otherwise, they never seem to come out just right. Do not lose the power of the moment of now by spending your energy fascinating on what may happen in the future. Live in the moment of now, the moment over which you have the power.

"Whatever you can do, or dream you can, begin it.
Boldness has genius, power and magic in it."
—Goethe

The obvious point is that when you have something to do, do it **now**. Procrastination makes it much harder. If you keep putting off a job, telling yourself you will do it later, you actually use more energy in feeding the "later" entities than if you just went ahead and did it. If it is something that tugs strongly at your conscience, then the thought is frequently entertained, *"Oh, I must do that."* or, *"I should be doing this."* You play with the thought; you fascinate with it. That is why this little control game that the personality plays usually uses far more energy than actually would be consumed by just doing what you are supposed to do in the first place. For some, the conscience may tug so strongly it makes them feel guilty.

AN APPOINTMENT IS A COMMITMENT TO THE SOUL

Are you among the many who find it so very difficult to be on time, whether it is for class, work, an appointment, curtain time at the theater, dinner, completing a report or project, or whatever you have committed yourself to do? If so, then perhaps you have wanted to break the cycle. Be aware that in making an appointment for a certain time, you establish a law, and at the same time **a commitment to your own soul** to be present at a particular place at that appointed time. If you are unable to keep the appointment because another and stronger desire has arisen, which is a demonstration of priority values, it only reveals a lack of control of the inner attitudes of your mind. *"Outward manifestations are revelations of inner attitudes of mind."* You have allowed additional laws to be established by the personality that counteract the original commitment.

USING DISTRACTIONS TO CONTINUE TARDINESS PATTERN

If you try to break the cycle of being habitually late, you may have noticed that each time you try to be early, something invariably seems to come up that you feel needs your immediate attention. Invariably, unless you make a very determined effort, you get sidetracked. What is taking place? Well, you are never without choice, so you allowed yourself, through the choices or priorities you established, to be late. No one else is to blame, though you may frequently tend to put the cause outside yourself.

Tardiness usually follows a very definite pattern. In other words, a certain tape has been programmed in the subconscious and since the subconscious is the magnetic mind, it draws to it all the experiences necessary to guarantee the continuity of being late. This is why all those little things seem to go wrong at the last minute when you are madly dashing about consciously trying to be punctual. The sabotage efforts that face you while trying to get to an appointment might include the last minute telephone call you think is so important to make, misplacing your car keys, having to stop on the way for gas because you "conveniently" forgot to fill the gas tank the previous day when you had time, going back into the house to make certain an appliance has been turned off, and so forth. These are simply the manifestations of personality laws established to obstruct the soul Law of Promptness.

If you say from the self level, *I won't be late again,* you guarantee the experience because the personality has been given control. It does not want to let go. That is why it sets laws into motion which cause distractions to make you late. Procrastination guarantees all the experiences necessary for its continuity, then justifies the pattern to which you have become addicted. The personality is trying to prove it is in control, so it justifies its position. If it had total consideration, there would be nothing to defend, and, therefore, nothing to justify. The extent to which the personality will go in its battle for supremacy over the soul is dependent upon our control, or lack of it, over our own mind.

THE "LATER TAPE"

Those who are under the control of the *"I'll do it later"* tape are those who cannot control their desires. The *"later"* game is the procrastination game because later rarely comes. The *"later tape"* is just an excuse not to do something. It is a con game against facing personal responsibility. A person knows that inwardly. By not facing our responsibility at the moment, the chances become slimmer that we will ever face it later. It means we are still the victim of our desires. So, people who are habitually tardy or who procrastinate, being bombarded with total unfulfilled desires, cannot commit themselves to a time because the desire does not yet know what it wants for its fulfillment. In other words, the mind does not want to commit itself because it wants to be free to fulfill whatever desire pops up at the moment. If we could see in another dimension, we would see the entities hovering to draw energy as a result of our not wanting to make the effort to control our desires.

TAKING CONTROL OF OUR DESIRES

We are constantly bombarded by choice—bombarded by the desires of yesterday. Remember, we are the instruments through which The Divine is expressing and that divine expression is known as desire. We establish the Law of Obstruction as a self-preservation device. Because the effort has not been made by the mind to control itself from the effects of bombarding contrary desires, we procrastinate on the things we know we should do. And because of this procrastination, we direct energy to other conflicting desires and build walls of obstruction. To be free to accomplish what we desire to accomplish, it is reiterated that it is absolutely necessary to gain some degree of control over the mind. Move from letting the levels of procrastination speak and guide you to letting them just flit by in a split second. Just be the "bystanding mind."

We are never free from desire for we are never free from God. The Divinity is expressing through our forms. Therefore, never being free from desire, or the divine expression of God, it behooves us to take control of the limited patterns of our desires. For without doing so through a total acceptance in consciousness known as Divine Will, we become a procrastinator, dividing the temple of our soul from our personality. In that division we do not long stand; rather, we fall into the darkness of delusion through our errors of ignorance. The personality has to come into alignment with the soul.

PERSONALITY GLORIFICATION LEVEL
LACKS CONSIDERATION

The self-glorification level loves to make its late grand entrance, no matter whether this is an inconvenience to others, or whether we are embarrassed by the attention given a latecomer. This is a demonstration of the lack of consideration that level of consciousness has not only for our soul, but for others. We must become aware of the negative energy we get from people who are inconvenienced by our procrastination and know there are instead positive ways to get energy. We must also guard against vicariously enjoying it when others are late.

FASCINATION BY WAY OF PROCRASTINATION

We cannot be in fascination without demonstrating the Law of Procrastination, for *"He who fascinates procrastinates and goes from temptation to fascination by the way of procrastination."* The reason one fascinates and procrastinates is an effort by the human mind to entertain itself with visual pictures so that it does not have to accept what is rising from its own soul consciousness and dictating what is right to do, because it is right to do right. Every individual is aware to some extent what his or her path in evolution is because the experiences in evolution are indelibly recorded in the memory par excellence (the heart seed atom). Therefore, to try to block out what it must do, the personality fascinates in a realm of delusion and procrastinates on what it knows it must do. In time—some day in eternity— we will do what we know we must do despite the battle between our personality and the infinite eternal soul.

MAKE FRIENDS WITH ADVERSITIES

Without discipline of the mind there is no Light, no illu-mination. When you truly face this discipline, what then is your obstruction? The obstructions in life are revealed by your pro-crastination in your efforts, which possibly have a history of untold centuries. Ask yourself honestly, *what is my greatest ad-versity or dislike?* Whatever it is that you dislike the most is your greatest adversity. Sit back and ponder the truth—*What has be-come my greatest dislike?* These are the lessons that you did not pass in prior incarnations. Seize the opportunity of this lifetime to make friends with your adversities so they will no longer be your attachments. Make the effort in the here and now to view the obstructions wisely.

MOVE THROUGH JUDGMENT GRACIOUSLY

There is always a voice from heaven to guide you, but you must learn to pause and be at peace. You must learn to gain control of those things that have controlled you for so many centuries. What you are waiting to gain is waiting for you, and what you have to lose has already served its purpose in your evolution. Judge not what waits on your horizon, for in the judg-ing is your struggle. Each thing judged waits as your child to judge you, and every law transgressed waits patiently for you. Let it come and flow into your consciousness graciously for you in truth are moving through it. Be encouraged that you are making some effort to awaken within you the demonstrable truth there is no escape from any thought, act, or deed. Be encour-aged in your prayer for peace in all your thoughts. The struggle is never greater than your prayers to God to get through it. Put peace in each thought and feeling. The good going from you will return to you.

RELEASE THE CHAINS OF FEAR AND OVER-IDENTIFICATION

You cannot hide thoughts and feelings. You feed them thrice the energy by your fear. They become even more blatant than before. All minds fear for fear is the authority of the mind over the eternal soul, but its authority is only temporal and in a constant process of change. Throughout the universes you have journeyed already. The more you identify with the earth realm and its materiality, the more difficulties you will have in your journey onward. Learn the wisdom of not over-identifying with form, for the pain in your evolution is the direct effect of your over-identification. You are in truth the universality of consciousness. Pray for broadening of your horizons so that your passing from moment to moment shall not be so painful.

Ever seek the *cause* of the experience you are having. Do not work on the effect. Work on the cause of obstructions which are the effects of procrastination. Remember, you have already long endured what plagues you and impels you to continue in the pattern.

Through an acceptance of the death and birth cycle which is constant in creation, you will gradually but surely be released from the whole and the chains that over-identification have upon you. Because of lack of control of your mind, you experience the forces of your own emotions through over-identification. Instead, identify with constant change. Accept the coming as graciously as the going—the loss, the gain. Only a fool tries to stop or stand rigid in the Law of Constant Change. Be flexible and from the flexibility in consciousness you will begin to identify with God's kingdom. Be prepared that when you make the slightest effort to change, your kingdom of thought forms will scream and your pain will become greater. Each time you do what you know you should be doing, the forms, in keeping with what you have done, build a wall of obstruction known as procrastination. You shall pass through it by giving to God your greatest gift, the gift of self. By giving that, you give the kingdom that has made a slave of you.

CHANGING FROM PROCRASTINATION TO PROMPTNESS

Promptness reveals character and the ability of the personality to control itself. Energy follows attention, so do not give energy to being late. Instead of saying you will not be late again, better to say to yourself, *Be it in Divine Order, I will be on time.* Divine Order is important so the subconscious will refrain from rebelling. That will raise your level of consciousness out of self to a more neutral level. It sends some energy to higher levels of consciousness where care and consideration can rise and express. When you care more about considering your soul and its freedom, and in turn, considering and respecting others, you will gain control over the "late" entities. Then, when a distraction, or the voice of *I'll do it later* arises, you will be in control. After affirming you will be on time, *be it in Divine Order*, you must make the effort to truly be on time and be firm in not giving in to those thought forms that are screaming to be fed. You are the victim of the level and destined to the bondage of obsession until you have had enough through suffering, and the change is made and the soul freed. Would it not be worth the effort to program a new tape in the subconscious? You can talk to it and explain in a kind but firm manner that when one makes an appointment or date, one makes a spiritual commitment.

When you have truly made a spiritual decision to change your level of consciousness from procrastination to promptness, you will then feel, with the courage of true conviction, that you are greater than that old level of procrastination. You will begin to exercise self-control, and you will no longer fulfill your desires of the moment but will set priorities that show consideration for others. You will no longer need to gain attention by making your grand late entrance, nor will you need to continue to feel guilty or embarrassed because of the excuses you have made to justify your tardiness—actually, your lack of self-control. In fact, you never needed to justify in the first place unless you were concerned about what somebody might think of you. If you are honest with yourself, that does not matter.

CONSIDERATION AND ORGANIZATION—
IMPORTANT FACTORS TO PROMPTNESS

Promptness not only considers the rights of another soul, but it is also an expression of our ability to organize ourselves. For without organization in our lives, we have chaos and confusion and nothing but problems. If you are not organized, there are desire priorities which are the obstruction. Organization establishes priorities, otherwise, we are like a rocking chair, going back and forth, and getting nowhere. *Shall I do this? Or, shall I do that?* We must concentrate enough to follow through to completion of something rather than wasting too much time trying to make a decision on where to start. Just do it, instead of vacillating or moaning over what you really should do, for that only leads to frustration, self-pity, and loneliness. Procrastination is very draining! It is possible when a person is really striving for organization, he or she will continue to think he or she is not getting organized. These are the thought forms at work trying to gain the attention which is energy necessary for them to stay where they are. They do not want to move onward. Only through the Law of Repetition is the Law of Change made possible.

It is tiring to indulge in laziness and wishful thinking that someone will do it for us. And if the object of our procrastination is an adversity, we will continue to call it forth. It is draining to feed the thought forms. Being free of these forms, your energy may be used to complete the job. Did you ever wonder why you have such a good feeling when you do things on time? It is because good is God.

WITHDRAWAL FROM ADDICTED PATTERNS

We have a duty to our soul to free it from the addicted patterns of mind. Being late is so deep rooted in some people that it can be likened in degree to that of the drug addict in his or her effort to continue to support the habit. How much self-control do the addicts show when they compute they need a drug? The mind finds security in all of its addicted patterns because to the mind, familiarity represents security. A soul cannot be free to express its divinity when the form, the mind, chokes its very expression by its various patterns of addiction.

Refusal to make a time commitment is only one example of the many ways in which we literally imprison our souls. The principle of freedom from all the self-levels of addiction is the same, and includes the practice of self-control, awareness of self from moment–to–moment, continuity of effort, being at peace, and serving selflessly. The result will bring unity and harmony between the conscious and subconscious minds, enabling *"withdrawal"* from a pattern of addiction.

COOPERATION, UNITY, AND APPLICATION ARE INSEPARABLE

When you are expressing the soul faculty of unity, your various levels of consciousness are working in a cooperative effort and this allows you to apply your spiritual wisdom. However, when you are in fascination, you are focusing on one level of consciousness and that leads to procrastination because all of your energy is spinning around and around, and not moving forward.

If we do not make the effort to discipline our minds to fulfill the commitments we make to our soul, whether it is to be prompt, to be organized, to serve in a particular way, or whatever it may be, then we open ourselves up to the more negative invisible thought forces which reinforce that tendency on our part. If we make moment-to-moment effort to discipline or control our thoughts and to express continuity of the new pattern, we attract spirit helpers from realms of Light who encourage and strengthen us and help lift us to higher states of consciousness.

Cooperation, unity, and application are inseparable. Spiritual application means *"total expression of the being,"* putting the totality of your being into your efforts. Application is the very instrument through which The Divine being moves, ever responding to you. In your endeavours in life, through the faculty of application, the energy flows unobstructed. But first, you must become aware of the levels of consciousness within you that you may assure yourself that all levels of consciousness will cooperate and unite. The various levels of consciousness all want to maintain their varying degrees of authority within you. That is why tolerance must rise supreme so that the levels of consciousness shall all bow in humbleness to that authority, moving you on to ever-increasing and expanding success in life. Without application there is no Light. **Perhaps the saddest example of procrastination is that of putting off the application of spiritual teachings.** Energy cannot express itself until it is applied or directed.

As stated at the beginning of this "game," procrastination is the device which employs devious ways and mechanisms of your own self-will, controlled by the fascinations of your own mind. With procrastination there is a lack of unity in the levels; therefore, without control over the mind you become a victim of uncontrollable desires. With application of the soul faculty, you are greater than the level. With procrastination, the sense function, you are the victim of it and are destined to the bondage of obsession until through suffering you have had enough, then change is made and the soul freed.

BREAK THE BACK OF PROCRASTINATION

The efforts, no matter how small, made to discipline your mind will bring you just reward in due time. However, you alone must make those efforts. You alone must become aware of the multitudes of forms that are in truth the armies of your past efforts. You must encourage your soul to rise and take charge. It takes constant repetition to evolve; otherwise, discouragement will rear its ugly head. Discouragement is the last effort made by the patterns of yesterday to keep control of your life. Pause to think. Become aware, awake, and alert to what in truth is really happening.

Life was designed by the Great Architect to be enjoyed. Every experience is the living demonstration of the level of consciousness that is receiving the most of the divine energy flowing through you. Let that level be a level that lifts you to the heights of joy and happiness. It is within your power to gain control of your mind. It is within your power to break the back of procrastination, to free yourself from the Law of Obstruction and be the living demonstration—a Light in the world for all to follow. We all follow someone. Whether we think about it makes no change in that truth, for we are followers and our following takes us into many experiences in life. We know deep inside before we follow whether it is a detour, dead end, or a way. Let your life be a way upward, a way onward that you may follow the principle of joy and eternal freedom in this the moment that is truly yours.

*   *   *

*"Today I reap the harvest of yesterday
and plant the seeds of my tomorrow."*

Game 16

The Bellyaching Game

Key Players:

Sense Functions:
Complaining, Dissatisfaction, Fear,
Frustration, Greed, Judgment,
Selfishness, Self-Pity

Counterbalancing Soul Faculties:
Acceptance, Duty, Gratitude,
Personal Responsibility,
Tolerance, Value

How the Game is Played:

The Bellyaching Game is the complaining and manipulative way that the personality seeks to not only make others take the responsibility for what you experience, but to want them to correct things according to your desires and demands. When you depend upon others to supply your needs, whatever they may be, you live in continual fear that they will not deliver.

COMPLAINING IS AN EXPRESSION OF INGRATITUDE

One of the easiest ways to recognize ingratitude is to listen to the complaining. If you know those who are continuously griping and complaining that this is not being done, or that is not being done, or whatever they receive is not exactly what they judge they should get, etcetera, then go inside *your* computer and look at every area of your life. See if the law has been established any time within you to call forth this experience. Speak the truth that you may be an instrument, not only to free your own soul from that type of illusion, but an instrument to free the soul that is speaking to you.

Let us not be quick to judge those who complain, or those who do not show gratitude. Let us not forget for a moment that the potential for expressing this level exists in all of us. Whatever level exists in one exists in everyone. We and we alone choose what level of consciousness we will express on.

The crumbs of life are the essence upon which the loaves of life are built. You have the opportunity each day to demonstrate gratitude for the crumbs of life. Whenever you have an experience and you permit your mind to dictate that it was a good experience, but there should be more, you direct energy to the throne of judgment. Then the energy necessary for the little crumb, the essence to grow and become a loaf, is dissipated by your choice of the mental superiority over your spiritual being. We continue to live in unfulfilled desires because of that one simple transgression of Gratitude, the Law of Supply. Conversely, when we appreciate, we apply that appreciation to the crumbs of life. Being grateful for the crumb, we establish the Law of Acceptance which guarantees we will receive the whole loaf, a continual supply in principle.

Life, the great mirror of all experience, reveals to us in a multitude of ways that whatever goes out in our universe shall return to us, because energy follows attention; and whatever it is that we place our mind, our thought, our attention upon, we tend to become. Like attracts like. Therefore, when a person is truly grateful he or she emanates a rate of vibration that goes out into the universe and brings back its kind, like kind. Gratitude is a very powerful attribute of the soul.

We must not blame God for our lack. We must accept personal responsibility that we do it to ourselves. As we continue to complain, a feeling rises within us that we are lacking, and this feeling of lack increases in our consciousness. Recorded in the subconscious mind as lack of what we desire, we establish the Law of Greed. The more we complain, we experience ever increasing lack. When we believe we are without, we are always without in keeping with the dictates of how we think we will get what we believe we need—telling God how it will be. The self-concern of wanting "my way" brings frustration. Instead, experience the joy in life by ceasing to tell the goodness how it will come into your life. *"Thank you, God, I have a right to the goodness of life, but I don't have the right to dictate what the goodness of life is, for the goodness of life flows through me."*

Have you noticed that the people who are **not** grateful are the ones who seem to have the greatest difficulty with God's divine abundant supply? The function of greed is not limited to money. It is not limited to anything, for it encompasses everything. When we stop complaining, we will start experiencing what we desire. When we are no longer concerned about what someone else is doing, we will be freed from the frustration of not doing what we want to do. Our mind is in a constant process of programming. It is also in a constant process of defending the programs that are in it. Why live in the delusion of lack when in reality abundant good is demonstrated by The Divine throughout all nature? Each denial that we make not only establishes our destiny, but each denial is a cloud between our true being and the realm of truth.

WHAT IS THE REMEDY FOR THE BELLYACHING GAME? How do we counterbalance the energy going into the mental game of the personality so that the soul can express?

OUR DUTY IS TO SERVE THE LIGHT

First, let us digress a bit to give some understanding of the triune soul faculty of duty, gratitude, and tolerance. The foregoing mental games have established that our first duty, the real duty is to The Divine that is expressing through us. Spiritual responsibility is the most important duty in our eternity. The vehicle itself, that is, the physical, mental, astral, and etheric bodies, are simply automobiles that we are driving. The real "you" is the power, the fuel. An automobile does not go very far without gas in it. In truth, we are that power expressing through these vehicles.

Our duty is to serve the Light. *"Duty becomes direction when you use wisdom."* We cannot understand ourselves unless we have *duty* to our own spirit, which is the true self, *gratitude* for its expression, and *tolerance* for those levels of consciousness that are so difficult for most of us to grow through.

The great delusion of the mind is to try to work on somebody else. It is a total waste of effort and only retards the day when you are going to reach your own freedom. The moment you judge how another should be or act, you have stepped on their evolutionary path and shall pay the price with them. A wise person tries working on himself or herself first, then shares that understanding, *when it is solicited*, and by doing so, continues to work on himself or herself, not on someone else. This is why unsolicited help is to no avail and is extremely detrimental. When you go to work on yourself, you go through the triune soul faculty of duty, gratitude, and tolerance, and you rise to a level where you see the good in the person that you wanted to change. Now, by seeing that good and becoming the good in yourself, you will attract that goodness from another human soul, or an animal.

We have a duty not only to your soul but to what the soul has taken on in this time of incarnation, including family responsibilities. When we have been given much in spiritual understanding and duty calls to give back by serving in a spiritual capacity, the giving must be at the expense of our many greedy desires bombarding our consciousness for attention. For the call of duty does not usually wait until the moment it is convenient for us. When we serve God at our convenience, we are, in truth, serving our personality. In responding to the call of duty, if we find ourselves weighing it against our other desires, then we have missed the opportunity to really serve and, thus, express gratitude for what we have been given. Respond to the call of duty with the soul and not the mind.

When you truly recognize the duty to your own soul, it makes you grateful for the opportunities that come to you, no matter how painful or depressing, because they have allowed you to grow. You are grateful to God for allowing you to have those particular opportunities, and yet the opportunities become responsibilities. They are lessons to be learned. A very helpful affirmation to soothe the pain was given by the spirit teacher: *"O God, I am grateful for all life's experiences, especially the difficult ones, for I know that they are in truth my greatest blessings."* A beautiful truth, for it is the tough ones that are so painful that force you to make some changes in attitude, and by that, free you from the bondage of the personality.

When you recognize and accept your first duty is to your own soul, and you are grateful for its expression, then you begin to realize that each person has different duties and a different set of responsibilities. This understanding and acceptance develops tolerance.

We would be well advised to listen to our spirit friends who tell us it is easier to work on ourselves while here on the earth plane. Our physical body buffers us from being so locked into certain levels of consciousness. On the spirit side of life, you are magnetically drawn far more strongly to spirits who think the same way, and it is more difficult to break away should you want to progress.

SEND GRATITUDE, NOT COMPLAINTS

Every soul faculty and its corresponding sense function is at the opposite end of a pole, a continuum. The mind sees in opposites, so when the thought of self enters, a faculty in that instant becomes a function. For example, gratitude becomes greed; faith becomes fear. The soul is grateful for the crumb, but when the mind or personality gets it and dictates how it should show gratitude, it becomes greed instead. *"Gratitude, not greed, is the path of joy."*

You are only giving lip service to gratitude when you are playing the "Bellyaching Game" for gratitude is not something you lightly say, *Well now, thank you, God, I am very grateful.* Then you turn right around and complain about something. That is a contradiction and you become a house divided. The separation only widens between the soul and the personality. *"Griping, bitching, complaining, and blaming are the pillars that uphold the realms of diabolical delusion."*

Yet despite the fact we have many things to be thankful for, we do not always express it. When good things come, we want them to keep coming and that is the way it should be. It is our divine right to have the goodness of life, but we tend to take things for granted. As the old saying goes, *we do not appreciate the water until the well runs dry.* The moment we permit our mind to take something for granted, we have no gratitude and the door of supply closes. Value is the application of the Law of Gratitude, so taking someone or something for granted shows we have no value for the person or thing, and *"that that we have no value for we guarantee to lose."* For example, if you take for granted your weight reduction, you start gaining again because the personality has taken charge. When you close the door of gratitude, the Light cannot get through for you have cut off the continuity of the Law of Supply. Everything requires energy for success. Things left on the back burner will burn up if we do not take care of them. Actually, what we take for granted, we abuse through the lack of total consideration, for that which does not have total consideration does not have the divine faculty of care or kindness. Gratitude is a demonstration of the faculty of care, and the application of the Law of Appreciation.

BE GRATEFUL TO YOUR SPIRIT GUIDES

As part of their service to humanity, our guides and teachers come from the spirit realms and spend some time with us each day. They never deprive us of the lessons we need, but they help us to get through them. They form a holy partnership with us. Because most of us have not yet reached sainthood, those loving spirits listen to a great deal of garbage rattling around in our heads. Stop and listen to yourself occasionally. If we find it difficult to tolerate our own thoughts, surely we can be grateful that those souls are willing to listen and help us. The commitment of our inner spirit band is for the length of our earthly stay. Send them frequent loving thoughts of gratitude.

WE RECEIVE AS WE SEND OUT

Let us try thanking the Universe, thanking God, in advance for whatever it is that we want. Remember, there is no credit in the spirit world, no visas or master cards. You pay in advance. You make the changes in consciousness first before rising to a higher plane.

In the Gospel according to Matthew, Jesus said, *"For to everyone who has will be given more, and he will have more than enough, but from the man who has not, even what he has will be taken away."* (Matt: 13:12) I heard this quoted often as a child and it was interpreted to me as meaning God gives to the rich and takes from the poor. We know that cannot be for God is totally impartial. We and we alone set laws into motion to bring to us all of our experiences. To be otherwise, would be a denial of personal responsibility.

The Bible can be interpreted literally or it can be interpreted metaphysically on different levels. So I like to think that one possible interpretation of this parable shows the Master Jesus explaining how the Law of Gratitude, known also as the Law of Supply, really operates. *"For to everyone who has"*—who has what? Who has gratitude. *"To him more shall be given, but from the man who has not, even what he has will be taken away."* To the man who has no gratitude, nothing can be added. He will deplete what he has because he is not replenishing his supply by directing his energy toward gratitude for what he already has and is not expressing acceptance for what he wants.

We are like radio receiving sets. We must send something out in order for like kind to return. Think of gratitude as a radio frequency, just as faith, courage, compassion, forgiveness, gentleness, kindness, to name a few of the soul faculties, may be considered frequencies. The faculties and sense functions send out energy on their own individual frequencies.

MOVING BEYOND DISSATISFACTION TO GRATITUDE

It is through gratitude that God's love flows unceasingly. When you have that inner joy within you, you express love and are grateful for what you experience. Unhappiness, on the other hand, is motivated by the thoughts of selfishness and lack of gratitude because you do not think it is enough. To the mind, it is never enough, for the mind can only be satisfied momentarily—only the soul is ever fulfilled. When the mind says it is not enough, you can rest assured God will support that negative affirmation and will bring the experience necessary for the uneducated personality to learn its lesson. In your immaturity, you complain because you want your own way. If you are complaining that you are in need, if you are complaining that you are limited, then in those moments, ask yourself the simple truth, *O God, am I grateful, or am I, through an error of ignorance of my mind, dictating to you, and in so doing, unable to receive?*

How do we get beyond our dictate of dissatisfaction with our supply? We must flood our consciousness with the truth that God is the true and only source of our supply. Be grateful for the crumb instead of asking, *Is that all there is?* Tell God how abundant things are for that establishes the Law of Abundance. *How great you are, God, for multiplying my supply.* When we give up the thought of denial, we will receive the principle of acceptance. If we give up self-will, we gain divine will.

* * *

"Stand guardian at the portal of your thought that you may experience the freedom and joy of your eternal soul."

Game 17

Conscience Deafness

Key Players:

Sense Functions:
Deception, Judgment, Pride

Counterbalancing Soul Faculties:
Consideration, Discernment, Honesty,
Intuition, Justice, Personal Responsibility,
Reason, Truth

How the Game is Played:

The game *Conscience Deafness* is played when particular tapes in the subconscious mind are playing so loudly that we turn a deaf ear to the promptings of our spiritual conscience.

DIFFERENTIATING BETWEEN THE EDUCATED AND THE SPIRITUAL CONSCIENCES

We all have two consciences. We have the created or *educated conscience* of the human mind. The *educated conscience* is what we are taught is right or wrong. It is that which we have earned in this present life experience as an effect of centuries of evolution. Culture, social mores, family values, political persuasions, economic conditions and other factors enter into the forming of an educated conscience. The educated conscious is subservient to pride. It is capable of cheating, deceiving, stealing, and dictating, depending upon the values we have been taught.

How one's values affect the expression of the educated conscience is illustrated in the example of a young person caught stealing who had no problem justifying why he stole from the wealthy. Upon questioning, he replied, *"They have more than they need. They can afford to let me have some. They aren't going to miss it."* There was no guilt connected with perpetrating this crime to satisfy his desires. The statements were made with a clear *educated* conscience. It is the educated conscience that creates in varying degrees many psychological and ethical problems, antisocial behavior, and/or criminal acts for untold millions of people.

We experience moment-by-moment the divine expression known as desire. Unfortunately, for us, until we learn the difference between the suppression of desire, the education of desire, and the fulfillment of desire, we will continue to live in the mental realms of frustration and trigger painful personal struggles or act out in unacceptable ways toward society. With the educated conscience there is judgment because there is a ribbon of comparison over it. The educated conscience is the servant of pride. It works to preserve what is in the computer.

The other conscience is known as a *spiritual sensibility* that accepts the Law of Personal Responsibility. This spiritual conscience is the demonstration of Divine Truth. It is in fact *"a spiritual sensibility with a dual capacity, knowing right from wrong. It does not have to be told."*

Some people have a greater expression of conscience than others, depending upon how free their soul is from the bondage of their personality. How does conscience know right from wrong? It knows where we have been, where we are, and where we are going. It knows the games we play. It knows our true motivation, for like the eye of eternity, the conscience never sleeps.

Spiritual conscience dictates reason. It is your conscience that knows reason for that is the spiritual counterpart of the divine scales of balance called justice in your own heart. The spiritual conscience does not exist in your mind. The conscience of your mind is what you have created as conscience. Your conscience of Divine Truth is in the deep recesses of your heart which is in truth the door to your own eternal soul. It does not consider just this short life or incarnation that you presently remember. It has total consideration and knows your journey in eternity. You do not have to tell it. You do not have to believe it, for in your heart you already know it. When you control the vehicle of mind, your personality, you can express your spiritual conscience, and you will be fulfilling the laws you have already established by your soul. You will be doing what is right and in the best interests of others.

"Conscience is the voice of God in the soul. No one truly obeying this voice will meet with permanent harm."

—Andrew Jackson Davis

RELEASED ENERGY CREATES ON MULTIPLE DIMENSIONS

Color is a very important vibratory consideration. As light green is the vibratory wave of conscience, choosing that color, we will be guided into right thought and right action in the so-called other dimensions. These other dimensions around and about us are like a vast jungle that we are expressing through—dimensions that most of us are unaware of. When we speak forth a word, it is energy released from our being and we create on more than one dimension. When we express our feelings, we must realize thoughts are more than forms, they are the causes of forms. It takes conscious awareness that we are not just dealing with the physical world. So when we speak our word out into the atmosphere, it behooves us to be choosy with the life-giving energy—express from the level of spiritual conscience.

STANDING BEFORE THE JUDGMENT SEAT

No thought is ever lost. It is recorded in eternity, and the day is guaranteed for all form to go before the judgment seat of conscience. When you hear the verdict, know that it is not God that judges, but it is the divine principle called conscience. So in truth, each moment of each day, you stand before the judgment seat, though you know it not with your conscious mind. You stand before the judge and each moment you choose between the Eternal Light of Surrender and the darkest of self and self-concern.

How just and fair are the divine laws of the Universe? You are never left at any given moment without choice. When you say to yourself, *I know what is right but I am too weak*, this only reveals to you a device of your personality because you do not yet want to make the effort you think will be required. You say *someday, someday*. Delaying only makes the struggle more difficult because you alone have chosen to feed the energy directed through the negative thought forces of "someday," or procrastination, to the demons you have created. Remember, their only survival is the energy that you direct through that negative aspect called fear and procrastination. We fear what we do not understand, but we can understand by freeing ourselves from our own self-concern.

THE LEVELS OF INTUITION

Intuition is a part of the spiritual conscience. Flowing through reason, it uses the superconscious mind of the soul. It is a natural or divine knowing. Intuition may be experienced as a feeling or a sensing. The original sense is a sense of feeling and from that original sense of feeling has come the sense of sight, hearing, taste, and smell. And this is why the sense of feeling precedes thoughts of mind.

Intuition will manifest from whatever level of spiritual consciousness you are on. If an intuitive person is on a high level of consciousness, he or she is going to bring that spiritual consciousness into play. Charles Fillmore, co-founder of Unity, taught that, *"Through the power of intuition, man has direct access to all knowledge and the wisdom of God."* Intuition can be impressions received from one's own soul or from the higher spiritual teachers. It can also pick up what is on the ethers; therefore, it can be a material as well as spiritual consciousness. Again, this depends on the level to which one is receptive.

FILLMORE DESCRIBES SPIRITUAL CONSCIENCE

In *Keep A True Lent* Fillmore describes beautifully the spiritual conscience:

There is a divine goodness at the root of all existence. It is not necessary to give in detail the place of abode of each sentient part of this central goodness, for it is there, wherever you look, and whenever you look. No man is so lowly but that at the touch of its secret spring this divine goodness [that it] may be brought to light in him. This goodness sleeps in the recesses of every mind and comes forth when least expected. Many stifle it for years, maybe for ages, but eventually its day comes, and there is a day of reckoning. This is the law of universal balance—the equilibrium of Being. It cannot be put aside with transcendental philosophies or metaphysical denials anymore than it can be smothered in the force of the blind passions.

Man is never without a guide, no matter how loudly he may be crying out for leading. There is always at hand a sure torchbearer if he will but follow the light. It is too simple, too easy! Man has formed in his mind a far-off God who talks to him from some high mountain in invisible space. By thus looking afar for his God, he ignores the spark of divinity shining in his own being.

Herein is man fooled into believing that he can do the things that are not in harmony with his ideas of goodness and yet escape the consequences. He presumes that God is too far away to behold his shortcomings and he loses sight of the fact that God is right with him every moment.

This is the meaning of the old saying that a man and his conscience are good friends as long as the way is smooth, but when it grows rugged they fall out.

HOW WE BECOME DEAF TO OUR CONSCIENCE

Our spiritual conscience constantly strives to express itself. It knows right from wrong; however, if some of our tapes in the subconscious are very strong, if they have been fed a great deal of energy, and if they are playing loudly at the time our conscience is trying to speak, we cannot hear our conscience, and in time, we become totally deaf to it. We no longer sense it, especially when a certain tape is playing. Nevertheless, the spiritual conscience itself continues to try to express itself, to get through to the conscious mind that something is wrong, something is not beneficial to the unfoldment of our soul.

DISCERNMENT AND THE LOVE OF HONESTY

In "letting our conscience be our guide" it is clear that many people mistake the spiritual conscience for their programmed acceptances of what is right or wrong for themselves. We are not the things of life. We are the essence of the intelligence of The Divine. Let us flow in ways that will do justice in our days and years ahead. It is our conscience that judges us and if we are to know the difference between the spiritual conscience and the educated conscience, we must use spiritual discernment. What is necessary to discern? Honesty and reason. Discernment, then, is the revelation of difference for it casts the light of reason and honesty upon our limit of God. It is not the limit, it is the light that reveals the limit. Let shadows go that we may be in the Light. Do not let the darkness tell you it is too much effort. *"Thank you, O God, for leading me through honesty in what I have trapped myself in."* You will never know a greater love than honesty—not in all eternity.

* * *

"Pearls of wisdom are the tears of conscience.

* * *

"Whoever has felt the prick of conscience has been spoken to by the Holy Spirit. Whoever has sat at the feet of his own inner convictions has been aware of God's presence."
—Charles Fillmore

* * *

"The exploration and understanding of intuition will be a central part of spiritual psychology. Intuition is the voice of the nonphysical world. It is the communication system that releases the five-sensory personality from the limitations of its five-sensory system, that permits the multisensory personality to be multisensory. It is the connection between the personality and its higher self and its guides and Teachers . . .

"The five-sensory personality processes only the knowledge that it gathers and substantiates through its five senses. The multisensory personality acquires knowledge through its intuition, and, in processing that knowledge, aligns itself, step by step, with its soul."

—Gary Zukav, *The Seat of the Soul*

* * *

Game 18

The Sell-Out Tactic

Key Players:

Sense Functions:
Fear, Judgment, Laziness,
Partiality, Pride, Self-Pity

Counterbalancing Soul Faculties:
Courage, Peace,
Personal Responsibility, Principle, Truth

How the Game is Played:

The personality plays *The Sell-Out Tactic* when it expresses partiality instead of showing the courage to stand up for principle. The granting of special help or favors to some and not to others is motivated by the fear that we will incur their displeasure and suffer the loss of an attachment or tarnish our self-image of pride—a sell-out to our own self-love.

THE CHOICE BETWEEN PRINCIPLE AND PARTIALITY

As we walk on the path of light, we become increasingly aware of the necessity to transcend the duality of personality and to put greater effort into expressing principle, the path to peace. Since the mind is dual, being a part of creation, it can only know the disturbing flux and flow of creation.

When effort is made to still the mind, a small voice from within speaks forth the truth and we know from the very depths of our being what is right. Beginning this process we often loose track of the small voice of our spirit for it becomes muddled in the loud ramblings of our mind. If we have some control, however, we can test the situation. The question we must ask is: *If this decision is right, will it apply to all other like situations and people? If it is right for one, is it right for everyone? Am I willing to help a person that comes to me in need of help, or am I willing to only help those that I judge it would be advisable to help?* One will put you into personality, and the other will guide you on through principle. Which shall it be?

In James 2:2-4 (Lamsa Version): *For if there should enter into your synagogue a man with gold rings and costly garments, and there should also enter a poor man in soiled clothing,*

And you should attend to the one who wears the beautiful clothing and say to him, sit here in a good place, and say to the poor man, stand up there, or sit here before our footstool,

Are you not then showing partiality and thereby giving preference to evil thoughts?

If you have something to do for someone, and you are truly willing, ready, and able to fulfill the need of an individual that you know, and you are truly ready, willing, and able to fulfill the same need of another individual under similar circumstances, or twenty individuals, then you are on the path of principle.

"One should never grant the right of difference at the sacrifice of principle."

Personality, on the other hand, is the door we open for the shadows of the past to enter the realms of consciousness where they may satisfy their needs and obstruct the Law of Goodness known as principle. If you put self into a situation, you are in personality. When you are expressing through personality, you are expressing partiality. *"One who sees personality never finds principle."* As the spirit teacher put it, *"When man serves man, he is in personality. When he serves spirit, he is in principle."* You cannot be in principle while you are in personality because they are opposites and the energy being directed by thought cannot go in opposite directions simultaneously.

How can you perceive correctly when you are in principle? if you are in principle, you are not concerned about principle. And secondly, you are not making the judgment that you are certain that you are in principle. Truth, which is principle, needs no defense.

MOVING FROM MAKING JUDGMENTS
TO ACCEPTING PERSONAL RESPONSIBILITY

The prerequisite to selling-out is the making of a judgment. It is judgment that breeds the poison of personality. We sell out to the judgments of the "have been's." It is not outside, it is inside. The attachment (the judgment we love) is in our head and it reflects outside. It is our head that we can change. That is what we can do something about. The deception is that it is outside.

It is judgment that causes us to fear that a loss will take place if we stand on principle. Without judging the effect—a presumption by the personality as to the outcome or loss—there can be no fear or sell-out. A loss may be an attachment, a feeling of comfort, self-image, or pride. Intimidation or fear, laziness, and the need to be liked may be added to the list of causes for selling-out to personality, which only reveals we are controlled by the mind and not by the soul. In moments of self-pity, we may review a catalog of situations in which we have sold-out principle. When we sell-out, we become the instrument to drown our own soul and also the soul of another.

Wherever there is personality, there is always dissension. With dissension you have no unity. Without unity, you cannot have success in any endeavor.

When we accept personal responsibility for all our thoughts, then we do not get caught up in personality. For when we accept the fullness of personal responsibility, we can discern the difference between transgressing another's path and standing on principle. If, however, we choose to depend on our own mind rather than on the Light within us, which awakens personal responsibility, we are trapped by the mind of another. When you sell out to the desire to please another, you can never trust yourself. If you cannot trust yourself, you cannot trust others. However, when you rise in principle, you free yourself from judgment and rejection, you move into peace and acceptance.

HOW WE SELL-OUT

What are we afraid of that we are not willing to stand up for principle? You cannot please everyone. It is a total waste of life. What are some everyday examples of selling-out?

A person may cast a vote for someone that he or she truly feels would not be the best candidate for the job because he or she has something personally to gain from it. Or, a person may have promised to help someone, only to renege when badgered by a third person to help him or her instead. A judgment based upon past experience that the third person's emotional forces will be heaped upon us, and the fear of dealing with those forces can cause us to sell out. Another example is showing partiality in hiring an acquaintance over a better qualified person because, again, we do not want to face someone's emotional forces. We want to be perceived as "the good guy." If we relax the rules for a friend, or whatever twist the game of sell-out may take, a part of us always knows when we sell-out. We feel bad and dump it on the first person that comes along.

What is right for one should be right for everyone in keeping with one's efforts. It does not matter what someone thinks about us when we stand up. When we are not sure we are right, it reveals our pride is at stake. Pride is a key player in selling-out. When we support the darkness in another without speaking the truth, we pay twice. First, for not granting the truth to another, and secondly, by not being true to our own spirit. So if we stand on the rock of principle, our right of being, we will never again be concerned about what anyone thinks, let alone does.

You must first deny God before you can sell-out. And, of course, when your faith is not in God, your reliance is upon your mind and that is all you can grant to another. You deny God as your sustenance, the source of your supply. The moment you put somebody in the place of God, you sell-out. You do it to yourself. When you sell-out, you sell-out to the forces of darkness in yourself, and support the same level in another. In truth, you have given power over you to another individual. Ask yourself, *What thing is so valuable in my consciousness that I would sell-out my light of reason? It has taken centuries to get to my present level of unfoldment?* Do we allow our mind to tell us that we have need and that another person has something to offer us? Are we afraid that if we do speak out we will not be able to control our emotions? Or, that we will "lose" in the relationship? Is it difficult for us to be assertive without becoming emotional?

You must first sell-out to your own intimidation forces to sell-out to another's. If you support another's forces, you support your own inside. Intimidation forces express through one's emotions, so the payment of getting free of intimidation is the control of one's own emotions. Until you make the decision not to be intimidated, you will always sell-out principle. It is the "easy way." People who do not communicate are easily intimidated. They do not speak up because of fear of retaliation. Communication would clear up the intimidation feelings. To ask is to receive but our attitude blocks our receiving.

BEING THE VICTIM OF IMPOSITION

If you sell-out, you guarantee the Law of Imposition. Why be a victim of imposition? If a person is put down or taken advantage of and does not speak up, that person is supporting the transgression. It is the responsibility of the person who has been unfairly treated to correct the situation immediately. The excuse that it may be inconvenient is no justification for refusing to accept the responsibility—the ability to respond to the act. *"Silence on crime is endorsement."*

Sometimes, however, we may make the conscious decision not to speak out after weighing the consequences of incurring the offender's wrath and potential vindictiveness. Fear of someone's retaliation is one of the worst bondages, for *"fear born of emotion compromises."* Test the situation by asking the question: *Is it a minor enough infraction that it is in the best interests of all concerned to let pass now and deal with later when the climate is less emotionally charged? Can I use humor to get my point across?* It is fear and fear alone that gives power to things outside ourselves. We do not want to battle someone's personality because we know an uneducated personality demands to defend its position. All functions of the mind have to be defended because functions are not truth. Truth just is. Truth is a soul faculty. Truth needs no defense. If we feel we must defend something then it is not truth that we are expressing.

THE NEED TO BE LIKED

How many times during the course of a day do we sellout? When people gossip and express all kinds of negative levels, remember, it is the divine right of the listening ear not to hear it. It is also the divine right of the listening ear to change the subject. Of course, it is more difficult to close the hearing than to change the subject. But, if we hesitate to change the subject, then we are being controlled by our fear of offending the individual, and reason is not flowing.

We pick certain people to consciously manipulate into liking us. Why do we choose those particular people? We must first have the value for wanting someone to like us. It may reveal we are lonely. We view the comparison of our strengths and weaknesses in trying to get someone to like us. We may do this because we want what we have judged they have and have judged we have not. In that thinking we will never get what we think they have. To free yourself, work on your mind so it does not matter whether others like you or not. Otherwise, you become first the victim of your own likes and dislikes only to become the victim of another's. When you make any man or woman your god, you sell-out for your reliance is limited to personality.

"The desire to be liked is stronger than the desire for reason."

BECOME AWARE OF YOUR WEAKNESS

Beware when people prey on the weakness of another, for they are only romancing the love of self. For example, we may puff up another individual for his or her accomplishments. Remember, we only "puffivate" another to sacrifice them for our self-gain; we "puffivate" others to weaken them and then we strike. Likewise, others may sense our weakness and work on it. Beware of where they are coming from so you will know where you are going down in consciousness.

If you demonstrate through priority, being awake to your true motive to stand on principle and dissipate soulless forms, you gain. If not, you lose. So, you either stand on principle or you choose temptation and continue to be a slave to the grand sell-out. If you choose to be tempted, you identify with your creations and go out on a limb. As long as you remain on the limb, you have to pay the price, that is, as long as you are tempted. Giving in to weakness is the sell-out to what you have created. In other words, choosing to serve what is past. You make that choice moment-by-moment, and because you make the choice, you are never without hope of changing.

"When our fear of man is greater than our love of God, personality becomes our king and principle our slave."

You must become aware of your weakness when the forces of darkness are working on you. Only through the weakness can the forces of darkness take you out of the Light. If you give up the constant thought of self, self, self, you will win the war within. Otherwise, the battle goes on. Unless we are in personality or self, there is no possibility of self-deception, of selling-out. What do we sell-out? **We sell-out our soul.** So when working on yourself, be honest. There is nothing or no one worth selling-out your soul. Work for the Light and not to please people. However, be certain it is for the Light that you are working and not simply using the Light to justify your actions.

DEMONSTRATING RESPONSIBILITY AND COURAGE

Only through communication will you gain the understanding that wisdom may cast her light of reason, which will transfigure you and free you from the bondage of self-deception. It takes courage to stand up for principle, to stay on guard and not slip. *"Courage is the unwavering commitment of the soul to principle."* We do have that great responsibility to demonstrate courage in accepting there is one God, one truth, one love, one law, and to know that any soul who stands on the rock of principle will be dedicated to the Eternal Light despite the mind's justification not to change. That great responsibility extends to treating each and every soul that it encounters in keeping with the impartial Law of Merit. And in accepting the right of all, we will not sell-out our own right.

*   *   *

"He who seeks the praise of man loses sight of God's true plan."

Game 19

Universal Motherhood

Key Players:

Sense Functions:
Credulity, Manipulation,
Sympathy

Counterbalancing Soul Faculties:
Compassion, Consideration, Honesty,
Love, Peace, Reason

How the Game is Played:

The game of *Universal Motherhood* is played when the soul faculty of compassion, trying to express itself, becomes obstructed by the magnetic field, and instead of being guided by reason, the intense drive of the personality rises with its need to run the business of everyone but its own.

THE UNIVERSAL MOTHERHOOD PROFILE

Universal motherhood is a need within a person to gather, to garner, and to control all things of its interest. When we are trapped in universal motherhood, compassion leaves the guiding hand of reason and goes into credulity because the judgment is made that we must decide what is right for another individual. We must then ask ourselves, *What is my need to believe so readily, to be convinced so easily that I alone have the right to control another person's path? Why is my need to "mother" or control so great that I cannot allow others to grow? Why can I not allow others the experience and lessons their souls have merited without interfering? Does my personality demand that I run the universe because I can't run my own life?*

Although the level of consciousness has been termed *universal motherhood,* do not be misled that it applies only to women. Men play the game as well. Emmet Fox in *Find and Use Your Inner Power* gives a fine profile of "Mr. Atlas":

> Not satisfied with his own many troubles (and Mr. Atlas is certain to have a great many of his very own), he has to go about worrying over everybody else's problem too. The Greeks picture him carrying the whole world on his own shoulders, bowed down under the intolerable weight.
>
> Mind your own business, Mr. Atlas. Hoe your own row, scrub your own doorstep, and that will give you quite enough to do—if you do it properly. Do not try to carry the burdens of the whole world. Such a policy will destroy you and will not help the world.
>
> Leave something to God. After all, it is He who is responsible for the world, and not you.

Not ready to play favorites, Fox describes "Mrs. Fix-it":

Nothing discourages her; to mere hints she is impervious—she means so well. She doesn't interfere in cold blood, it is simply an instinct with her—*she must try to fix it.* She has been interfering from the moment of her birth, trying to put everything right, and, needless to say, usually making things worse, doing more harm than good in the long run . . . Her basic error is love gone wrong, as love is so apt to, when not balanced by intelligence.

THE DYNAMICS OF UNIVERSAL MOTHERHOOD

When we are in personality, we are separated in consciousness from our other bodies, causing us to feel a sense of loss, of being scattered, feeling rejected, not cared for and feeling no one understands us. If we are out of self, we will not have these feelings and, therefore, no need to control others, nor will we feel the sticky need to be wanted, the need to please, or the need to be liked. Are we spending our lives trying to be what we are not to get someone to like us because we dislike ourselves? If we are out of personality, we will have no need to be a "people pleaser." Needs of this kind are distortions by the personality of The Divine awareness within us; for in truth we are a part of everything, everywhere, at all times;—we have always been; we will always be. The distortion of our relationship to The Divine causes us to place a higher value on human love, recognition, and acceptance than on God's unconditional love, and to play the mental game of trying to get others to like us. To what further depths can the personality possibly go to deceive us and keep the truth from our acceptance? What happened to honesty?

As stated in the game of *Playing Judge*, the instant we compare, we are in judgment. We compare our strengths and weaknesses with those of other people and then make a concerted effort to get others to like us because we have judged they have something we would like to have. In our comparing, we forget that everything we think we desire is possible for ourselves. *"O God, that, too, for me is possible should I choose to make that effort."* We must know what it is we really want in life. It is because we do not know what it is we really want that we have such a struggle. We cannot know until we are honest with ourselves.

Sadly, universal motherhood is widely practiced by many parents, and sometimes is at the root of the ambivalent relationship between man and woman. The smothering role first played by the parents is then carried on by the children in subsequent relationships in their lives. This practice has implications for those in the helping professions in that they are trained carefully to avoid treating their clients and patients in a way that would foster dependency.

WHEN COMPASSION LEAVES
THE GUIDING HAND OF REASON

When you feel compassion for a soul, you must make the effort to be at peace so that you may objectively observe that the experience the person is having is an effect of laws that person has established; and, if you do not make that effort, then you cannot find the cause, nor can you be the instrument through which the cure can be revealed. When in the universal motherhood level of consciousness, you do not see what laws another has set into motion to cause his or her experiences. Therefore, the soul faculty of compassion becomes the blindness of the sense function of sympathy. Our uneducated personality in its misguided love does not want the person to have to pay for his or her transgressions of the law and so a protective pattern rises to shield, and at the same time, control another's soul. We may be afraid to challenge the transgressions of another and instead support that person's level of deception to protect our own deception from being exposed.

We are all God's children. It is the insanity of the personality to think it owns another being—an eternal being. Children are not extensions of their parent's personality. Their soul belongs to God. A parent has no right to steal it. We have no right to smother or possess another soul.

When we are possessive, we become fearful of losing what we possess. We may not want to enforce discipline for fear a child will grow up and not be under our control. A mother in self-will may be saying she wants humility for her own soul but not for her child when she decides something is good enough for her but not good enough for her child.

"There is no more finely polished mirror for parents than their child." We must help our children to grow up rather than demanding to relive our personality through them or another soul. We must get out of the glory train of attachment to our fruits of action. If you do not care to give your children what they need to be free, they will grow up not to care for you. They will see you as an instrument to fill selfish, greedy desires, and in extreme cases, that could be the only time they will have anything to do with you. You will be used as you used them. *"God, help me to do what is right. I must give up my need to control another soul and play God."*

You help others to help themselves not by doing the job for them, but by pointing the way; for to do it for them renders them helpless and dependent upon you. That is how we control others and perpetuate the smothering pattern. For example, a wife supporting the license of her husband because of her need to control makes a cripple of him by making him dependent on her. The wife's personality is fed for its own glory. She lets her husband have his own way—the way he thinks he wants—to keep peace and harmony, and he becomes trapped, wallowing in his own self-pity. It is a game of victimization. When you truly love unconditionally, you make great effort to show your loved ones their traps. They suffocate because you are blocking their nostrils of reason. They cannot breathe. After awhile, they scream for life. Ask yourself: *Who am I putting* *where God belongs? In God's rightful throne, who have I put there? Am I **empathizing**—projecting my being into the being of another in order to better understand that person and share in his or her emotions, thoughts, or feelings—or, am I **sympathizing** through lack of understanding and emotional involvement?*

Compassion, under the guiding hand of reason, knows the Law of Non-Interference. It is sympathy that interferes. *"Compassion has the light of reason; sympathy has no understanding."* What are we doing when we sympathize with another human soul? Are we helping them to grow out of their level, or are we helping them to stay in it? Usually what sympathy does is to help a person stay in the level they are in and it puts us in that level also. Sympathy for one who has transgressed the law throws us under the transgression of the law of that person's payment system. By supporting that person's transgression, we pay the price of the transgression also.

EXPRESSING CARE THROUGH SELFLESS SERVICE

"One who cares for others, in truth, cares for oneself." Each time you make the slightest effort to help another, you reinforce your own spiritual strength. And you will always be guided to be at the right place at the right time to abort a disaster, or to take an opportunity to do something good for someone. It is the way to grow spiritually. It is called selfless service and is the only path to spiritual illumination. Serve the soul, not the personality is the teaching of all the great Masters.

Whereas universal motherhood is concerned with controlling all things of its interest, selfless service is working without the self-motivation. It means you really care about a person struggling through his or her disasters. You empathize on a soul level. If you turn your back on the struggles of others, you will not only see the day when others turn their back on you and your struggle, but you guarantee the day when you will need help. The kindness you give to another always returns in your day of greater need. The more you serve selflessly, the deeper you awaken.

CONCLUSION

It is a law that our attachments do in time become our adversities. The law ever seeks to balance itself, just as water reaches its own level by its own weight. All we have to do is to be honest with ourselves and see how the law guarantees her own balance and is driving us determinedly into our adversities to free us from our attachments. The law of the magnetic field is to hold, bind and in time destroy itself. Therefore, universal motherhood seemingly serving a bad purpose in one way serves a very good purpose in another way by eventually bringing balance and freedom.

The quality of help we must give is best described in the saying, *"When motherhood becomes brotherhood, the children will grow up."* When universal motherhood (the need to control and run another's life) becomes brotherhood (the respect for the rights of others), the children (the thought forms) will grow up (will be transformed into angelic forms). The soul faculty of compassion will be freed from the magnetic field and become expressed through a balanced electromagnetic field and then we will have the brotherhood of man, the heaven on earth.

* * *

"Let no man call God his father
who does not call man his brother."
—Andrew Jackson Davis

* * *

"Compassion is the key which locks the door of pride
and frees our soul that it may soar to heaven's heights."

*   *   *

There is a power greater than I
Expressed through all the earth and sky.
Its many forms we see without
And wonder why so many doubt
This God of love the humble know,
For they have found the greater goal
Which all may have if they but seek
To help the lost, the sad, and weak.
Thy will I find expressed divine
When all of life is seen as mine
And I am ready and willing to share
The part of me that's known as care.
                    —*The Wise One*

Game 20

Playing with Spiritual Teachings

Key Players:

Sense Functions:
Arrogance, Deception, Discouragement,
Distraction, Fascination, Intolerance

Counterbalancing Soul Faculties:
Awareness, Encouragement, Reason,
Self-Control, Tolerance

How the Game is Played:

The game of _Playing with Spiritual Teachings_ points out
how the personality deceives and enslaves by taking spiritual truths, fascinating with them, twisting them, using
them to arrogantly control or reform others, and unwisely
opening the psychic centers before unfolding the soul faculties.

GOING ON THE SPIRITUAL SMORGASBORD

It takes a very strong personality, wisely directed, to stay on the spiritual path. Never let anyone convince you to the contrary. We all know what spiritual philosophy can do for those who use it wisely. We also know what it will do for those who abuse it. Many students—we are all students of life—go on the spiritual smorgasbord from one philosophy or one religion to another, and another, and another, which, of course, is their right. Because they are looking outside for what is waiting for them inside, they will never find what they are really after until they make the change and accept the truth that they cannot get it outside. It takes commitment to stay with one path long enough to plant the seeds, see them sprout and grow.

"Truth is for honest seekers, not for those of idle curiosity."

WHEN THE INTELLECT TAKES HOLD OF SPIRITUAL TEACHINGS

Many people go to metaphysical or spiritual awareness classes, or to one of the New Thought churches, and their **intellect** takes hold of the teachings. They have not had prior exposure to free thought. They may have been programmed in religions which teach fear and control through rituals and dogma, and they become fascinated by what they are learning. Here is the danger: When the **personality** has determined their spiritual awakening and does not give an ounce of consideration to the "have been's"—tapes in their heads from that which they were taught before coming—they pay a terrible price. Fascinating with and analyzing philosophy opens a living hell inside. That dive into hell can be unbearable. Besides the rebellion of the "have been's," there can be considerable guilt connected with changing one's religion or spiritual thinking. The easiest way to free oneself is to flood the consciousness with positive affirmations that God is at the helm and you are being guided in the way that is right for you.

"When one is chained to dogma and creed, the soul of reason is ever in need."

The true purpose of a spiritual awareness class is to help people help themselves; to help them think more deeply. This is an especially relevant approach for the New Age of Aquarius. We have the divine right to know truth because there is a part of each of us that is truth.

An awareness class should not tell anyone how to think or what to think. It is a sharing of a certain path upon which, if one applies and demonstration has proven, the student will find truth. When we find truth, we respect the rights of all individuals of all expressions, because that is what truth does. Truth is everywhere; it wears many garments and *"deceives the wisest **minds** of men, however, it does not deceive their **souls**. "*

Become aware of your motive for studying things of a spiritual nature. It must stem from a sound mind and a pure heart if your soul is to gain. We may deceive others but never the spirit or God within. Some students who become converts to a particular philosophy or religion and who let their **minds** grab hold of the teachings, become arrogant in asserting theirs is the only right path. Jesus condemned the Pharisees' spiritual pride which was manifested in ostentation. (Matt. 6:5; 23:5) When the dark side of the personality takes hold of spiritual philosophy, it is self-destructive because it not only becomes arrogant and intolerant of the beliefs of others, but uses the laws to control others and to blame outside for what is going on inside. It is understood the more you permit your **mind** to entertain the question of spiritual truth, the more thought forms you create.

In intellectualizing spiritual teachings, the mind "qualifies" what it receives. Therefore, it would be naive not to be very aware that some people can and do twist the universal laws. They take the spiritual philosophy out of context to support established patterns and use it to avoid personal responsibility.

TOLERANCE FOR DIFFERENT VIEWS

Reformers have no tolerance for the struggle of others because there is no understanding within themselves; consequently, they stunt their own growth. There is nothing worse than reformers for they are suppressing, not educating or broadening their horizons. It takes a titanic personality to suppress. It takes a humble soul to educate. May the divine infinite mercy save us all from the reformers!

Developing the soul faculty of tolerance for those who differ from us must begin by first being kind and granting to ourselves the right of choice. For if we do not grant to ourselves the right of choice, there is no possible way that we can grant it to another. We can only give what we first have, and if we do not first grant ourselves the right of choice, the right of difference, we cannot give that, or grant that, to another human being. That which we attempt to impose upon another is only the revelation of what we are imposing upon ourselves.

Think! What kind of God would it be, what kind of goodness would it be, that would not permit the snake to crawl the ground, or that would not permit the ant to be equal in principle to the angel? The only difference is the form through which The Divine, Infinite, Formless, Intelligent Spirit is expressing.

There are many factors involved in spiritual unfoldment and work, and one of the pitfalls is to try to force upon another soul one's religious convictions. This seeming need in the human mind to force a belief upon another reveals that one is not secure in his or her own convictions. Confirmation is needed. Their personality receives confirmation by converting everyone else in the universe. Whatever you have found your truth to be, if it is secure in you, you will not need to depend upon someone else to support it. It is yours and you know deep within, for that Light has awakened in your consciousness.

If we choose to see the limits within ourselves, rather than making the effort to broaden our horizons, then that is how our life shall be. When we meet anyone who is not in keeping with the limits we have set for ourselves, then we cannot feel good for we have already limited ourselves on how we will permit ourselves to feel good. Let us not be so insecure mentally and emotionally that we must impose upon another the restrictions, the limits, and the suffering that we have imposed upon ourselves.

LET THE TEACHING ENTER YOUR HEART

Spiritual philosophy works when it enters our heart; that is when we use it, for the soul expresses through the heart. That is when it serves us well. It is when we play with it with our heads that it starts to become abused. What our heads do is to take their own set of judgments and desires, and using the philosophy, they go to work to justify judgments that they refuse to let go of. Therefore, if we keep feeding the judgment form energy, in time we attract entities of delusion from the astral realms, and that is how we become the victim. This is why we cannot treat a spiritual philosophy with the mental realm; eventually, we become the victim of self-created forms. Take heed, for the thing we serve will demand that we turn our back to the Light. That is what our mind does with those things. But when the teachings enter our heart, we will see in front of us the Light that will clear a pathway through our evolution.

TRUE RELIGION UNITES GOD AND HUMANKIND

The purpose of religion is to unite God and man and woman, and that is the true religion that breaks down the barriers between man and woman and their fellow-beings. It brings to us the consciousness of the eternal union between the Heavenly Father and His child. The origin of the word "religion" is from the Latin meaning "to bind together" in reverence. If a religion is truly spiritual, it adds to another religion; it does not take away.

All religions are in the world to serve One God, for there is only One God. There cannot be ten, twenty, or thirty Gods. Different religions call God or Infinite Intelligence by different names and worship this higher power in different ways. It is the same spirit of which we are all a part. There is no separation to Truth and so there is no separation to God Itself.

It is Truth that forms the universal brotherhood by showing we are all one body and one spirit (Eph. 4:4) in God, and what is done to the least in that body is done to the whole. Religion teaches us to love the good and to serve all who are striving after truth. None of us is perfect, so if we really accept life lovingly and empathetically, we shall expect no more of those close to us than we can demonstrate in our own living.

There is no set way to the so-called Ultimate or The Divine; for creation, by its very laws of duality, guarantees variety of form. Therefore, there is no philosophy or religion or set way that will work for everyone because there are many different levels of consciousness being expressed. In time we will all find the way, but there is no particular way for everyone at any given time.

Are the teachings of such prophets as Mohammed, Jesus the Christ, and Buddha varied, or is the difference only in interpretation? One of the spirit teachers answered the question this way:

> The question in reference to the prophets who have visited your plane of expression is not a new question in the minds of the masses. The divine spark known as truth, known as eternity is one! It is the misunderstanding of the receivers who find a contradiction and doubt in the teachings of old, which are truly the teachings of new. Truth is simple and unconcealed. When we receive truth, our minds, which are guaranteed to be dual, start the opposing forces into motion and we experience what is known as confusion. The teaching of Buddha or the Christ or any of the prophets is one and the same teaching. There is one life, one law, one love; it is unbroken and eternal. We are not going to God, we already are a part of God. It is our minds which need

awakening, for the tendency of the
mind is to hold to form, to bind.

QUESTIONING THE MOTIVE FOR SHARING
ONE'S SPIRITUAL UNDERSTANDING

*"It is through the sharing of the truth with another soul that
one is moved from mental theory to spiritual application. That is why
blessings are shared, never sheltered."*

A person does not benefit the world unless he or she first
benefits himself or herself. You cannot teach another what you
have yet to teach yourself because it will fall on deaf ears. It
states clearly in the Bible, "O physician, heal *thyself.*"

If we wish to share, we must be honest with ourselves and
ask, *What is my motive for sharing my spiritual understanding?* If
we are motivated by the desire to seek recognition, personality
glorification, confirmation of our beliefs, or another gain which
is self-related, then we are in deep water. We simply must become aware of which desire is motivating us so our soul can be
free. Have we fallen into the pit of spiritual arrogance by trying
to force upon another our own convictions?

The desire to share our spiritual understanding **when it
is solicited** is not a bad thing at all for desire is the expression
of The Divine. It becomes detrimental to one's soul when one
is no longer aware of the motive for so doing, for then one can
no longer control it. When it is so subtle that we become its
slave any time it desires to pop into our brain, then it is a sad
day for our soul. When we cannot say no, then we have fallen
into the pit of pits. Just a little bit of self-discipline and self-
control will free our soul from the bondage of the personality.
It is very important that we become aware of what is motivating
us, what is **really** motivating us. Are we the captain of our ship,
the master of our destiny? Or, have we given that great power
of mastership away to certain programmed tapes of desire that
we have become so addicted to that we can no longer recognize
what is happening to us when it happens?

Each soul is prompted to do what is right for him or her to do. Some people are prompted to mention their understanding to another individual. They must go by their inner prompting. If they are motivated by a spiritual level of consciousness, they will not be concerned to any extent whether the person accepts or rejects it. They will be free because the motivation is from their spirit and, therefore, they are not attached mentally by the sense functions to the effect.

TAKING THE PAINFUL INWARD JOURNEY

"When of my God I seek to know the purpose of my life, the answer comes, the pain to grow, and willingness to strife."

Let us at this point consider what is involved in staying in the Light and taking that inward journey on a treacherous path of our subconscious mind. Never underestimate the personality as a vicious enemy to battle. We must descend in order to ascend. The dangers exist within ourselves. To reach the spark known as Divinity that is within us, we must go layer by layer down through the subconscious levels. There are many pits, many psychological, traumatic conditions that have been suppressed since early childhood. To go into the deeper, inner levels of mind without guidance is not recommended. Who, shall we ask, is so illumined to know this moment every thought one has, every thought one has ever had, every act one has ever done, every feeling one has ever known? All of those things lie waiting in the memory par excellence (heart seed atom) and through that dimension we must pass to enter the levels known as Light.

Our journey may take us on a "spiritual high," where all is viewed euphorically, only to have us plummet down into an uncontrollable emotional state, a state which may come without conscious awareness that an old painful tape is playing. Clearly, when we descend into the personality, we must "handle with care" so-to-speak, not exposing too rapidly the defense mechanisms which may be very fragile. This is why the ideal way of teaching and unfolding is in giving and receiving the philosophy in bits and pieces so that emotionally it can be better handled to insure changes in consciousness.

In the Divine Plan we are guaranteed all the experiences necessary to free our soul and, of course, we cannot free our soul until we clean out the garbage stored in the subconscious mind. How we go about it is critical in developing emotional maturity. Be aware that the closer we get to declaring our divinity, the battle of the "have been's" will intensify. However, one consolation regarding the Law of Creation is that *"by its coming, it will go."*

We reach a crossroads where the material is pitted against the spiritual; where the mental is pitted against the Divine Spirit; or a combination of the two. Will the soul rise and emerge the conqueror?

FACING DISCOURAGEMENT ON THE PATH

When you express control of self, you are gaining control over the many forms you have created. Without conscious control of the mind, you become distracted by the passing panorama of thoughts and events. It is then easy to be pulled off the spiritual path by distracting temptations. This leads to discouragement which can take a soul from the Light. Discouragement faces all students on the path for it is the reluctance of the personality to bow to the formless.

When we understand the true cause of discouragement, then we are well on our way, through application, to freedom from that level. It is true in any study or endeavor that we experience different planes of consciousness, discouragement being one of the most interesting and complex. Whenever the mind makes effort to study any subject, it makes decisions and judgments concerning the completion or victory of that study. Often the student is not consciously aware of doing so. That mental process is instrumental in breeding discouragement. Especially in the study of life and spiritual principles, the mind is quick to garner and to gather for the sole purpose of use and control. In spiritual studies, laws are revealed, making a person aware of having had the same experience before. Though the subject or circumstances may differ, the principle is the same. One then fears to look back at yesterday to see that each time he or she moves in that delusion of being in desire, it always ends without his or her total control.

When there is no immediate improvement, or when you slip, the thought forms want to tell you it is a losing battle— *why not just give up?* You will be constantly tempted when on the spiritual path. Because truth is the most valuable thing in all eternity, the price tag is very high to the mind. You are tempted by your weaknesses. The more you grow in the Light, the clearer your weaknesses show up.

Someone close to you who is not on the path may tempt you to step off the path. Frequently this is a problem with couples where one partner feels in competition with God for the other's time and attention to spiritual studies and meditation. Therefore, we must buckle up and strengthen ourselves in preparation for the temptations, the many falls and little rocks in the way. It is only the personality that denies God's divine right of expression, dictating there can be no thistles on the path. We dig ourselves into a deeper hole if not careful. Do not rush the climb for then the subconscious rebels more forcefully. Remember, slow steps are sure steps under the guidance of reason, and also an entity can only take us out of the Light through our weakness. Therefore, it is critical to make the daily effort to stay in the Light.

EVERY STEP COUNTS

If you want much out of life, you must put more into life. Not everyone is ready to give up everything and walk in the Master's footsteps. *"Half a soul with God is better than no soul at all."* In other words, a halfway measure where you are spiritually growing, where you are very interested and wanting to put the teachings into practice, but not yet ready to give up everything and put yourself clear under, still makes you a welcome partaker in God's kingdom. You will receive from the level of consciousness to which you have gravitated. No effort, no matter how small, is ever wasted. Some people think they have to give it all up and go around with long faces. This is not true. We should be joyful and enthusiastic.

PLACING VALUE FOR TRUTH AHEAD OF JUDGMENTS AND DESIRES

The personality always holds us back until we take control of it. The struggle in awakening on the spiritual path is in the giving up of the dependence on the mind, which can only be a gradual process. It means we must accept a power in the universe that the personality cannot control. The grand deception is that we get what we have through the efforts of the personality. Once you get past that deception, you are on the way to freedom. You can measure your spiritual growth by how you allow the judgments to cry out.

"If you aspire to function in a universal body, you must think in a universal way."

If you have a judgment tape that is stronger than your love of God, it may be the weakness through which an entity works to take you out of the Light. Sadly, if one succumbs, one frequently does not return to the Light in this incarnation. Know your weaknesses because that is the only way the forms can get to you. Remember, you are not here to serve your judgments, but to have value for the Light.

It cannot be stated too strongly that you must be eternally vigilant for you are constantly facing the bondage of creation or freedom. No thing can have higher value than your seeking truth. Only **you** can find truth. If **creation** is a higher priority, you will be stuck in creation. You have to face all the priorities of creation—desires, dictates, and so forth—that you have established. The things that are your lessons are the things you have flunked in prior incarnations. They will never be greater than your ability to overcome them, no matter what the thought forms tell you. **Everything** works out when you truly put God ahead of judgments and desires.

Remember, each desire creates a separate entity—a living entity without soul that takes on the form of your desire. That is why it is taught not to suppress desires; educate them by shining the light of reason over them, or fulfill them. Every time you push back a desire, you guarantee the day when it becomes so strong you cannot control it. Students may want to leave the Light because the Light gets in the way of fulfilling their desires.

Ideally, the "bits and pieces" teaching system reaps greater benefits. Otherwise, the emotions will not change if faced with too much Light too rapidly. Delusion will keep the door of application shut, and then, of course, transformation does not take place. Hence the teaching, *"If the Light is too bright, 'tis best we not see it now."* The path of Light is only as tough as your uneducated personality makes it. When we truly start to awaken, no illusion can stand in the way of truth. *"Illusion melts like snow at high noon, for joy and the fullness of life live in truth."* Truth is not something you read about in a book. It is not something that your ears hear. It is not something that your eyes see. It is not something your hands feel. It is something that your soul knows. *"Truth is simple that it may confound the **seeming** wise."* The Light of Truth and the love of it brings everything to the person who demonstrates it. *"Truth is taught through indirection, demonstration, and example."* Truth may only be demanded of oneself. Seekers of truth can think only of **all** life.

"Appearances are deceiving but truth is revealing." Discern the difference between appearance and truth. Falsehood is half truth. Truth is the fullness of life. Truth is not something you can play with like a toy. It is greater than the A-bomb. Truth is a Living Light that must be carried in the lamp of honesty. There is nothing like the honesty of the heart to lead us up to heaven. There are no free ways to truth. It is a single path, winding, twisting and turning up the mountain to the eternal Light. Do not seek truth unless you are willing to work for it. Lessons get more difficult as we evolve so we must work harder at control.

The soul can rise to any level that it has reached throughout all eternity. A person may rise to a level within a split second because he or she has already experienced it. Once having experienced a level, we repeat the experience.

THE FORMIDABLE FORCE OF THE PERSONALITY

To reemphasize some points already made, the following excerpt taken from *The Tibetan Book of Living and Dying* leaves no doubt as to the formidable force of the personality (ego) and the task that lies before the conquering soul:

> To end the bizarre tyranny of ego is why we go on the spiritual path, but the resourcefulness of ego is almost infinite and it can at every stage sabotage and pervert our desire to be free of it. The truth is simple, and the spiritual teachings are extremely clear: but . . . as soon as the teachings begin to touch and move us, ego tries to complicate them because it knows it is fundamentally threatened.
>
> At the beginning, when we first become fascinated by the spiritual path and all its possibilities, ego may even encourage us . . . but as soon as the teachings begin to touch us deeply, unavoidably we are faced with the truth of ourselves. As the ego is revealed, its sore spots are touched, and all sorts of problems will start arising. It's as if a mirror we cannot look away from were stuck in front of us . . . Ego goes on to conjure up all sorts of doubts and demented emotions . . . ego is so clever that it can twist the teachings for its own purposes . . . yet however hard ego may try to sabotage the spiritual path, if you really continue on it, and work deeply with the practice of meditation, you will begin slowly to realize just how gulled you have been by ego's promises–false hopes

and false fears . . . You realize that for years, your ego, like a crazy con artist, has been swindling you with schemes and plans and promises that have never been real and have only brought you to inner bankruptcy. When, in the equanimity of meditation, you see this, without any consolation or desire to cover up what you've discovered, all the plans and schemes reveal themselves as hollow and start to crumble.

CHOOSING GOD AND FINDING GOD

The teaching is given: *"He who **chooses** God **finds** God, and in finding God paradise is revealed."* Is there a difference between **choosing** God and **finding** God? Why do the scriptures say *"many are called but few are chosen?"* Few are chosen because few are ready to choose God. After finding God, a person may still choose personality over God and, therefore, not be fulfilled because he or she is not expressing God. We are fulfilled only during moments when we are in divine will rather than self-will. It would be wise to ask, *God, what is my cross that keeps me from finding thee?*

Churches teach about God. But revelation by itself is not fulfillment unless we make a choice **after** the revelation to express in divine will. Clearly, finding a thing does not mean being in it. For example, you may find a beautiful ring yet may not wear it. We are all on various rungs of the ladder of eternal progression. There are no two flowers identical and there are no two petals upon them that are identical. This is also true in the unfoldment process.

SPIRITUALIZING ONE'S THINKING

How does one spiritualize one's thinking? It is by becoming aware of what one is thinking. How many people are consciously aware of the thoughts of their own mind in ten short minutes? We have sold out our divine right to creation and have allowed ourselves to be influenced by whatever thoughts are swimming in the atmosphere. Many of the thoughts we are controlled by do not even originate in our being. We just become receptive to that level of awareness and we act accordingly. For instance, we may be drawn to something displayed in a window because of the strong desire vibration left there by the previous onlooker. So strongly influenced by the other person's desire, we may even purchase the item, only to wonder later why we bought it. Clearly, we sold our rights to the material world.

Therefore, the best way to spiritualize your thinking is to make the moment-by-moment application of awareness of what **your** thoughts are. You will not have to worry about how your **mind** can attain spiritual awakening because it is a total waste of your energies. It is your **heart** which is the vehicle through which your soul expresses itself. When your heart is truly open, you will not have to worry about **how** the law works, for you will be **applying** the law.

Spiritual awareness is not possible without daily application of the principles or laws. As we make a little effort each day to still and to quiet our minds, we will slowly but surely become aware of dimensions in which we are moving that we have yet to be consciously aware of. When we place our attention through concentration upon spiritual values, those spiritual values grow and increase in our life.

Wisdom is total spiritual awareness. The Light can only glow through application. People apply the laws in many ways. No one is to tell a person how he or she must apply law, because that is his or her individual right; but without application there is no Light. Energy cannot express itself until it is applied or directed. The Light is dormant like The Divine. God is like a great slumbering wisdom, just waiting to move. It takes will to make the move. However, when we do make the move, The Divine keeps us going.

Proper breathing is indispensable to spiritual growth. You cannot control a thought without breath. If you are not using air properly and speaking your word knowing it will not return unto you void, it cannot return. It is so very important to stop over-serving the water center, which is where the emotions live.

The energy flowing through you must be kept in balance. Do this by devoting part of your energy to mundane, physical work. Otherwise, the energy would be out of balance into the mental realms. Wherever your attention is going, that is where your energy is going.

OPENING TO PSYCHIC AWARENESS

It is advisable not to pray to see in these other dimensions. You may see too much before you are strong enough spiritually. The Light can blind and you can suffer unbearably. Instead of praying for clairvoyance, pray for divine guidance, and then whatever is best will come to pass. Pray for clairsentience, clear sensing, that you may clearly receive that guidance.

The great danger of opening to psychic awareness, or communication with the various dimensions, is if it comes before a fuller expression of the soul faculties. Then it is indeed not beneficial because the awakening and opening of the psychic sense exposes us to the Astral World, the mental world, and the mass thinking of the earth plane. Those things are not particularly pleasant. Thus, it is not recommended to use various crutches for unfoldment, such as Ouija boards, crystal balls, and other means of opening the psychic centers without first making the effort at control of your thoughts to raise the consciousness; and by that effort, contact the highest spiritual realms possible. Any time individuals depend upon anything exterior to themselves for spiritual unfoldment they are becoming dependent cripples to the thing that they are depending upon. Remember, nature and creation are designed to be a tool of man and never his master. Therefore, in unfoldment do not rely upon anything outside The Divine within you. The Divine within you will impress you and guide you to whatever you may or may not need for study and application. It is not just the studying. That is not the difficulty. It is the application.

It should be pointed out that when most people start on a spiritual path, only the three lower chakras or energy centers are open—the root, the spleen, and the solar plexus. It is possible, and frequently occurs, that a person will have psychic awareness stemming from the solar plexus chakra. This indicates that a person may have psychic and mediumistic ability without necessarily being a spiritual person. Like attracts like; therefore, that person will not be attracting on high levels. The desired pattern is to continue to raise one's level of consciousness through application of the soul faculties; thereby, in time the four higher chakras or spiritual centers that grant clear communication with one's higher self will open, and the helpers from the true spiritual realms will appear.

Sadly, many will go only so far and not put forth the effort to reach for the highest. Although every servant is worthy of his or her hire, those who channel solely for the money will not attain spiritual heights, and will in time find their abilities, and possibly their health, waning. So often they then begin to "fake it" for the money. Our spirit guides and teachers make a commitment to stay with us for our entire journey on the earth plane no matter how far off the path we go. They do their best to inspire us to do what is right for our own soul's growth. They cannot interfere; however, they will help us pick up the pieces when things go awry if we are receptive to them. Even when channelers or mediums misuse their psychic abilities, the guides will try to get through to give as much help as possible to the people who come to them.

AURIC POLLUTION

It is much easier to be spiritual if you associate with very spiritual people, so choose carefully to whom you give your life-giving energy. It is unwise to involve yourself with someone not demonstrating support for the Light for the simple reason you have to enter their level of consciousness. It is known as "auric pollution." If you find yourself in this position, for your own spiritual survival, do not allow your emotions to cloud what you are working for. Stay in principle and not personality. In short, be careful where and to whom you expose yourself. The faculty of encouragement, the handmaiden of reason, must be used wisely and frequently to flood the consciousness that one may see more clearly. As we accept that the quality of our lives is dependent upon what we are thinking, we begin to take responsibility to gain control.

THE STUDENT-TEACHER RELATIONSHIP

Perhaps a few words are in order with respect to the student-teacher relationship. These are words of wisdom expressed in a séance by a universal master teacher:

> The mind of man creates a shadow, and although the spirit guides and teachers want to help, it is like a steel wall to penetrate. All steps in one's spiritual progress are major steps. There are no minor ones because each step is related to the future in order to reach completion.

> The ego is a vicious enemy. Some students think they know it all. If you are a teacher, place that person in a ray of light. That would instigate radiation of the soul so it can express itself. If a person is not willing to listen, step out and go your way. Draw back, leave them in the Light, knowing the seed has been sown. If it lies on dormant ground, that is their choice. In time, the seed will find the fertilization it needs to progress.

> As a teacher, you have the responsibility to help a person over the threshold. The student must first open the door. As the student progresses and the power of Light and sensitivity is strengthened, you will be aware of his or her action.

The Bible teaches *"Ye shall be known by your works."* You need not speak. Let your Light shine. It helps individuals to know there is something beyond.

Jealousy is a vicious viper. Look upon light as you constantly move. Encase yourself in the Light and you will not encounter anything negative— thought patterns that would subject you to something that is not a part of your makeup.

The world is filled with catastrophic conditions, but a purification process is taking place for there must be an equalization of the material and the spiritual.

Remember to always give time to God and when the call is put out, it shall be heeded by God. The physical mind must be at ease to let the soul have its freedom to follow your choice. We cannot just serve and not do anything else. The test of life is to conquer both the material and the spiritual. Worldly possessions are your rewards and as long as you don't glorify them, they will not control you. The same is true with spiritual gifts. Don't compare your talents with those of others. Don't create a facade. Truth must come to the front. You will be uplifted to realms of glory if you follow this law. It may make you feel you don't want to return to earth, but this is a responsibility you must carry out.

The door is being opened. There
are no hidden secrets. Teachers are trying to help you facilitate your spiritual
progress. The main key is to follow
natural laws of God and meditate on a
daily basis. Meditation keeps your
teachers close to you and if there is a
waning away, it may help you to get back
to more discipline. The presence of
your teachers magnifies the power of
your efforts. Set a regular time.

Do not be discouraged initially at your efforts to unfold
and awaken, or to view the stepping stones of unfoldment as
the final plateaus of eternal life. Above all, do not view experiences as *you*. View them for what they truly are—expressions
that come and in time shall go, no matter what you may decide.
View life in the beauty and the joy that is truly there. Do not
continue to choose to suffer when through a microscopic effort
you may be free. The law is the Law of Continuity. Use the law
to raise your consciousness. You are already using the law to
remain where you are. It is the same law; just direct it upward,
not outward.

In closing this chapter, we again quote the wise Rinpoche:

... The more you listen, the more
guidance you will receive ... listening
is a far more difficult process than most
people imagine; really to listen in the
way that is meant by the masters is to
let go utterly of ourselves, to let go of
all the information, all the concepts, all
the ideas, and all the prejudices that our
heads are stuffed with. If you really listen to the teachings, those concepts that
are our real hindrance, the only thing

that stands between us and our true nature, can slowly and steadily be washed away . . . the more and more you listen, the more and more you hear: the more and more you hear, the deeper and deeper your understanding becomes . . the deepening of understanding, then, comes through contemplation and reflection . . . As contemplation slowly unfolds and enriches what we have begun to understand intellectually, it carries that understanding down from our head into our heart . . . and puts into action the insights we have gained and applies them directly . . . to the needs of everyday life.

THE JOY OF SERVICE

We must be honest with ourselves in identifying our true motives, not the apparent motives for studying spiritual philosophy. Can we in all honesty say it is for the joy in the effort that we serve God? Joy does not mean pleasure or enjoyment. The soul faculty of joy is an expression of harmony in all levels of consciousness. When this takes place, the functions and faculties are in a perfect balance and the experience of the fulfillment of all good takes place on all levels of being.

May that which is the joy of the spirit become part of your life, a part of you that cannot be taken away, but only added to. Your spiritual rewards are far more precious than the gold and silver of earth.

* * *

"No one can carry your burden,
No one can lift your load;
But angels of light wait patiently
To tell you their stories of old."

*   *   *

MAKING AFFIRMATIONS WORK

The reason many affirmations do not work is that we do not give them our rhythm or beat. We must put our beat and harmony into an affirmation or The Divinity does not respond. Rhythm is power; it is flowing with the divine stream of life. When we go with it, we will go the source of life itself. We cannot capture The Divine. It is formless and free—flow with it. The moment we get results, use that as a stepping stone to the next level of consciousness.

Rhythm is repeating the same goals time after time, day after day, until finally they have been reached. We make it drudgery because of lack of practice. Repetition is indispensable to rhythm. We cannot have harmony without rhythm. Rhythm is the life of the spoken word and the law governing wealth.

*   *   *

Game 21

Meditating Without Purity of Motive

Key Players:

Sense Functions:
Deception, Delusion, Distraction,
Need, Self-Glory

Counterbalancing Soul Faculties:
Common Sense, Concentration,
Patience, Purity, Surrender

How the Game is Played:

This game of *Meditating Without Purity of Motive* is played when we begin meditating for mental gain rather than for soul unfoldment. As a consequence, we are trapped by the deceiving thoughts of need, becoming the victim of those many entities who are on the same level of consciousness.

CAN MEDITATION BE DETRIMENTAL?

Is meditation for everyone? So much has been written about its benefits—its greatness, its beauty, its joy, but little has been said about its potential detriments if we enter meditation for mental gain rather than for spiritual unfoldment. Clearly, meditation is not for everyone because not everyone is willing to give up the glorification of the personality. In such cases, they go into delusion and not into a true meditative state. For some, meditation can be a form of self-hypnotic trance that defeats its purpose for that does not bring about changes for the better in one's life.

Such negative possibilities should compel one to definitely examine his or her **true motive** for wanting to meditate. If it is for mental interest, believing that we **need** to gain something better, then we will be controlled by a level of consciousness known as **need**, for the mind has judged and dictated **need**. We then not only become receptive to that level within ourselves, but we now become the receiver of all the realms of consciousness that are en rapport with that level, not only on the physical earth realm but in the astral and mental realms as well.

The detriments can be especially serious when we disregard reason and common sense and meditate too long or too often per day. The so-called danger in extended meditation is the tendency of the mind to create. The mind not only creates but it possesses, and when we are in meditation we are highly receptive to whatever level we are expressing at that time. Therefore, to extend a receptive or meditative period beyond twenty to thirty minutes in any given day is extremely dangerous, for most people are not in control of their mind. They can, and often do, become possessed by a predominant, insistent thought from their own subconscious mind.

When we go "overboard," the first thing that happens is that the bridge, the door between the conscious and the subconscious minds starts to open to the level of consciousness where the suppressed desires exist. Those suppressed desires start to rise. The conscious mind, not being familiar with its other part, the subconscious, interprets those desires to mean many different things, but they are always self-fulfilling. Consequently, instead of unfolding in spiritual concentration and control, the person becomes the real victim of his or her own suppressed desires, perhaps of many years ago.

HEARING VOICES AND SEEING SPIRITS OF DECEPTION

Frequently in this process of misguided meditation, we believe we hear a voice or voices. The earliest experiences are the voices of one's own suppressed desires. As time progresses, and greater effort is made in continuity for the experience, we begin to hear the voices of those from the astral realms. And, because we, our personalities, are in a level of self-interest, we lack total consideration for our higher levels of consciousness, thereby establishing a rapport with those entities within our own mind, and without in the universe, whom we believe are wise and looking out for our best interests. Not knowing what they are, these desires may appear to be illumined guides and teachers. They appear as discarnate spirits, but actually have nothing to do with spirits in any sense or form. They have a great deal to do with suppression of the desires, and yet the conscious mind is deluded by itself for it is not aware of itself.

So when you **think** your guides and teachers are telling you how great you are, what good work you are doing, and what everybody else should be doing, and that friends of yours are either great psychics or great healers, it is highly questionable that this is clear communication. Stop and say to yourself: *Now this thing that talks to me is telling me that this friend of mine is a great healer, and that friend of mine is a great medium or channeler, and that friend of mine over there is a great something else.* Then ask yourself the question, *how is it they never tell me that the people I dislike are great healers and great mediums?* Ask yourself that question.

So-called spirits may enter a person's aura or universe and be from the realms of deception. They may not be what they pretend to be and, therefore, it behooves us to judge the tree by the fruit it bears. We cannot experience a deceitful spirit unless we have expressed energy at some time in our lives in the realms of deceit. That which is within us is attracted to us, and that is why the teaching to *know thyself and you shall be free.*

Many delusions can be very frightening and become very difficult to control. So, let us use, not abuse, reason and common sense about meditation. Any voice that enters your consciousness that is not instrumental in its dictates to help you to stay in the Light, that is not serving and doing good in the universe, is not an entity of Light, but it is an entity of darkness that will feed your selfish desires.

THE SUBCONSCIOUS GARBAGE CAN MUST BE EMPTIED TO EVOLVE

It is important to understand that no matter whether our motive for meditating is pure or impure, when we start to unlock levels within the depths of our own subconscious, the things that have been suppressed may come out in symbology, visions, and so forth. If an individual has had severe traumatic experiences that have been suppressed beneath the conscious level of mind, the traumatic experiences must be brought to the fore. In other words, our house must be put in order so that our conscious mind may tap into what is known as the superconscious or soul level.

Therefore, to be a clear channel to our own spirit, it is absolutely necessary to empty the garbage can known as a multitude of experiences that we have had in this short earth journey. When a person, level by level, is uncovering those experiences, like attracting like, he or she will attract at those times entities from the astral realms who are in harmony or rapport with the experience of that past that he or she is reviewing and expressing.

Some people do not see visions and so forth, but they start to have different emotional experiences. Some become highly sensitive and cry at the drop of a pin. This indicates they are going deeper inside themselves to reach their soul. You must go down to go up. The way is to go down inside the self and clean up all of those suppressed desires, all those hopes, all those fears, and all the day dream wishes. This is the way we find ourselves— a painful process indeed. It is not God's fault that we have wandered out into the wilderness and now all of those things are distracting us.

THE TRUE PURPOSE OF MEDITATION

Before entering into a process of meditation, it behooves a person to ask: *Am I ready, am I willing, and do I have the patience to accept a greater authority in my life than my own suppressed desires, and to be receptive and honest in that answer?* Until we can put God or goodness first in our thoughts and acts, we will not enter true meditation.

The true purpose of meditation is to attune the spirit encased in the body with the Universal Spirit in a clear, unobstructed way. Through meditation the soul is expressing The Divine, the God that in truth we are all a part. This process requires that the personality be aligned with the soul so that the mind is still, that is, in harmony with peace, the divine neutrality. The inevitable result from regular meditation is freedom to know that which is right and to act upon it without any doubt.

Meditation, properly done, is a total **surrender** and a beautiful experience of your true birthright. When you enter that realm of Light, you become that Light, and there you know and do not have to be told, for there you are one with everyone. Without surrender, you are trapped in so-called meditation, not only trapped by the deceiving thoughts of need that are in the consciousness, but you become the victim of those many entities who are on that level of consciousness.

If you are in a level of consciousness known as selflessness, you are thinking about the growth of your own soul, and not your own selfish interests of what will just make you happy. And it is for this reason we should meditate. Meditation can be instrumental in freeing you from self-related thought. Twenty minutes out of twenty-four hours is a small gift to our soul. We are reluctant to give the self because we are secure with it, whereas, we cannot assess what we feel or think is the unknown. Yet we all must give up the self someday and accept this "unknown" which is something greater than the self. *Why should I change? Why should I rock the boat in my secure little life?* Whether we like it or not, we are all changing.

THE TECHNIQUES OF MEDITATION

"We sit to meditate; we stand to agitate."

It is more beneficial to meditate at a set time than to meditate when one feels so inclined. The law is very clear. We get from a thing what we put into the thing. Therefore, when God is the most important thing in our thoughts and in our acts, then God, The Divine, shall guide our lives and they shall indeed be well ordered. We know that like attracts like and if one does not feel the value of system and order, then one shall not find system and order in his or her acts and activities. You attract from the universes those entities that are as reliable as you are yourself, no higher than your highest aspirations, and no lower shall your experiences, your guides, your teachers, your helpers, your mentors be.

Once a day for twenty minutes is recommended, preferably in the morning hours to take maxim advantage of the power and energy of the rising sun—the time when the power that makes for enlightenment is on the increase. What is more important, you are turning your thoughts to God before the confusion and cares of the day set in—a time when it should be easier to concentrate because the mind is reasonably quiet, a time to set a peaceful stage for the rest of the day. It simply becomes a part of you. Set aside a specific time, which in effect, is an appointment with your spirit guides and teachers.

It is said that God knocks at the door of our heart once in every twenty-four hours. However, we often fail to hear this knocking of the Divine Presence who continually seeks entrance into our heart because we are so busy with the mundane affairs of our lives. The Divine Presence can make itself known to us when daily, in solitude and quietude we open the door of our hearts so God can enter. God may then be heard as the still small voice of our own spiritual consciousness. Privacy during meditation is essential, for a sudden intrusion while abstracted in thought can produce a shock to the nervous system.

The meditation posture in the West differs from that taught in the Eastern philosophies. Here it is only necessary that the spine be erect and the body completely relaxed—no strain or tension, hands and feet uncrossed. Breathing should be slowed to about half the normal speed. A cleansing breath and a power breath are beneficial.

Cleansing Breath: Make the mouth into the shape of a pea, inhale as much air as possible. At the same time visualize the breath as energy permeating your entire being. Exhale through the nostrils as slowly as you inhaled. Learn to enhale the vibratory wave of peace, learn to release the vibratory wave of peace. Do this three times. This can be practiced safely at other times, not only before meditation.

Power Breath: This is to be done only before concentration following the cleansing breath. Close the right nostril with the fourth finger of the left hand. Inhale through the left nostril to the count of four. Close the left nostril with the thumb of the left hand and count to sixteen. Exhale through the right nostril to the count of eight. Keep the left nostril closed. Inhale through the right nostril to the count of four. Close the right nostril and count to sixteen. Exhale through the left nostril to the count of eight. Repeat three times This exercise should not be abused.

CONCENTRATING ON PEACE

"Silence is the savior of the soul and peace the expression of its love."

In what way is it possible to be en rapport with God or peace when our minds are so filled with the mundane problems and experiences of the earth plane? If one will truly make the effort, and if one will truly have the wisdom which is patience, and the faith which is strength, then one shall indeed enter the peace that passeth all understanding. The reason that this is difficult for some is because the mind is so very full of thoughts of passing creation where so much time is spent. To still the

the mind is to attune oneself with The Divine. It is in silence that God does His greatest wonders. In all your getting, get self-control. Be aware of all your thoughts, for your thoughts are creating your lives. They are the seeds that you are planting in fertile soil and you will make a garden of beauty or a jungle of hell.

Peace calls forth harmonious action of the inner mind and will attract its like kind according to the Law of Consistency. It is through the vibratory wave of peace that all things are harmoniously arranged in your life. Remember that all of our experiences are effects and never causes. Look wisely at these effects; they are the doors back to the cause.

Peace is the power itself; peace is called God. It brings balance into the inner mind, the personality. In other words, in concentrating upon peace we, in time, become that peace. Or, if not on peace per se, fix your thoughts upon some great truth, such as, love, gratitude, the oneness of all life, the ever-present spirit of the universe, or beautiful scriptural texts. Some find it helpful to concentrate upon the breath, while dissociating themselves from awareness of the rest of their physical body, their emotions, and their mind, realizing unity within the divine self.

It is recommended to concentrate on peace rather than to concentrate on an object that pulls you to the mental realm. You want to go beyond to higher states of consciousness. It is not a matter of mental strength, for concentration is not a mental activity. Concentration is beyond the power and control of the human mind; it is the human mind that must surrender. The less mental effort in your meditations, the greater the spiritual Light you would find and receive. Concentration should be an effortless receptivity to peace, moving from the thought of the word peace to the feeling and to the experiencing of it—a time of silent contemplation to lift the soul up into the realization of its own inner unity with the Divine Source. It is when the conscious thoughts are in harmony with the subconscious magnetic patterns that we express balance or peace. It is at that point that we are receptive, through the superconscious mind or odic field, to the Divine Intelligence.

When you truly let go, you experience true concentration which is the **key** to all power. Concentration by itself is not all power, but is the **key** to all power for that is the process in which your soul enters the united whole, your true being is awakened and aware of its own inseparableness with the Allness. If you are not experiencing the greatness, the beauty, and the joy of meditation, your mind is trying to control the process. You cannot pass through the doors of concentration into the realms of meditation and still entertain self-thought and self-interest. Concentration and meditation are vehicles but will not work without selfless service. You must surrender the authority and superiority of your mind and let God in.

MEANING OF THE ACTIVITY DURING MANIFESTATION

There are three parts to daily meditation. These are concentration, meditation or stillness, and manifestation or communication. In concentration, we focus our thoughts serenely on a single point. As we concentrate on that point, the mind becomes calm and we naturally move into a state of meditative tranquility. This is an alert condition, but one free of the distractions and cares of daily life. It leads to a state of clarity in which we either gain insight into ourselves, or we receive spirit communication.

The question may be asked, are the impressions, feelings, sights, or sounds that we receive during manifestation from our own spirit, or are they received from guides and teachers? Many people are unable to be en rapport or in tune with their own spirit. There are discarnate entities who have been attracted to us according to laws we have set into motion. They are enabled at times to impress our minds through telepathic communication; therefore, usually, but not always, the impressions, feelings, sights, and sounds that we receive are from our spirit helpers. For most people a thought impression is more quickly understood than a soul impression. However, as you go deeper and deeper into your silence, a great Light shall rise from level to level until you become consciously aware of your own spirit. When that day comes, you will know beyond any doubt what is from your spirit and what is from other spirits.

What are the seeming noises, sounds, and disturbances during our efforts to find silence that do not come from our spirit helpers? These experiences emanate from a level that we are tapping within ourselves; it is the door before the silence. It is the outer silence. The sounds are the sounds and the motions of our body. Each part of our anatomy is playing its tune. If we listen intently, we will know which part of our physical anatomy is out of tune or out of harmony. We are a great symphony, a great orchestra; each part of our body is playing its tune. We are becoming aware of our being.

FREQUENTLY ASKED QUESTIONS ON MEDITATION

During meditation should one concentrate upon the psychic centers of the psychic body?

It is most detrimental to most people. When we concentrate upon a thing, we become the thing concentrated upon and what is more important than God, or peace? Many people try to find a short cut to going back home, because that is what we are doing in truth. To concentrate upon activating the various psychic centers of the psychic body can and often does trap one in psychic astral realms. It is especially dangerous if the mind concentrates upon the solar plexus. Never below the heart is the great rule. This affects us not only while we are in the flesh but when we leave this earth realm. It is much easier to **grow through** those dimensions while yet in flesh than it is when we have left the so-called clay.

Should you discuss your meditation experiences with someone who is interested? Or, should you keep your own meditation experiences to yourself?

The greatest counsel that one can ever receive is the counsel known as silence, for silence is the power itself. However, there are those who need an expression of the experiences that they have in meditation. Choose wisely with whom you express those experiences for you will trigger certain levels of mind known as envy and jealousy, and in so doing, you shall rob yourself of future beneficial experiences.

At what age should children begin to meditate?

It has been recommended by many who have practiced it, that children may start meditating in their third year. A child who is placed in daily silence to think only of peace for ten minutes a day will be helped to maintain a rapport with The Divine.

Do all people have nonphysical guides and teachers and, if so, where do they stand during our meditation?

Yes, all people have a basic inner band of five spirit helpers. When you sit to meditate, visualize your Master Teacher standing behind you in an elevated position; your Doctor-Teacher of Philosophy standing to your right; your Chemist standing to your left, your Protector (usually an Indian) standing in front of you; and your Joy Guide (usually a child) standing between the Protector and Doctor-Teacher. The help you receive from them in everyday life is ever in keeping with your efforts to walk a spiritual path. They will never make cripples of you by interfering with your lessons. Their commitment is to walk with you on your entire earthly journey. Other spirits may come from time to time to assist in a specialized way, depending upon what you are involved in. Some may simply want to use you as a channel to complete their work.because of a rapport they have with you.

Are there certain foods that we should eat that would prepare us for a better body for meditation?

That is entirely dependent upon the computations of your inner mind. If somewhere in the inner mind there are programmed patterns of belief that dictate a certain type of diet would be beneficial to the purification of meditation, then for those who have those patterns, it is not only wise to use those diets, but it is necessary unless they can change the patterns of mind. The mind controls the body and that which controls a thing is greater than the thing that it controls. Work with your mind. Then, you shall be receptive to The Divine and control what is known as matter.

CLOSING REMINDERS

Let us remember that pure and true meditation is not detrimental—it is what you do with it. Without surrender, you are trapped in so-called meditation, not only trapped by the deceiving thoughts of need that are in the consciousness, but you become the victim of those many entities who are on that level of consciousness. The wise have always known to be patient, to see what grows from the seed before digging it up. Therefore, take another view concerning your efforts in meditation. See what is growing from the seed you have planted, but give it a chance to grow, water it faithfully, and care for it. The caring for it is the degree of surrender you can attain during the process, and the watering of it is the organization necessary to do it on a regular basis, not permitting it to be dictated by the fluctuating desires of the human mind. Any voice that enters your consciousness that is not instrumental in helping you to stay in the Light—the Light that is serving and doing good in the Universe—is not an entity of Light, but is an entity of darkness that will feed your selfish desires.

If the motive is pure, and if you will sincerely do your part in being still, the manifestation is inevitable. The teachers assure us it is simple in truth to be still, to be silent, to let the great God of All flow freely. Speak to the levels of mind and declare the truth of truth. *"I am spirit, formless and free, whatever I think, that will I be."*

When we meditate for the right reasons, the mind becomes still. *"When the mind is still, the Light doth dawn within, because the stillness of the mind is the sleep of the self."*

In reaching for truth, no effort is ever in vain. If you do not reach a high point today, just know that you are exercising your strength to enable you to reach a higher point tomorrow.

> *"When the lips are sealed in silence,*
> *And the ears are closed secure,*
> *Peace within has found its glory.*
> *The soul will play the perfect score."*

Game 22

Questioning Life Eternal

Key Players:

Sense Functions:
Doubt, Judgment, Justification

Counterbalancing Soul Faculties:
Faith, Personal Responsibility

How the Game is Played:

In playing the game of *Questioning Life Eternal*, if we are unable to accept that things of the spirit can only be discerned by the spirit, the personality then demands proof, to its satisfaction, of eternal existence.

QUESTIONING LIFE ETERNAL

One of the many levels on the spiritual path in which we will find ourselves, if we have not already, is the level that doubts what it cannot physically see, hear, sense, or taste. In time, all of us must, if we have not already, face that level of consciousness. When we are honest with ourselves, we have to admit there have been times when we questioned the existence of God and an afterlife. In those moments when we are questioning the existence of spirit, we are questioning the existence of our own eternal being.

> *"Man insists on questioning God,*
> *yet God in humility never questions man."*

There is no phenomenon that by itself will prove beyond any doubt that life is eternal. It is the mind that judges and decides what is truth. The mind, despite its constantly changing judgments, demands scientific evidence. The material science of this age traces everything to physical causes which are perceptible to the human mind. When we ask for so-called scientific proof, we are asking for facts that will be satisfactory for a time to the judgments we have already made. It is our mind that is making the demands, not our soul, because our soul already knows.

PAYING THE PRICE OF THE MIND'S DEMANDS

When our mind demands that we have absolute proof of life eternal, in keeping, of course, with our mental judgment, then we set every law into motion necessary to pay the price before we attain it. For in the realms of spiritual dimensions there is no credit, there is no pay later. We pay and pay in advance. We do not pay with the coins of the earthly realm. We pay by facing every mental obstruction that we have created that has blinded us to see and see clearly. The seeming sadness is that we do not know what the price will be. So we start on the journey. We take a few steps along the path and we decide the struggle is too great. We say, *That's too much to demand of anyone.* Understand that before our eyes open to the greater Light, they must first see clearly the lesser light. The greater Light is the light of the eternal spirit, and the lesser light is that of the limited mental world.

When our minds make the judgment that we have made the effort and have yet to receive, that is when we begin to question the validity of our own eternal existence. It is not our soul or the Infinite Spirit that questions, for it is beyond question. It just knows, and that which knows, has no need to question. It is known as faith—to be able to accept without the need of the justifications of the mind. Without faith in the Cause that gave us life, how can we have faith in anyone or anything?

COMMUNICATING WITH THE GOD OR GOODNESS WITHIN

"No one has ever seen God." (Jn. 1:18) The only God we will ever know is the God within our own being, and our perception changes as we unfold. It is not the responsibility of someone else to prove to us that God exists. That is our number one responsibility, and it is ours personally. When we have difficulty communicating with the God or goodness within ourselves, it reveals that our mind is very active, and every time that we attempt to get through to that peaceful, beautiful space in consciousness, something is in the way. Instead of a peaceful thought, a disturbing thought form plagues us. We believe we are the judgment form and that belief binds us to creation. It is in that false type of thinking that we fear death. We observe the life cycle of the plants, animals, and humans and we fear death because we believe we are the physical body, rather than the eternal spirit which is formless and free. On the other hand, some people fear immortality because of a deep-seated error that God is a vengeful God. They are afraid to inquire about life beyond the grave, because they are afraid of God.

People who doubt or reject the idea of the existence of God first make a judgment. Many times it is based on what they have been taught. It is that judgmental conception of God that they reject. Frequently, they have not moved in consciousness beyond thinking of God as a being in human form. In Genesis 1:27 it clearly states, "God created humankind in his image." What is his image? God is spirit. God is not a white headed man sitting on a throne judging us. We house a spark of that Infinite Intelligence or Divine Spirit within our human forms. As God is eternal, so is the God part of us.

ACHIEVING PERSONAL DEMONSTRATION OF ETERNAL LIFE

Only in the controlling of the thoughts of our mind will the great peace, the great harmony, which is our true being, rise in our consciousness that we may have the personal demonstration of our own eternal life. Absolute understanding of life eternal will come when we give up the constant illusion of the thought of self. When that effort is made and we have that experience, we will no longer have the need of our mind to doubt and to question life eternal for the Light of our soul, the faculty of reason, will shine over our mental realm.

Remember, things of the spirit can only be discerned by the spirit. Therefore, in considering the possibility of immortality, we have to call on the inner voice of our own soul. If we have not found the truth, it is only because we have closed the door against it. When we study pure spiritual science and honestly practice its laws, we will receive confirmation of the existence of God and the truth of our own divinity through firsthand experience. The science that all of the spiritual masters have taught and demonstrated for centuries is the principle that the basic cause of everything is the imperceptible and all-powerful Spirit. That path of inner awakening will remove any shadow of doubt as to why we are here, what we have to do, and how long we will be here.

WE BLOCK OUR VISION OF GOD'S ANGELS

The more firmly convinced one is that immortality is a fact, the more naturally that person will believe that communication between spirit and earth is not only possible, but is in perfect keeping with natural law. In every generation since there has been life on earth, there have been means of communicating with those who have gone before. The purpose of spirit communication is to help us to choose wisely the laws that we set into motion, and to bring comfort in knowing that our loved ones live on.

The only thing that keeps us from seeing angels is the thought of self. It is a curtain that blocks our vision. When we give the gift of self, we will then see God's angels. By giving the greatest gift the personality can give, we will be given the greatest gift—freedom from the fear of death, a vision of life eternal. We will move from God being an abstract idea to hearing the celestial melodies of His Word, the Holy Spirit.

ALL THE GREAT TEACHERS TAUGHT LIFE ETERNAL

"Remember that he who loves himself more than he loves Me shall lose himself to find Me. But he who loves Me more than he loves himself has found the truth, eternity."

The soul, which belongs to purer spheres, incarnates into the dense earth realm to acquire necessary experience to unfold its faculties. Coming into such denseness has been likened to entering a tomb. So birth is much like a death, and at the end of our earthly existence, the discarding of the worn-out garment that we call a physical body, is like a rebirth back to a higher plane. While on earth we remain entombed, so-to-speak, if we do not make the effort to return in consciousness to more refined planes of Light.

The greatest work of Jesus' ministry was the triumph over death. His other works—healing and emancipating us from errors of ignorance through correct living—are subservient to that end and necessary first steps in the great demonstration.

All the greater teachers taught that life is eternal. As Krishna says in the *Bhagavad Gita:*

> The truly wise mourn neither the living nor the dead. There was never a time when I did not exist, nor you, nor any of these kings. Nor is there any future in which we shall cease to be. Bodies are said to die, but that which possesses the body is eternal.

*   *   *

"Life is eternal and wise ones act accordingly."

THERE IS NO DEATH

There is no death! The soul lives on for aye,
   'Tis but a changing to another sphere,
E'en though the body passes back to earth
   The soul lives on, in spirit life, as here;
It will expand, and thrive, and ever grow,
   And still retain its influences o'er
Those left on earth, until they, too, shall go
   To join those who have merely gone before.
There is no death! 'Tis but a higher growth,
   The soul continues to another scene
Devoid of all encumbrances of earth—
   Shorn of all pain and suffering so keen;
And while we'll miss its daily presence here,
   And from its sweet companionship are torn,
We will be blessed, inspired and comforted
   By its o'er shadowing love, in heaven born.
There is no death! 'Tis but a change of form,
   Enabling the soul to reach its own,
And there expanding with each cycle made
   As it ascends near to the heavenly throne;
Our life on earth is but a transient stay,
   As onward to a future life we tread,
And, having gained experience of earth,
   We then pass on with those the world calls dead.
There is no death! For life can never die,
   Life is as potent as the truth itself,
It lives forever, through eternity;
   And when, in turn, the summons comes to us
To pass unto the land that lies beyond,
   We should not sorrow, but should e'en rejoice
That we've gained our freedom from earth's bond.

                        — I. C. I. Evans

Game 23

Redemption Without Effort

Key Players:

Sense Functions:
Belief, Deception, Fear,
Ignorance, Laziness

Counterbalancing Soul Faculties:
Acceptance, Application, Effort,
Personal Responsibility, Wisdom

How the Game is Played:

The game of *Redemption Without Effort* is played by the personality when it refuses to accept that salvation comes only by character, choosing instead to labor under the false assumption that the soul will be saved by belief alone in Jesus.

THE TRUE MEANING OF SALVATION

Many theologians interpret "salvation" as a deliverance from sin and from the penalties of sin and death; a saving of the soul through the atonement of Jesus. In proselytizing, the followers of this orthodox religious point of view frequently ask the question, "Do you believe in salvation by Jesus?" An answer to this question may be found in the writings of Charles Fillmore, co-founder of Unity, who said "The belief that Jesus in an outer way atoned for our sins is not salvation. Salvation is based solely on an inner overcoming, a change in consciousness. It is a cleansing of the mind, through Christ, from thoughts of evil."

Joseph Leeming in *Yoga and the Bible* explains the confusion regarding the meaning of salvation:

> Precisely what salvation may mean, as so often happens in theological matters, is not always very clearly understood. This is partly due to the fact that the English word "salvation," derived from the Latin, does not convey the meaning of the original Greek word used by the writers of the Gospels. This word was much closer to the meaning of the term employed by Jesus.
>
> The Greek word—*soteria*—means simply "a safe return." That is all. Our prodigal wanderings in the lower worlds at last completed and our lessons learned, the time has now come for a safe return to the realm of the Father from which we descended long ago.

Geoffrey Hodson in *The Hidden Wisdom in the Holy Bible*, Volume I, elaborates upon the Parable of the Prodigal Son. (Luke 15:11-32)

> The prodigal son's repentance is descriptive of that stage of maturity at

270

which the discovery is made that nothing that is outside of him can spiritually satisfy or 'save' any human being. The search for fulfillment then begins to be directed inward and upward, away from the particular to the universal, and from the lesser, human self to the greater, divine Self of the universe as a whole. Symbolically, the prodigal son repents of his former errors, discovers the true path and begins the journey home.

Leeming points out the universality of the parable:

In the parable of the prodigal son, Jesus epitomized the story of all humanity. This is the story of the descent of the soul from its original home in Sat Desh, the real country, of its wandering for many ages in the lower worlds, and of its eventual return to its Father's house.

All other great Masters have told the same story in various ways. It is a story that they must tell in carrying out their work of teaching men that they are spiritual beings who are now living in a very imperfect world, far lower than that from which they originally came.

"All things are delivered unto me of my Father: and no man knoweth the Son, but the Father; neither knoweth any man the Father, save the Son, and he to whomsoever the Son will reveal him." (Matt. 11:27)

Using Matthew 11:27, Hodson in *The Christ Life from Nativity to Ascension,* gives a very plausible explanation for the tendency of Christian orthodoxy to misinterpret and misrepresent the inner meaning of the words attributed to Jesus.

This error, constantly repeated, arises from the custom of applying essentially impersonal ideas to persons. The phrase "neither knoweth any man the Father, save the Son, and he to whomsoever the Son will reveal him" illustrates this practice. These words and others occurring in the New Testament have been taken to suggest that the Lord Jesus Christ was and remains the only mediator between man and God, and furthermore that all born and living outside the Christian faith are bereft of this mediation and so cannot know the Father. The very opposite, of course, is true. All men of all times and races are spiritual beings by their very nature and existence. The one Spirit known in Christianity as God dwells in each and every man, is, in fact, the Source of human existence and the assurance of salvation, meaning evolution to "the measure of the stature of the fullness of Christ."

In *Becoming a Spiritualist*, H. Gordon Burroughs simply says:

Christ never spoke of God as a personality; Christ never spoke of God as a being with personality. He spoke of Him often as his Father and Father of us all. He demonstrated this universality of manifestation in everything he did. He said unto the world, "Let all who are heavy-laden come and drink of the waters of the well of life freely." He did not designate a few; he did not say to this group, "You alone may drink of the waters of life." Neither did he condemn those who were healing, giving peace to the hearts and minds of people by means other than those he taught. When the report was definitely brought to him that there were others who were casting out demons and he was told by what method, he said, "Forbid them not," because they, too, were demonstrating the law, the manifestation of God, and were doing the bidding of the Father.

Our good forefathers who landed on Plymouth Rock in the early history of our country boasted of religious freedom. However, because they did not have religious freedom, they left the countries in which they had been born and brought over with them the same intolerance that they had left. Consequently, an ironclad religious system was established in this country, based on the precept, "If you believe, you will be saved; and if you do not believe, you will perish and have everlasting torment."

"For God sent not his Son into the world to condemn the world; but that the world through him might be saved.

"He that believeth on him is not condemned; but he that believeth not is condemned already, because he hath not believed in the name of the only begotten Son of God.

"And this is the condemnation, that light is come into the world, and men loved darkness rather than light, because their deeds were evil.

"For every one that doeth evil hateth the light, neither cometh to the light, lest his deeds should be reproved.

*"But he that doeth truth cometh to the light, that his deeds may
be made manifest, that they are wrought in God."* (John 3:17-21)

Taking the above verses and considering the meaning of
the key words *saved, condemnation,* and *belief,* Hodson submits:

> *Saved* implies the existence and
> threat of a danger, in this case presum-
> ably condemnation of the souls of man-
> kind. Literally read, the scriptures
> might be construed to mean souls are
> condemned for unbelief . . .
>
> The word *condemnation* requires
> interpretation in this light; for the sense
> of the word, as Jesus is presumed to have
> used it, implies, not condemnation by
> God for unbelief, but rather, it is sug-
> gested, for an unillumined state, a
> purely materialistic outlook and con-
> duct based thereupon. Condemnation
> in this sense might be inferred from the
> scriptural words *"light is come into the
> world, and men love darkness rather than
> light, because their deeds were evil."*
>
> The word which in these verses is
> translated as *belief* is not to be under-
> stood as credence affirmed from blind
> faith; for such belief, while perhaps con-
> sidered worthy ecclesiastically, can have
> little or no power to produce the inte-
> rior illumination and its effects upon
> conduct to which Jesus apparently re-
> fers. Thus, it is to be presumed that
> Jesus means a belief founded upon per-
> sonal, direct spiritual experience. This
> is to be attained by elevation and pen-
> etration of the mind into those realms

of human consciousness where the Christ nature of *"Son of God"* is established in man. The whole passage, thus viewed, becomes a description of the effects of such direct knowledge resulting from mystical illumination to the point at which the *"Word which was made flesh"* becomes directly known. The result is a veritable transfiguration, both of the mind and of the conduct of life. In such a case the individual can in no sense come under condemnation, whether by God or by man. Ultimately, as the twenty-first verse indicates, deeds rather than words, conduct rather than affirmed belief, constitute the final test of an individual's worthiness.

Elizabeth Sand Turner in *Let There Be Light* explains that for centuries people have labored under the false assumption that they would be saved by belief alone. If this were true, why would God have sent Jesus to teach us how to live?

... Christians today hold that their salvation is assured because they accept Jesus as their redeemer. But when Truth becomes active in consciousness ... it is understood that worship, manifesting in righteous living, is all that can protect ...

The crucificion of Jesus became the foundation of the Christian doctrine of salvation by the blood of Jesus. Christians generally believe that Jesus gave His blood on the cross as a sacrifice for the sins of every person, and that when one accepts Him as Saviour one is saved by His blood (the doctrine of vicarious atonement).

THE ROLE OF THE MASTERS

Jesus as well as the other Masters came to this earth to give liberty to captive souls, to awaken and revivify souls that have lost touch with God due to the long reign of the personality over the soul, and to deliver them from their bondage to this world. The Masters themselves have attained salvation, and their teaching and guidance can and do lead others to salvation.

As H. Gordon Burroughs points out:

> The message of Jesus cannot be accepted without accepting the message of other great teachers who came before him. All gave to the world a new dispensation; all in like manner interpreted the message according to the needs and understanding of the people at the time in which they lived ... the message is one and the same.

Whether you accept Jesus as a personal savior or not, or whether you accept him as a teacher or philosopher, the important thing is that he gave to the world very definite knowledge and he demonstrated his philosophy by applying natural law. As the crowning effort of his life, he materialized to his apostles after his crucifixion proving the continuity of life.

Leeming explains the real meaning of *"These things I say, that ye might be saved."* (John 5:34):

> When Jesus told those whom he accepted as disciples that they would be saved, he meant that he would show them how to find the Way back to a reunion with God. He would give them the keys to the kingdom, and would put their feet on the path that would lead

them to the abode of the Father, who
loves them with an infinite Love and
awaits their return.

The salvation of individual human beings was what Jesus
offered to those who listened to his words. He knew that it is
the will of God that humankind, without exception, attain salvation.

JESUS EXPLAINS HE IS A WAY-SHOWER TO SALVATION, NOT A "WIPER" AWAY OF SINS

In receiving the inspired words for *Jesus and Mastership*,
James Coyle Morgan, includes a present day clarification on
salvation. It is written in the first person with Jesus speaking:

One person asked me, "Lord, will
those who are saved be few?"

I questioned, Saved from what and
by whom?

He answered, "Saved from sin by
you and God."

I think it should be made clear to
everyone right now that I do not save
anyone, as such. I came to show each of
you how you can save yourself from suffering the pangs of hunger, feelings of
lack, fears of all kinds and the results of
indulging in the false pleasures of trying
to satisfy your fleshly desires. I have told
you and shown you by these healing
works that God wants only good for you.
Every person can be as happy, healthy,
strong and prosperous as he desires, if
he will do one thing that will bring this
to him. That one thing, or one way, is to
turn within to God to find and express
his true Self, his Christ Self, the I Am,
the Father or whatever you want to call

that which is within each of us and is to be expressed in the outer way of life.

You ask if only a "few will be saved," and I say, as many as want to be saved and find their way to God will be saved, from themselves. Many will say they are saved, many will call on man and many will call on God to be saved, without making a true effort. Only those who open this one door to their own salvation will find it. A person can only determine for himself the course his life will take and just how soon he will save himself and rise above all limitation. So you can answer your question for yourself and let others seek their own answer.

WHAT DOES SALVATION SAVE US FROM?

"I am the door; by me if any man enter in he shall be saved." (John 10:9) Here Jesus is saying through the I AM, the Father or the Christ Spirit, within him, he is the teacher or door to the way to be saved from errors of ignorance resulting in sickness, lack, limitation, misery, sorrow and other unhappy fruits of our actions. If we apply his teachings of natural law, we can save ourselves from the dire effects of our transgressions. *"Be ye doers of the word, and not hearers only, deceiving your own selves."* (James 1:22)

It is not in God's plan that we should suffer. Jesus showed us the way of righteousness, meaning the right or correct use of universal principle. The teachings of Jesus teach us how to live a better life by regaining conscious possession of our soul faculties so we do not have so much to make restitution for. The highest God-knowledge and power is needful sometimes to make restitution and reparation to others whom we have sinned against; for mortals it would seem impossible, but to the Divine within us all things are possible. The teachings of Jesus help us not to make the mistakes in the first place.

When you believe in Jesus the Christ as your teacher (your savior), you are accepting his will. You are walking in his footsteps. He does not throw away everything that you have done and make it all right for you. You must pay the penalty for the things you have done which deviate from the law of God. But if you walk in the footsteps of Jesus, you will be free of mistakes, or you will make fewer, depending on how sincere you are. And each time you ask for forgiveness, you will try a little harder not to repeat the thing. There is no escape from the exact consequences of wrong deeds and thoughts except through the knowledge and application of the Truth given us by Jesus and the other great Masters. Even though we appear to fall into error again and again, each time we should courageously rise as though we had not fallen.

The Mosaic law was a revelation to the Hebrews of moral causes and their physical effects. *"Whatsoever a man soweth that shall he also reap"* (Gal. 6:7) is the tenor of the whole Levitical law. He who defrauds and cheats will suffer loss either in this age or in another. He who deceives will be deceived. He who slanders will, in his turn, be bitten—it may not be by a slander but by a scourging, physical disease.

LET GO OF REPENTED ERROR

When one has thoroughly repented of an error and turned from it, he or she should let it pass completely out of mind. Continued remorse is contrary to the principle, "only the Good is true." Regrets and sorrows over the past must be banished wholly from consciousness. *"Thou shalt forget thy misery, and remember it as waters that pass away."* (Job 11:16)

DOES HELL FIRE AND BRIMSTONE EXIST?

Is there a place in the spirit world where hell fire and brimstone exist, where unbelievers are damned for all eternity? In a séance, my grandfather said he has searched and searched in the spirit world but has never found such a place. He did not find it because both heaven and hell are not locations; they are states of consciousness. We create our heaven or hell, consciously or unconsciously, as we obey or disobey God's unchangeable laws. We cannot evade the results of our misdeeds.

Regarding the heavenly world, H. Gordon Burroughs wrote:

> The story has also been told to us that heaven is a place foursquare where the streets are of transparent gold, the gates of the temple of the city are studded with precious jewels, and there is a throne about which angels throng and sing hosannas to God. (This story, by the way, was never given to us by Jesus of Nazareth.) . . . A place of absolute idleness would be a waste of God's great time in His vast universe: furthermore, it would grow very monotonous throughout eternity to sing songs and play harps.
>
> We want to know something of the heavenly world to which we are going, and the only way we can have absolute knowledge is to talk with some one who has been there; so we make it a part of our religion and science to investigate, through mediumship, the nature of that other world. Much knowledge of that country has been brought to us; we are told that it is a world of reunion, a world of understanding, a world of constant endeavor, a world not of chanting and idleness but of labor, of doing. We are told of the influence upon us of those who have gone Beyond as we sojourn in this life and of the joys that they attain in watching over us, in guiding us, in communicating with us.

There was a time when attempting to investigate God's heaven was not done. We were taught not to ask questions, since we should believe. That time is past . . . There has never been a time in the history of the human race that God has not spoken directly to the children of earth. He has spoken to the founders of every religious movement of which we have any knowledge. God spoke long before Christ came to the earth. The message of psychic truths was being given to the world long before our scriptures were written; the ancients of Egypt and India were giving to the world direct knowledge pertaining to life here, life after death, and the development of the soul, the "spiritual man". . . According to all Christian interpretations . . . It was possible two thousand years ago for spirits to manifest and communicate with the earth; but the claim is made that it is not possible today. If we attempt to make it possible, it is said we are being misled; therefore they close the door and the human family cannot find from these sources the answer to the question of life.

When we leave this material plane, we are not going to change immediately. We are going to be the same person, not one bit better or worse, five minutes after death than we were before. We shall find ourselves minus our physical bodies, but just the same person in surroundings that we have earned and created by our efforts while on earth. After adjustment in the

Spirit World, we begin our further progression.

We know these things to be true: many things that played a part in our earthly manifestation that we thought did not count, we shall find *do* count; and conversely, other things that we thought did count, we shall find do *not* count.

THE TIME TO ENTER THE PATH OF SALVATION IS NOW

The path to salvation is one that must be entered during one's lifetime. It is not something that should be postponed until after so-called death. Let us not deceive ourselves in relying on salvation after death for we experience in the spirit world what we have earned in this lifetime. The Apostle Paul taught the same truth when he wrote to the Corinthians: *"Behold, now is the accepted time; behold, now is the day of salvation."*

Leeming writes:

It is not intended that we should merely resign ourselves and hope for salvation after death. The safe return can be made, and according to the divine plan of the Creator, must be made while one is still alive. This is done by following the age-old path of the Masters. Of this, the masters, including Master Jesus, have assured mankind over and over again. To each and every one of their disciples they say: Come, let us return to our own home. Why live in a foreign land?

DID JESUS DIE FOR OUR SINS?

"For God so loved the world, that he gave his only begotten Son, that whosoever believeth in him should not perish, but have everlasting life." (John 3:16).

Since we are manifestations of pure spirit, made in the image of God (spirit), spiritual death and eternal damnation cannot exist for humankind. We are immortal and eternal by our very nature. Only the physical body is shed like a worn out garment at the time of transition to a higher life.

Jesus sacrificed his life upon the cross to demonstrate the continuity of life, not to save us from our mistakes or so-called sins. If we transgress, we, and we alone, must pay the price. It is known as accepting personal responsibility. Would we honestly be willing for our friends or loved ones to suffer for what we had done while we enjoyed life? The soul wants to pay its own debt because it wants to do what is right because it is right to do so. It is only the uneducated personality that believes we can do anything we wish and then throw the burden on the shoulders of Jesus, and pass into the next life without any payment at all. It is the personality that becomes absorbed in the fascinating panorama of creation and loses all recollection of the Father. There have always been those who were willing to live as they pleased, thinking that at the last moment they could profess to believe and slip through somehow.

It is the epitome of laziness to expect something for nothing; to expect all will be done for you. It is known as redemption without effort—redemption by belief rather than by action. Salvation comes from the improvement of our character. That is the master key. We improve our character by studying and obeying the teachings of Jesus and all the great Masters.

As H. Gordon Burroughs reminds us:

> Heaven is not gained by a single bound. Life is the ladder by which we climb, and experiences are the rungs upon which we ascend . . . Man is not a sinful creature; he does not need vicarious atonement. All he needs is to unfold himself, to learn how to use the faculties God has given him . . . We would not have our people bow in fear to any angry God, but would have them honor Him in love and understanding.

"The greater the truth, the simpler its tenet."

* * *

"Modern Spiritualism is pre-eminently an educational movement. We have abandoned the idea of being saved vicariously through the merits and suffering of others.

"Nature has implanted within us Infinite Possibilities, and launching us out on the great sea of life, figuratively speaking, says: "Go out into the world. Make something out of yourself!" Ours is the privilege either of meeting death as bankrupt souls, mental and spiritual paupers, or as souls, rich in mental and spiritual attainments. Which shall it be?

"Spiritualism is a religion that consists of doing good and acting honestly toward one another; a religion, not of forms and ceremonies, nor of long prayers and longer faces, but a religion of kindness, justice and good works; a religion that will make life brighter and more livable, and will bring back smiles to the lips and happiness to the souls of all who understand and live up to its highest teachings."

—Reverend Thomas Grimshaw

* * *

Game 24

The Soul Talent "Put-Down"

Key Players:

Sense Functions:
Discouragement, Judgment,
Pity, Pride

Counterbalancing Soul Faculties:
Beauty, Effort, Gratitude, Harmony, Imagination,
Inspiration, Quality, Rhythm, Spontaneity

How the Game is Played:

The *Soul Talent "Put-Down"* game is played when the personality abuses the soul talent by either "picking it apart" or making no effort to use it at all.

USE, DO NOT ABUSE, YOUR SOUL TALENT

Everyone has talent. It is a matter of what we do with it. The expression takes many forms and varies in quality. Nevertheless, talent is available to us, and if we do not express it, we alone are the obstruction to its further development. It is interesting, according to the spirit teacher, that so few people accept their soul talent even when it is revealed to them. They know deep inside they have a natural feeling for a particular expression, but block their use of the very thing that is natural to them.

A soul talent is something that we earn. It is not something that a gift-giving God has given to one and not to another, for that is contrary to spiritual law. Whatever the soul talent is, it means that soul has spent centuries in incarnation upon incarnation perfecting that particular **service** to the Universe. In other words, soul talents are the lessons that we passed, and passed very well, in prior expressions.

To enter the earth plane with all the effort one has already made and to abuse that which has taken centuries to acquire, to blatantly abuse it by the lack of using it, surely is the error or all errors. The law is not only just, kind, and compassionate, but the law of the Universe is infallible and clearly states that *lack of use is abuse.* That which we abuse shall be taken from us, not by a gift-giving God, but by the Law of Lack of Use. Just think: we abuse the goodness that is constantly flowing through our universe by the lack of use.

TALENT IS BEYOND THE SHADOWS

When we permit our minds, from our limited earthly experiences, to judge that we cannot do this and we cannot do that with the talent that we have, then it is tantamount to placing before ourselves one single page of a gigantic book, with that being the only page our judgments will allow us to read. That surely is a great sadness for the transgression is to let the *"have been's,"* the judgments, the shadows of the past, restrict our talent. Talent is beyond a shadow of the past, for talent is that which is. It is never dependent on what someone else thinks. We restrict it by what we think.

We must let the shadows of the past go so we can live in that which we have earned in this great eternity. Do not look around and envy what another has earned. The Divine Intelligent Power that is being used by others is available to us, for what one experiences, all can experience in principle.

TALENT IS THE PREROGATIVE OF GOD

"Did you ever find a thought of man as good as an idea of God?" Talent is not the prerogative of our minds; it is the prerogative of God. The mind, perpetuating its deception, is unable to satisfy its ever-consuming thirst. Not being able to accept something greater, it is thrown into a state of frustration. This "grounds" the energy of one's body, leaving the individual to forge deeper into the mire of self-pity, denying the lifeline to an even greater degree. It is indeed a vicious cycle. The longer the personality has ruled, the more difficult it will be to change. However, when it bows in humility so that the powers that be can work in pursuing one's soul talent, there is greater opportunity for the power of peace to flow freely. As it flows, healing takes place. Harmony is the Law of Health. Harmony is also an important ingredient in art, for in harmony there is an interrelationship of forms, color, sound, and rhythm.

MUSIC AND COLOR ARE THE LANGUAGE OF THE SOUL

Music and color are the very language of the soul for they are vibration. When you look at any painting or color, there is a musical note that is sounding in the universe from that color. If you would pause and be perfectly still, you would hear the sounds of all color. If you would pause and be perfectly still, you would view the color of all music, for there is color and sound all around you, permeating your very being. You may feel it and you may hear it if you still the mind. Still it that you may see and feel the great beauty of life herself. Still those thoughts of yesterday, still those fears of tomorrow. Be in the moment of your own heaven. It is a moment that is so precious. It is a moment that is so dear and valuable to the soul. Forget tomorrow and do not judge tomorrow. Live the fullness of your life by being in the moment of neutrality.

MUST HAVE GRATITUDE, NOT CRITICISM, FOR TALENT TO FLOW

The spirit teacher said, *"That which you earn deserves payment thereof."* In fact, he went further to say that it is a blatant transgression of divine law not to earn your living from a soul talent. *"Not only do the workers win, but the wise workers live the best of all."* However, when there is a lack of gratitude, closed by the personality, it will not yield financial or other rewards. You must have gratitude for what you have earned. The personality cannot see the centuries it took to achieve the talent because the personality did not create it. So you must quit picking apart your soul talent. The audacity of the prideful personality to pick apart the soul, or an object created by the soul! Whoever has great pride also has phenomenal demand for perfection. It is equal. A person suffering from pride and its concomitant need for perfection must bow the personality to acknowledge that it did not create a soul talent, nor does it sustain it. The talent is sustained by God. Pride will always find something wrong. Pride tells the soul how to do its talent. That is what keeps the talent from flowing.

Criticism reveals an attachment to the fruits of action, so if pride insists upon rising to "put down" your efforts, it is well to affirm something like: *"O God, help me to see clearly in all your universes that there is nothing in form that is perfect, especially pride."* You do not need to strive for perfection. It is quality, not perfection that you should seek. The personality and pride demand perfection. The soul strives for quality. Remember, you are doing God's work and God's work is quality. Emanate that vibration, and raise your level of consciousness to attract still higher quality. Quality is the effect of pure energy used exclusively for the purpose of creating the form of your desire without contaminants of past experiences—judgments of the past. Relying on the limited judgments of the mind, we discourage and reject the promptings, the inspiration, coming from a higher source, the soul. We close ourselves off because fear rises to preserve the dominance of the personality over the soul. Inspiration, flowing through the soul faculties of reason and consideration, must be free to consider all.

"God is the epitome of quality and without quality there is no good; without good there is no God; without God there is no inspiration; and without inspiration there is no true art." As inspiration comes from God and God works through people, it follows that we are all channels. Ideas are the effects of inspiration. The artist seeks to imitate what is in God's mind. And so we are inspired not only by our own eternal being, but by the soul expression of others, and by many things in nature. The degree of receptivity differs from person to person, depending on one's freedom from the entertainment of negative thought forms. The greater the degree of control we gain over our thoughts, the greater our receptivity to inspiration.

When you over-identify with self, you not only become the obstruction to inspiration but also to all good in your life. For in self, you are in separateness. In truth, you are not separate, for we are all one, but the mind deceives us into believing we are separate. The personality refuses to bow and change because of its need to control. When there is no flow of inspiration, we get discouraged; however, *"discouragement is a fool's paradise."* We then go into self-pity. There is no production efficiency when in self-pity. You cannot move when in self-pity because all of the energy is depleted out through the "brain." When the personality and pride bow, and you are grateful for your talent, then abundance will flow because gratitude is the Law of Supply or Fulfillment. We have a responsibility not only to ourselves, but to be clear channels for pure, unaltered art for the listening ear and viewing eye.

WORK UNDER CONTROL OF THE SOUL

If your talent, for example, is painting or drawing, do not overwork it. The mind does not know when and how to let go. You block the flow when you are in concern. You establish a "re-do" vibration by living in the judgments of the past. That is why the effort must be under the absolute control of something greater—the soul and not the personality. It is the suggestion, rather than the detail, which keeps the door open to the spiritual realm of imagination. That is the difference between a so-called "living" and a "dead" painting. One closes the door to imagination; the other gives the key. It is when the artist is concerned with the effect of his or her effort that the indispensable ingredient for opening the door of imaging or imagination is stolen from the viewer. Beauty should be left to the eye of the beholder, rather than the mind of the artist stealing the beauty by overworking. If the artist takes all for himself or herself, there is none left to share. The viewer should be able to add to a painting with his or her imagination. Viewers, of course, vary in their need for suggestion. Learn when to stop. *Have I given enough?* Nothing returns when we take it all.

Again, we emphasize, for art to be art, the instrument through which it is being expressed must be free from the bondage of a mental world. To accomplish this freedom, the instrument must move quickly in spontaneity. In spontaneity we express inspiration and freedom from the bondage of the past— *the bondage of judgment.* The less time the artist takes to paint the picture, the more spiritual it will be and the more likely the viewer will tune in. Therefore, when the artist is in the spirit of spontaneity, working for a spiritual realm, then he or she is the instrument to help the viewer enter that spiritual realm. The mental realm offers rigidity. The spiritual realm offers flow. With God in your efforts, quality is revealed.

PRACTICE, PRACTICE, PRACTICE

Be kind to yourself and give your talent years of practice. Work at it and never mistake the stepping stones for the final attainment. Be willing to sacrifice whatever it takes to practice and practice. When you practice you feel good inside for you know you did the best you could. When you do not want to practice and yet still do so, giving it your best, you have gained control over the personality; and you get energy from your efforts. Whenever you change your thought, you move to another level of consciousness. Remember:

"God smiles through the angel's efforts."

ART IS IN THE SOUL OF GOD

"Inspiration is the smile of God traveling faster than the speed of light," and to receive that which is the Light one must become the Light.

*"Artist, paint your scene in part, knowing I AM **all** of art."*

As beauty is in the eye of the beholder, so art is in the soul of God. We can only be a part of, never the whole, for God is the whole, but we can be that which is in wholeness. There is no need to fear losing your individuality for you are a part and each part is different.

Art is not limited to painting, drawing, singing, acting, cooking, gardening, weaving, writing, designing, or any other field of endeavor. Art is the expression of the soul faculty of harmony, rhythm, and quality. It is an instrument through which the seeing eye or listening ear is enabled to open the door of imagination and enter the spheres of perfect harmony where peace reigns supreme.

*　　*　　*

"Inspiration is not limited to a few souls. All are inspired, for inspiration is the breath of God, by which man lives."

*　　*　　*

> *"When I consider the faculties with which the soul is endowed, its amazing celerity, its wonderful power of recollecting past events, its sagacity in discerning the future, together with its numberless discoveries in the arts and sciences, I feel a conscious conviction that this active, comprehensive, principle cannot possibly be of a mortal nature. "*
> —Cicero, 106 B.C.

A THREAD

In the spirit of truth we seek to find
A common link that will unbind
Man from the limits of his mind,
That will close the gap between
Science, philosophy, music, and math.
That will find the path
Of artists, poets, and sages,
Stretches across the ages—
On the same bridge.

For man is a speck on the ocean floor
Never ever knowing more
Than what he aspires to.
And when man aspires
To something outside himself
Then he receives true wealth,
For he has given up his thought of self
To a greater call—
The common wealth of all.

Then man's creativity begins to flow
Then man is inspired to know
That there is nothing new, except to those few
Who are willing to view beyond their own mind,
And accept inspiration from like kind
Who patiently wait to serve
To give to those who deserve
The pearls of wisdom, the lovely tune,
A technological boom.

From Michelangelo to the spacecraft Apollo,
From Plato to a Beethoven symphony
A thread runs through.
A thread that links through time and space
Advancements for the human race.
A thread no mind can erase,
So much power and energy does it encase
That man for centuries does it embrace,
And is moved upward toward Divine Grace.
                              —Beverly Houser

Game 25

Feeling Superior Over Animals

Key Players:

Sense Functions:
Cruelty, Delusion, Disrespect,
Intolerance, Selfishness, Teasing

Counterbalancing Soul Faculties:
Compassion, Gentleness, Kindness, Love,
Patience, Respect, Reverence,
Sensitivity, Tolerance

How the Game is Played:

The game of *Feeling Superior Over Animals* is played when the personality, unable to accept the divinity of animals, has the need to feel superior over their souls, and through mistreatment, acts irresponsibly regarding their evolutionary ascent.

RECOGNIZING AND RESPECTING
THE SOULS OF OTHER FORMS

There is a common misconception that animals do not have souls. If we think that we are separate from animals and plants, and that animals do not have souls, that is only a delusion created by our mind. It is our personality that must feel a sense of superiority over the four-legged creature. All animals have souls. However, there is a difference between the human form and the animal form in that animals belong to a group soul, whereas, humans have individualized souls.

Every four-legged friend comes into this incarnation with exactly the same soul essence, the same soul faculties as the two-legged human. The faculties are those attributes of the soul that we commonly call character—patience, courage, loyalty, gentleness, compassion, and so forth. The animal is inhibited in its full expression of these soul faculties only by the limitations of its form or mind. Nevertheless, animals have the same potential for expression as do humans. *All* animals have souls. It is only the personality that prevents us from accepting the divinity of the animal and forgets that God is everywhere present—in all living forms—and that the soul is merely the covering or body of the spirit within. The purpose of our soul entering the earth form is not only for our own soul's evolution but to be an instrument for the spiritual evolution of all forms with which we come into contact.

DEMONSTRATING THEIR SOUL FACULTIES

We know that animals are sensitive and show us compassion, protection, love and comfort. Their loyalty is strong in expression despite their suffering. They demonstrate it always. If you have ever cried around a dog, he or she will come quickly to comfort you. Animals have been used very successfully in the treatment of mentally ill children. Many humane societies around the country take puppies, small dogs, and kittens into nursing homes on a regular basis so there can be an exchange of affection in a non-threatening way.

In her wonderful book, *When Your Animal Dies*, Sylvia Barbanell speaks of the character of the animal:

> Neither could a dog cheat, lie, nor slander his neighbour. The scope of an animal's mind has a different range from the human one. But even within his more limited scale, he does not descend to some of the pitiably mean tricks that the inventive brain of man can devise. No dog has ever been born with the ability to plunge continents into darkness and despair. Only the brain of man has achieved such great ambition.

> Yet the dog, in his own sphere, can attain heights similar to the ones reached by lofty and noble human souls. Selfless love, service, devotion to duty, courage, sacrifice, compassion—all these qualities have been expressed time and again by the dog.

> He has laid down his life for his friend—man—and 'greater love hath no dog than this.'

> ... Compassion is undoubtedly one of the highest spiritual expressions of mankind. Because Jesus of Nazareth manifested such an abundance of this tender quality of love, it may be counted as one of the most divine virtues man has developed in his evolutionary journey through the ages. Compassion is veritably an expression of the soul itself. Yet this aspect of love has manifested not only through God's highest creation—man—but also through the despised rodent, the rat.

Barbanell tells the story of the man "who saw two rats running along together. He threw a stone which killed one of them. The other remained where it was. Upon investigation, the man discovered that the living rat was blind. It still held in its mouth the piece of straw by which it had been led by the other rodent."

Barbanell's book is filled with numerous heartwarming stories about animals, one of which is the story of Minkie, the cat "who used to play with a neighbouring cat. At the age of two, Minkie became totally blind. Constituting himself as a guide to the stricken Minkie, the other cat continued to call at the house and take him for a walk. Afterwards he would escort his playmate safely home again."

Silver Birch, that beautiful spirit guide who regularly worked with a group in England, had much to say about the animals. In speaking on compassion, he pointed out:

> . . . the hall-mark of spiritual attainment is compassion. Without compassion there is no spiritual progress. Compassion must be extended to all beings, to all animals, to all creatures, to every manifestation of the divine spirit that exists in your world.

Animal lovers all have their stories to tell of the "specialness" of their friends in fur coats. I am reminded of how Romiel, my German Shepherd, was instrumental in preventing an accident. One day I hurriedly backed my car down the driveway, got out and closed the gate. Romiel stood just inside the gate. When I got back into the car to drive away, I looked up and saw great concern written on Romiel's face—a very real frown. His head turned slightly, trying to peer around the car. His expression alerted me to look back and there was Penny, my other beautiful German Shepherd and his inseparable companion, standing behind the back wheels. She had gotten out through an opening in the fence and I had not noticed her. Romiel frolicked with joy when I put her safely inside the gate.

He licked, and licked, and licked her with all the love and affection a parent would bestow upon a child who had just been rescued. He expressed gratitude to me, also. Yes, they certainly can show genuine caring and love.

Some people, of course, demean an animal's love as mere instinct, obedience, and dependence, but the behavior of animals in the wild disproves that hypothesis. Elephants will act as midwives, assisting herd-mates in giving birth. Whales and dolphins will hold sick or injured companions above the water so that they can breathe, and wolves will bring food to injured pack-mates. Some animals show great distress and obvious mourning at the loss of a companion. My daughter's lop-eared rabbit Felix died of depression shortly after his constant companion Fanny, a female rabbit, died of a heart attack.

Much research is now going on with dolphins which clearly indicates their compassion for humans as well as their own kind. It has been demonstrated that the conditions of disabled people have improved when swimming regularly with dolphins. The latter show a remarkable ability to tune into individualized needs and to actively assist in their therapy.

OUR RESPONSIBILITY TO ANIMALS

As like attracts like and forms the Law of Attachment, we attract to us animals that mirror some of our strengths and weaknesses. As we become more aware of ourselves, we will be more perceptive of the lessons with which our animals need our help.

We have a great responsibility to the animals entrusted to our care to guide them along their evolutionary path. We do not own them, for in truth we own nothing. As God works through man, not to man, we are helping that *Greatest Servant of All* when we encourage animals to unfold their soul faculties and control their desires and emotions. We do this directly through training, love, kindness, attention, protection, and discipline without emotion and, of course, by growing ourselves. Our animals grow as we grow.

Study your pet. Companion animals are telling you where you are in consciousness. Pets absorb the vibration of the person who is with them the most. They are reactors. The problems we have with our animals are the problems we have with ourselves. So, if you want to know about an owner's problems, the animal reflects them. In relationships, the stronger personality will mask the personality of the weaker one. Discipline yourself and the animal will respond. Without discipline there is no respect. Without respect, there is no love. Whatever our mind thinks it can "con," it has no respect for. From our own weakness, the forces of darkness rise up in the animal. Do not allow love of the animal to allow them the license that will destroy them. Consistent communication about the rules of the house will grant emotional security to them. When we accept that we are not perfect, then we have no problems in granting discipline to the animal. There is no emotion in the discipline. Emotion will cause the situation to be worse. But we must first grant to ourselves that we are not perfect before we can grant that to our pet.

JESUS SPEAKS ON THE TRINITY OF ALL LIFE

Some consider it a tragic omission that the Bible neither really addresses the spiritual importance of animals as companions, nor our responsibility to the lower kingdom. However, we must remember that in biblical times, the level of consciousness was not at a point where animals were considered to be of spiritual importance to humankind. The people of that day did not recognize and accept their spiritual responsibility to them. Rather, animals were a source of food, clothing, and objects to be sacrificed in homage to their deity.

A few pertinent questions were asked of the Master Jesus through the trance mediumship of Elwood Babbitt, which are contained in the book entitled, *Talks with Christ*:

> "The church teaches that animals
> do not have souls. What is the truth?"
> And Jesus answered, "Dare man deny
> the trinity of all life, the oneness of the

body, the soul and the spirit; and if it is given to human life to have that trinity of purpose, can one say it is denied to the animal or the plant?. . . it is given equally even unto the grain of sand."

Furthermore, Jesus said, "Those who seek the comfort of love should seek it not only from their fellow man but through animals, for from animals comes another trinity of love that sustains man and gives him comfort. The animal gives and asks nothing in return . . . Man searches in his love for all the possessions of earth and does not recognize that the animal in his own household contributes to his spiritual development."

COMMUNICATING WITH OUR FRIENDS IN FUR COATS

One of the master spirit teachers once said that any sincere and honest spiritually-minded person seeking to find the truth that frees his or her own being should make great effort to study and communicate with plants and animals. There is a spiritual law that we cannot grant to another what we have not first granted to ourselves. Therefore, if we make the effort to find goodness inside ourselves, we will then find that goodness inside forms that are different from us, and in so finding it, we establish rapport.

This wonderful teacher further expounded that if we have earned the responsibility of having four-legged friends in our care, then it is in our best interest, and in theirs, to spend a few minutes daily talking to them, preferable in the early hours upon their awakening. He emphasized that:

We must learn to treat our friends in fur coats much differently than we have been treating our two-legged friends, for the four-legged friends are

simple, kind, and extremely sensitive.
Therefore, we cannot use our big egos
to commune with them. We must become as little children and sit down with
them and talk to them, and not be so
bloated in our nothingness as to entertain the thought that they don't understand, for they do understand. They
don't need to study English or any language to understand what you are feeling. They don't need dictionaries to understand what your thoughts truly mean,
for they are receptive to your true self—
not what you think you are, but what you
really are at the moment that you are
talking to them.

What happens when people sincerely make this effort to
communicate with their animals? They begin to free themselves
from their over-identification with their physical human form.
We limit ourselves constantly by thinking we are the physical
body. The physical body is simply a vehicle through which the
true self, our spiritual being, expresses.

To be free, we must make the effort to broaden our own
horizons and accept in consciousness the possibility of an equal
intelligence expressing through forms that are different from
our own. When we truly take an interest in what is expressing
through the form, not just the outside covering that differs so
drastically from our own, but what is motivating the form, the
Infinite Intelligence that is expressing through the form, we
will have a totally different perspective.

All people who have studied spiritual matters to any degree are very well aware that love is the power of The Divine;
that it is love that is, in truth, the communion with all forms,
whether they are in the physical cloak or they are in the spiritual cloak. And so it is the same with plants and with animals.

They respond to the only universal language the universe has ever known, and that is the language of love.

> Love is not sentimentality. Rather it is the experiencing of compassion which allows us to feel the essence of all forms of life. Through love we can blend with the aspiring consciousness of the animal, the plant kingdom, the very stones under our feet—and of human beings, however strange they may appear to be." *(The Embodiment of Love* by Peggy Mason and Ron Laing).

THE ONENESS OF ALL CREATURES

Mason also wrote:

> If it be thought that I have laboured the kinship of the human and animal kingdoms it is because it is vital to our progress and our survival that we recognize that the basis of life is inter-relationship on all levels in all kingdoms. And these include the subtle kingdoms of the ethers, the angels of the air and water, the nature spirits and devas on whose cooperation we depend, and whose alienation, by our own actions, can create havoc and catastrophe.

St. Francis of Assisi, the Patron Saint of the Animals, was so filled with the ecstatic joy of God that he was able to see the beauty in all things. Conscious of the Oneness permeating all things through their common creator, he beheld everything and everyone as brother or sister. He felt the same love for the animal and the flower as he did for man. And the story goes that St. Francis even felt embracing love for brother rat who ran over his chest when he lay dying in his hut.

Several years ago in a séance, St. Francis came through a medium and spoke of his love for the birds and the larger animals, the ones that are almost in extinction. He emphasized the importance of keeping at least a few in each species. Also, he spoke of the older and more vicious animals, the holdovers from the Atlantean Age, as having their rightful place. St. Francis said that instead of hunting, trapping, and killing, humankind must learn to explore the fascinating habits of creatures, and thus benefit. We have the animal to teach us and to bring comfort and help us.

In Job 12:7-9 we read, *"But ask now the beasts, and they shall teach thee; and the fowls of the air, and they shall tell thee; or speak to the earth, and it shall teach thee; and the fishes of the sea shall declare unto thee . . . that the hand of the Lord hath wrought this."*

St. Francis truly believes the world would not be a very happy place without animals. The singing of the birds and the occasional roar of the lion somewhere brings us together in a spirit of Oneness.

Perhaps it was such a sense of the oneness of all creation that Chief Sealth of the Duwarmish Indians spoke when he said, "What is a man without beasts? If all the beasts were gone, men would die of great loneliness of spirit, for whatever happens to the beast also happens to man. All things are connected. Whatever befall the beasts of earth befall the sons of earth."

Baba tells us in this way: "There is nothing in the world that has no heart which is incapable of feeling joy or grief. Whatever we do against others, in all the kingdoms, we do against ourselves. That means the Indwelling God."

St. Francis of Assisi, Chief Sealth and Baba, all from different backgrounds, nevertheless demonstrate the words penned by Samuel Taylor Coleridge in his poem:

The Rime of the Ancient Mariner

> *He prayeth well, who loveth well*
> *Both man and bird and beast;*
> *He prayeth best, who loveth best*
> *All things both great and small;*
> *For the dear God who loveth us,*
> *He made and loveth all.*

OUR PROTECTIVE RESPONSIBILITY

During the séance mentioned above, St. Francis was asked about any changes he may have observed with respect to properly caring for animals. He answered, "There is some change but not a great deal. The TV is pushing to have the animals spayed or neutered and this is helping to control the growth population. It is the poor unwanted animal that is so badly mistreated. And it is much better to put them to sleep than to have them roaming the streets with nothing to eat and no where to go." He also suggested that we can do much at home by sending our prayers for healing to all animals everywhere, feeling that the love and the peace are going to these animals the same as if we were praying for individual people.

Silver Birch is very outspoken about our protective responsibility to animals:

> Man's place in the world is not to uproot, ravage, destroy, kill or to maim. It is to live in harmony with the whole of creation so that the stronger helps the weak, the more knowledgeable helps the ignorant, and those who are in the Light should strive to decrease the area of darkness in which others dwell.
>
> When man wages war on other creatures, be they human or animals, he

retards his own evolution. Nature cannot be at peace when man is at war with them . . . All the species have their part to play in this world and in the next. Nothing exists by chance or accident. The perfect planning of the great spirit has ensured that every creature, every form of life, has its own contribution to make . . . All life is intended to be of mutual helpfulness, by cooperation, by service to one another.

Silver Birch also teaches that:

. . . if we are kind, this is registered in the group soul of animals and when there are new births, there will be trust for man and not fear. And in future generations trust in man and loyalty to him will be strengthened. If there is unkindness, then fear of man will rise.

Another teacher added that mental anguish can be more painful than physical mistreatment, and furthermore, lack of consideration for an animal may cause scaring for centuries to that species. Teasing, which the personality may quickly defend as harmless fun, is actually a power trip. It starts with the personality's need to feel superior over another soul—whether it be an adult, child, or animal. Persistent teasing can actually lead to physical carving up.

"When disrespect manifests, wisdom demands change and reason shows the way."

There is nothing spiritual about experimentation on helpless creatures. It is all in the mental realms of consciousness that this practice is continued when alternatives are available. When asked about this, Silver Birch replied:

> Even with the motive to help their
> fellow men, they are still breaking the
> law. How can that which is cruel be
> right? How can that which causes pain,
> which inflicts torture, be right? . . .
> There will be found remedies for all
> your diseases, but they will not be found
> by experiments on animals.

In our present stage of evolution it is necessary that certain animals be killed by other animals or by man. What is wrong and retards the evolution of the individual is cruelty, deliberate cruelty, for which the automatic penalty is severe.

Rarely does a day go by that the mail or newspaper does not bring some horror story of neglect, abuse, unnecessary torture in the name of a gambling sport, research, or uncalled for mass slaughter of helpless animals. Despite our outrage that these acts are not stopped immediately, we must still find compassion for those who perpetrate these acts because there is no escaping the Law of Divine Justice here or in the hereafter. Our spirit guides tell us there is a time for righteous indignation, but never to fight violence with violence. *"Vengeance belongeth to the Lord,"* the "lord" meaning law. We must first go into prayer and ask to be guided if we want to do our part to correct the situation. Cruelty to animals will some day disappear when spiritual principles have supplanted selfish desires and there is reverence, an attitude of honoring life. *"Reverence is engaging in a form and a depth of contact with all life that goes beyond the form and touches the very essence of each."*

ANGELIC GUIDANCE

In the Spirit World the highest angels that interest themselves in animals are known as Aqui (ah kwee), who are under the guidance of the Archangel Uriel. Some of them have chosen to care for the physical welfare of animals and they influence creatures by guiding their instincts toward finding food and shelter, producing offspring, caring for themselves when ill or in danger, and helping them in the death process to go to the animal Astral sphere.

Others of these angels from the Kingdom of the Shining Ones are responsible for guiding the progress and growth of individual characteristics in creatures of the animal world. They are particularly watchful of animals that express uniqueness of individual traits. In fact, these traits are highly guarded, cherished, and encouraged by the angels who want to cultivate in their charges qualities that will exceed the level of mere instincts.

THE PSYCHIC NATURE OF THE ANIMAL

One who has felt a closeness to animals may have wondered why it is that animals are more psychic than humans, generally speaking. Spirit teachers tell us that psychic qualities should be a part of every person's normal life, but we have tended to repress these abilities because of the tremendous pressures of leading a material life. Mediums of today are exhibiting what will be natural for all tomorrow as we move into a higher level of consciousness in the New Age. Animals have not had to face the stress connected with the economic and sociological problems that affect human beings.

My German Shepherd Sammi was so psychic she made friends with my spirit guides and teachers while still on the earth plane. She would go to them when they called her. When the animals I had prior to her coming into my life would visit from the Spirit World, she was very friendly toward them, too. So clearly did Sammi discern spirits, that occasionally she could not differentiate between the living and the so-called dead, barking and chasing after them. Most of the time, however, she apparently could tell the difference. Sammi would get a little confused when she rubbed against my husband's spirit body and there was nothing solid there. She then would look up at him rather puzzled. She simply could not understand why his body was so evanescent. As she was originally his dog, she was comforted by his visits to the kennel when I was away on trips. Truly she lived in two worlds. Once I asked the spirit veterinarian in my spirit band why this wonderful watchdog did not bark at spirits, only those in the physical body, and he explained it was because she could not smell spirits; therefore, there was no fear.

RECEPTIVITY TO SPIRITUAL HEALING

Animals are not only very psychic, but are more receptive to spiritual healing than human beings possibly because they are more trusting and their egos do not dictate the outcome. Sammi was a shining example of receptivity to spirit healing. About two years before her transition, Sammi became ill. Her condition was not correctly diagnosed. As a consequence little was done for her, nevertheless, she seemed to improve. Periodically, I would check with my spirit veterinarian and he made minor suggestions. Six months passed after the first signs that she was not feeling well, when again her condition became critical. This time the veterinarian on the physical plane gave a diagnosis of tumor of the spleen. He offered no encouragement that she would have quality life even after surgery because the cancer might recur. The operation was performed and a 4-lb tumor removed. When the pathology lab returned a negative report, the entire veterinary clinic staff was tremendously surprised. The spirit helpers then described how they had worked for over six months to change the chemistry of the tumor from malignant to benign. Many veterinarians from the Spirit World came daily, drawing energy from me and our surroundings. When their work was completed, it was time to remove the spleen and "tumor," which was more akin to a giant hemotoma at that point.

Sammi had another two years until it was time for her to end her earthly life. The cancer returned and my guides advised euthanasia. As she entered the other dimension, my husband was waiting to gently carry her to her new home.

In making the decision to release an animal from its ailing physical body, Silver Birch advises:

> Motive is the important consideration. If in order to end physical suffering, when any beloved animal is beyond

all earthly aid, you put a period to its
physical life, your motive is a good one;
and thus the motive qualifies the passing and helps. But if, with complete and
callous disregard for all the natural
rights of animals, you kill them, then
your motive is selfish. You do no good
to yourselves or to them, and they have
to be helped.

LIFE IN THE SPIRIT WORLD

What happens when our little loved ones in fur coats go
the Spirit World? We know that they live for mediums frequently describe spirit dogs, cats, horses, and birds as being
brought to someone in a circle by a guide or family member
from the other side. Peace reigns supreme in their sphere because the stronger and more aggressive ones learn they can no
longer harm the weaker ones. In this sense, it is therefore true
that the lion and the lamb lie down together. If they have not
learned to do so while here, animals must learn in the Spirit
World to be tolerant of each other. By the same token, humans
who have been intolerant of animals here may find themselves
working with them on the other side, not as punishment, but
in order that their souls may have the necessary experiences for
growth.

At some stage the animal and the human evolution inevi-
tably part company. The animal has to be left behind because
the higher you climb in your spiritual unfoldment when in the
spirit world, then naturally the more difficult it is for the animal to keep pace with you, and in the end it merges with the
group soul of its species, or subspecies. When the time comes
for them to return to the Allsoul, they begin to sleep more and
take less interest in their surroundings.

The efforts that we make to love, and care for, and to
advance the soul of our pet companions is never wasted because it has contributed to the evolution of the whole group
spirit.

When the animal returns to the group soul, we may think of it as a sacrifice, but in truth, as Silver Birch teaches, adds an important contribution to the group soul, that is, **if** the animal has been treated kindly and its intelligence and progress in constructive behavior has been encouraged. The more such sacrifices are made, the quicker the group soul advances toward the stage where it leaves the animal behind and earns the evolution that makes it ready for individual souls in primitive human forms.

Do all animals survive? Some spirit guides have explained that everything that has life has a spirit body. We are told that pets, over whom we show our affections, are strengthened in their natures. Our love does something for them that builds up a resistance beyond that of wild animals. They become so stabilized in their spirit bodies that they are able to survive for years. There are no barriers to divide humans and animals from being together in the next world when this association is mutually desired. These little friends in fur coats go to their own plane on the Astral where they are loved and cared for while awaiting our arrival to the world of spirit. Although we may not be consciously aware of it, our spirit guides do frequently bring them to visit us so that a continuity of the relationship will be maintained.

When animals go to another dimension, they sometimes are trained for what is known as "rescue work" on the Astral Plane. Their selfless service may consist of forming a relationship with a person who is confused about his or her recent crossing or transition into so-called death, yet is unable to easily relate to another human being. The animal (and many species are used) acts as a bridge between the person needing help and the spirit doctor, leading them to the halls of repose. And then, too, there are times when animals are needed to comfort other animals who are recent arrivals who are fearful of humans for one reason or another. Thus, in all of life the soul is given opportunities to unfold its faculties regardless of the kind of form through which it is expressing.

COPING WITH THE LOSS OF AN ANIMAL

Understanding what happens when our four-legged loved ones depart is most comforting, but how do we who are left behind cope with the loss? We are human and may still find ourselves struggling emotionally to accept the loss of our friend. When a person dies, there is a network of family, friends, and professionals to help loved ones through the loss. When a pet dies, the people left behind are often alone with their grief.

About a decade ago pet loss counseling began to evolve in recognition of the importance of our bonds with companion animals. Now the ranks of professionals around the country who are engaged in grief counseling are steadily growing. Some fine books to help both children and adults through the process are available, as well. The stages of grief that Dr. Elisabeth Kubler-Ross formulated in working with people are equally applicable in dealing with the loss of pets. Children may need special help to understand. This is important because it will help them in handling the transition of someone close to them, be it a relative or friend.

Remember the good times you shared with your pet. Each animal is unique. If you decide to get another companion, do not make the mistake of constantly comparing the two. Love each for his or her own special qualities. To provide a loving home for an animal is an opportunity to serve spiritually. And do keep the perspective that you will be reunited with your beloved friend when you, too, are called "home."

If you will make the effort to communicate each day with your four-legged friends and plants, you will see a greater God than you ever dreamed possible. You will become connected and feel a part of the All. Hug a tree—the Indians do it—but first ask permission to share its energy. Talk to the flowers. Do not be reluctant to kiss your dog or cat. And lastly, the Indianapolis Humane Society has a motto worth remembering:

Every tail deserves a happy ending!

EPILOGUE

Approximately every twenty-one hundred years our solar system passes through a sign of the zodiac. This time is the measurement of an age or dispensation. Therefore, to think of our present "New Age" as unique to history is a fallacy. Each new age is ushered in by cosmic influences. These influences or Ray-Lives are explained in the teachings of Djwhal Khul in the Alice A. Bailey volumes on esoteric psychology. *Esoteric psychology* is a study "based on the fact, the nature, the quality and interrelationship of the seven streams of energy pervading our solar system, our planet and all that lives and moves within its orbit." It attempts to explain why there is a predominate cosmic influence at each age. The Seven Rays are the great builders and they are the custodians of the plan of creation. They are streams of energy coming from the Godhead. Depending upon which ray is most active at a given time is our mental, emotional, physical, and spiritual progression potently affected.

In *The Seven Rays Made Visual*, Helen Burmester states:

> Many readers are probably well acquainted with astrological terminology, with the interpretation of zodiacal influences, and with the effects of planetary forces on human life. But behind and beyond and coming through the Zodiac and our solar system are the seven streams of divine energy, the Seven Rays, which emanate on cosmic levels from the Most High, the Absolute. In the process of manifestation, creation, and evolution, these Seven Rays express and transmit the qualities, characteristics, and purpose

of the Absolute, but each Ray has its own characteristics, quality, and purpose as well.

These Rays are the seven great builders of all that exists—from universes, galaxies, solar systems down to the subatomic level of protons, neutrons, and electrons. Their tremendous scope and interrelating network of energies and forces present a holistic approach and a synthesis of invisible and visible worlds. And it is the potent cyclic playing of the seven ray energies upon manifested life that produces the complex problems in national and international affairs as well as in our personal lives.

In the sense of the life principle intelligently expressing through form or creation, intelligent life is not limited to the planet earth. If we view the planets in terms of state of evolution or growth, Earth is about half way back up the ladder of progression. So we can be of good cheer in the knowledge that we are not just starting.

It was at the beginning of a new age two thousand years ago—the Age of Pisces—that Jesus, the Avatar, came to earth. The great teachings he gave to the world—the New Dispensation—laid the foundation for the incoming spiritual Age of Aquarius. As we now gradually move toward greater spiritual values, those ageless lessons of love and truth may be better understood and applied by the masses.

As Burmester pointed out, the Piscean Age, controlled by the Sixth Ray of Devotion and Idealism, has "strongly influenced and colored our civilization and religious life but its power is now passing out of manifestation to be replaced by the Seventh Ray of Ceremonial Magic and Order." The seventh Ray is the highest ray. The "magic" comes from the Christ Spirit within, which unfolds as the personality, through the control of one's thinking, comes into alignment with the soul. This re-uniting with the higher self is a coming to grips with the realization that whatever is to be accomplished individually has to come from within. The "ceremonial order" means that it is not simply a blind faith in something, for all things operate according to divine law. The order comes from within ourselves as we obey the spiritual laws.

Many will begin through self-discovery to find their own answers pertinent to their lives. Their inner spirit will actually appear to come forth as they, through meditation, prayer, and study, ask that all things be revealed to them. It is evident then, the Age of Aquarius will be an evolution of the spirit more so than an evolution of the material. It will be a time when those in the spirit realms can reach out to us much more easily and in a much more advanced way. We will communicate with them on a soul level as we evolve spiritually.

So, "from the point of view of esoteric psychology," Bailey writes, "evolution is the evolution of consciousness, by which the imbedded fragment of the soul within the personality progressively identifies its spiritual source and becomes at-one with it."

The spirit guides point out that many are realizing to such an extent that their destiny is in their own hands they are losing the influence of devotion and reverence that has been a part of the Piscean Age. Even in churches of all denominations a more secular approach can be observed. But we cannot afford to lose sight of Idealism and Devotion. If we are to be balanced, we must incorporate these attributes into the mystical and spiritual overtones of the New Age of Aquarius.

However far along that path toward perfection we may have traveled, unless we have reached the summit, we still make mistakes. Although it is a positive step to go within for guidance, we still need teachers on both sides of the veil to give encouragement, strength, and help in walking our new pathway of light. And we must take the time to "be still and know I

AM God," to feel that Presence within ourselves if we are to develop our highest potential.

The next fifteen or so years will be very crucial ones. In this transitional period between the two ages, we will continue to experience very chaotic conditions on many levels—many upheavals and much churning—natural disasters, accidents, earthquakes, climatic changes, floods, terrorist activities, drug abuse, crime, spousal and child abuse, immorality, emotional intensities, and much searching in unorthodox ways to find new approaches to all avenues of life. On the positive side, the spirit guides assure us these chaotic conditions will be met and conquered as we turn back to the God within. It is the Seventh Ray of Ceremonial Order and Magic that will eventually take us back. We will reach the full bloom of this spiritual evolution around the year 2085. It is important, therefore, for the growth of all religions that all persons with aspirations and devotion remain faithful to their ideals, while yet open to greater spiritual understanding. Now is a time of testing our faith in a higher power!

* * *

*"Truth is the awareness of the divinity within
that we express at any given moment."*

New Age Interpretation of the Lord's Prayer

Jesus taught "When you pray, go within to the secret place where only you can go to meet with and speak with your Father. When you go there in secret, your Father will hear you and reward you openly. When you pray, do not use beseeching or supplicating language. It is not necessary, for His will for you is good. You cannot change God; you can only change your thinking, your own attitude toward God and your good. When you pray, say something like this:

Our Father, who abides in His Kingdom within us,
Blessed Is Your name.
Guide us in expressing our highest and true Self
In all our thoughts, speech, and actions.
This will bring forth our good here on earth.
We have forgiven others as we have forgiven ourselves,
And we are no longer tempted to transgress Your Law.
We rest in Your love and peace.
Thank you, Father, for all our good. Amen"

(Reprinted by permission from *Jesus and Mastership*)

*"Jesus Christ belonged to
the true race of prophets.
He saw with open eye
the mystery of the soul."*

—Ralph Waldo Emerson

Acknowledgments

For permission to use copyright material, the author gratefully makes the following acknowledgments. These excerpts may not be reprinted without permission from the copyright holders.

Babbitt, Elwood, Channel One Communications, RR 1, Box 325, Strong, MA 04983-9801, for permission to quote from *Talks With Christ and His Teachers.*

Chaney, Earlyne, Astara, Inc., 800 West Arrow Highway, Upland, CA 91786 for permission to quote from *The Mystery of Death and Dying.* (Published by Samuel Weiser, Inc. Box 612, York Beach, MA 03910) *Astara's Book of Life* degree lessons are available by mail.

Harper & Row, Publishers, Inc. 10 East 53rd Street, New York, NY 10022, for permission to quote from three books by Emmet Fox: *Power Through Constructive Thinking, Around the Year with Emmet Fox,* and *Find and Use Your Inner Power.*

HarperCollins Publishers, Inc.,10 East 53rd Street, New York, NY 10022, for permission to quote from Sogal Rinpoche's *The Tibetan Book of Living and Dying.*

Lucis Trust, P. O. Box 722, Cooper Station, New York, NY 10276, for permission to quote from Alice A. Bailey, *Esoteric Psychology, Volume I.* (These extracts may not be reprinted except by permission of the Lucis Trust which holds copyright.)

Meditation Groups, Inc., P. O. Box 566, Ojai, CA 93024, for permission to quote from Helen S. Burmester's *The Seven Rays Made Visual: An Illustrated Introduction to the Teaching on the Seven Rays of Djwhal Khul and Alice A. Bailey,* published by DeVorss & Co., P. O. Box 550, Marina del Rey, CA 90294.

Acknowledgments

National Spiritualist Association of Churches, P. O. Box 217,
Lily Dale, New York 14752 for permission to quote from
H. Gordon Burroughs, *Becoming a Spiritualist.*

Oakbridge University Press, 6716 Eastside Drive, N.E., Suite 50,
Tacoma, WA 98422, for permission to quote from James
Coyle Morgan's *Jesus and Mastership.*

Psychic Press Ltd, 20 Earlham Street, London, WC2H 9LW, for
permission to quote from Stella Storm's *Philosophy of Silver
Birch*, and Sylvia Barbanell's *When Your Animal Dies.*

Radha Soami Satsang Beas, P. O. Dera Baba Jaimal Sing, Dist.
Amritsar 143204, Punjab, India for permission to quote
from Joseph Leeming's *Yoga and the Bible.*

Sigo Press, 50 Grove Street, Salem, MA 01970 for permission to
quote from George Trevelyan's *A Vision of the Aquarian
Age; The Emerging Spiritual World View.*

The Theosophical Publishing house, Wheaton, IL, for permission
to quote from Annie Besant's *Esoteric Christianity*; Geoffrey
Hodson's *The Hidden Wisdom in the Holy Bible, Volume I*; and
Geoffrey Hodson's *The Christ Life from Nativity to Ascension.*

The Philosophical Research Society, Inc., 3910 Los Feliz Boule-
vard, Los Angeles, CA 90027, for permission to quote from
Manly P. Hall's *Self-Unfoldment by Disciplines of Realization.*

Simon & Schuster, Rockefeller Center, 1230 Avenue of the Ameri-
cas, New York, New York 10020, for permission to quote
from Gary Zukav's *The Seat of the Soul.*

Unity Books, 1901 NW Blue Parkway, Unity Village, MO 64065-
0001 for permission to quote from Charles Fillmore's *The
Revealing Word*, also *Keep a True Lent*; Elizabeth Sand
Turner's *Your Hope of Glory; The Life and Teachings of Jesus.*

318

Index

A

abundance 172, law of 167,
   173, 204
abuse 162, 168, 286
   cup overflows 167, law of 168
acceptance 96, 100-104, 118,
   204, 216, Divine Will 96
   freedom from judgment 81
   right of all expression 26, 94
   law of 198
Acceptance the Divine Will
   without identification 33
Adam, 140
addictions 133, 193, 194
   to judgments 133
   to thoughts, desires
      defensive when revealed 24
addicts
   vicariously savoring 48
adversities 124, 156-163, 227
affection 145
affirmations: index of 335
Age of Aquarius 312, 313
Age of Pisces 312
anatomy
   sounds in meditation 260
angelic forms
   created by being at peace 13
angelic guidance
   of animals 305
angels of light
   forms of light 55
animal behavior 297
animal mind
   how differs from human 140
animals 294–310
   communication with 299, 300
   experimentation 305
   spayed and neuter 303
animals and Bible 298
animals, companion 298

animals survival 309
apology 183
application 194, 195, 243, 244
Appreciation, Law of 202
Armstrong, Martin
   "The Cage" 5
Arrival, Law of 50
arrogance 231
art 291
asking 217
aspiration 122
Association, Law of 56
Astral World 244, 253, 306
attachments 124, 156-173, 215,
   225- 227, belief: illusion 19
Attachment, Law of 40, 100,
   110, 129, 156, 170, 297
Attainment and Payment 126
attention: to become
   not overcome 59
attitudes 95
   being "in the forces" 20
Attraction, Law of
   spirit side of life 25
"auric pollution" 245
authority 142
awareness 230, 231, 243
   in guarding thoughts 11
   of identities 33
   of origin of emotions 20
   of what is talking to you—
      voice of light or darkness
      21; reveals motive 110
   to avoid belief in illusion 19
awareness of thoughts
   before going to sleep 133
   upon awakening 133

B

Baba on animals 302
Babbitt, Elwood
    Jesus and animals 298
Bailey, Alice
    sex and marriage 146
balance 126, 146, 227
Barbanell, Sylvia
    on animals 295, 296
beauty 291
"because"
    entering delusion 42
becoming 94
    directing attention 59
Beer, William Arthur
    Poem, "Giving" 169
belief 99, 100, 275
    illusion: attachment 19
    sustains illusion 28
belief, meaning of 274
Besant, Annie 15
Bibical Quotations
    John 10:34 3
    Proverbs 23:7 108
    John 4:24 3
    1 Cor. 15:44 15
        spirit and natural bodies 15
    Gal. 6:7 279
    James 1:22 278
    James 2:2-4 214
    Job 11:16 279
    Job 12:7-9 302
    John 10:9 278
    John 3:16 282
    John 3:17-21 274
    John 5:34 276
    Matt. 6:22 135
    Matt 7:1 61
    Matt. 10:39 106
    Matt. 11:27 271
    Matt. 13:12, 203

    Matt. 18:18 16, 158, 169
    Mt. 7:6
        cast not thy pearls 50
    Ps 55:22 44
blame 9, 42, 99, 199
blessing 182
    of forgiveness 177, 178
blessings, gratitude for 201
borrower 172, 174
Brain Broadcasting System 151
breathing 243; exercises 257
brimstone 279
brotherhood 227
brother's keeper 47
Buddha 234
Burmester, Helen
    Seven Rays 311
Burroughs, H. Gordon
    universality of manifestation
        272; heavenly world 279-
        281, 283; Jesus & other
        masters 275
bystanding mind 189;
    being the observer 21
    looking objectively 19

C

care 8, 202, care less—freedom
    from attachment 160
Cause and Effect, Law of 58
celestial forms
    lift consciousness 25
celibacy 147
"ceremonial order" 313
chakras 245
Chaney, Earlyne
    heart seed atom 108
Change:Law of Evolution 66,
    81, 90
change 82, 85, 88,102,103, 191
    bucking the tides of life 86
    introducing:

to measure growth 65
second try more difficult 91
Change, Law of
meaning of "Repent ye" 85
changes: thru repetition 87, 143
thru suffering 195
channeling 117
checks
imprint God is source 150
Chief Sealth:on animals 302
children 225; meditation 261
choice 208, 219, 232
in changing identities 31
path of light or darkness 111
right of 232
self-control: service 114
choosing God 242
chosen
"many are called, etc." 242
Christ Spirit 3
Cicero 291
circle of completion:
face responsibility 47
freedom from 47
responsibility:
detaching from form 46
clairvoyance 244
clutter 168
Coleridge, Samuel Taylor
poem 303
commitment 186, 187, 192, 194,
203
common sense:
freedom from illusion 25
communication 217
spirit 266
comparison
controlled by fear 56
compassion
88, 222, 224, 225, 226, 227
expressed by animals 296
complaining 198, 199, 204

concentrating on peace 258
concentration 135, 258, 259
key to all power 37, 259
concern 167, 172
born on throne of fear 70
rejection of Divine 23
condemnation, meaning 274
conduct 275
confirmation
needed for convictions 232
confusion 123
conquering soul 183
conscience 9, 186, 206–211;
educated 206
spiritual sensibility 206
conscious mind; electric 6
exercising control 5
task to control 6
consciousness
same levels in all 25
states of 110
consideration 7, 35, 104, 112,
120, 126, 127, 137, 160,
192, 193, 202, 253
of true desire 135
Consistency, Law of 258
Constant Change, Law of
flexibility in consciousness 35
contemplation 249, 258
continuity 170
essential to flow 150
Continuity, Law of 248
upward and outward 92
control 226; another's soul 225
taking control of personality
239
controlling 237
controlling thought by
proper breathing 243
convenience 115
serving God 201
converting 232

converts 231
conviction 99
cooperation 194, 195
courage 43, 87, 220
creation
  become observer 34
  charge over all 33
  of mind: separating truth 18
Creation, Law of 126, 149, 237
creative process
  in fulfilling desire 136
creative urge 147
creativity 146
credulity 222
criticism 160, 288
crystal balls 244
cup: overflowing 167

D

darkness 219
Davis, Andrew Jackson 207
deaf: related to judgments 57
death and birth cycle
  acceptance of 35, 191
deceit, realms of 254
deception18, 41, 215, 220,
  225, 239, 253
  bucking the tides of life 86
  how to counterbalance 26
decisions 55; regarding desires
  128; weigh for 72 hours 62
dedication
  examine motive for 111
deeds 275
defense
  against thought forms
    denying existence 13
defense mechanisms 236
delusion 159, 18
  created by suppression 132
  how to counterbalance 26

unable to separate truth 19
delusions 254
demons
  thought forms 12, 138
denial 42, 56, 95, 99-101, 129,
  170, 199
  Annie Rix Militz 104
  God denies nothing 98
  need 98; destiny 95;
  of right of expression 94
Denial, Law of 168
depression: from uncontrollable
  desires 137
desire 8, 122, 138, 206, 226,
  239;controlling motive 111
  influenced by others 243
  pit desire against desire 143
  suppressed 111
  controlled by another's 134
  opening footlocker 45
  saying no 135
  someone else will not fulfill
    134; stealing 122-125;
  the creative process 136
  time takes to fulfill 125
destiny 199; web of 18
diet and meditation 261
dignity 160
dimensions
  existence in three 40
disappointment 123
discernment 25, 65,
  210, 211, 216, 240
  spirit by spirit 264
discord; in consciousness
  effect upon nature 49
discouragement 9, 87, 195,
  237, 248, 289
  "have beens" 41
disembodied spirit:illusion by
  suppressed desire 131, 253
disrespect 162, 163, 304

dissension 215
disassociation 174
divine circle of return. 1
Divine Flow, Law of 108
divine guidance 244
divine inventory
    soul faculties 4
Divine justice 2
Divine Justice, Law of 181
    animals 305
divine law; response to prayer
    wisdom of patience 45
divine love 104
divine neutrality 101
Divine Plan
    for soul unfoldment 1
Divine Spirit 4
Divine Will 189
    Acceptance 33, 104
Djwhal Khul
    Seven Rays 311
doubt, question and fear 73
duality of personality 214
Duality, Law of 156
duty 62, 89, 200, 201

E

educating desires 127, 133
effort; spiritual 238
ego 142
    formidable force of 241
    functions to usurp power 141
    personality: energy tool 140
electromagnetic field 227
Emerson : explains faith 76; 316
emotional experiences
emotions 127, 168, 176,
    240, 245
    awareness of origin:
        being trapped 19
    kicking out responsibility 44
    in meditation 254

obstruction to flow 148
empathy, 226
empire vibration 159
encouragement 246
energy 123, 244
    balance of: between minds 7
    obstruction to flow 7
    released thru emotion 176
enthusiasm 150, 239
envy 260
esoteric psychology 313
eternal damnation 282
etheric body 10
ethers 209
euthanasia 307
    motive 308
    on animals 307
Evolution, Law of
    change 66, 81, 90
    evolution of form 62, 81
    change is inevitable 88
excuse
    meaning of function of 90
expansion-contraction
    principle re: change 88
experiences
    defined by spirit 10
    acceptance of right
        to express 26, 97
    delusion 26
    necessary to find God 130
    seeking cause of 191, 258
    view as expressions 248
exposure 133 communication:
    confession 67
expression
    right of experience 97
eye of eternity 134, 207
eye, single 135

F

faculty: how it can
   change to a function 202
faith 50, 70, 76, 99, 100, 126,
   129, 130, 134, 153, 170,
   173, 257, 265;
   Emerson explains 76
   number 5 meaning of 78
   power of soul 77
false gods 173
falsehood 240
fascination 131, 148, 189, 190,
   194
fear 70, 99, 128, 208, 230
   authority of mind over soul
   191
delusion 72
   foundation of functions 75
   judgment 56
   like a magnet 71
   of retaliation 218
   over fulfillment of desire 127
   releasing chains of 34
   remove by giving to God 72
   retards growth 74
   The thing I fear the most
   Job 71
   two fears neutralize 77
   use fear to free self 77
Fear, Law of 172, 129
Fillmore, Charles 208
   conscience 209-211
   salvation 270
   spiritual conscience 209
finding God 242
flow 172
Flow, Law of 149, 170, 172
forces: being "in the forces":
   nasty attitudes 20
forgiveness 62, 176-183
   affirmation 184

judgment 67
   of level of consciousness 177
foundation: number 4, 78
Fox, Emmet 3, 222
   "Mr. Atlas" 222
   "Mrs. Fix-it" 223
free will 2, 3
freedom 100
   from creation
      accepting responsibility 36
   in acceptance 97
   through forgiveness 178
   through selfless service 111
friction: law of
   for soul evolvement 2
friendship 104
fruits of action 159, 114
frustration 41, 131, 133, 144,
   193, 199, 287,
   result of procrastination 46
fulfillment 123, 124, 127, 242
Fulfillment, Law of 289
function: how changes from
   faculty 202

G

Gabriel 48
garbage 237
generosity 167
gift of self 166, 191
gifts 166
Giving, Law of 166
givingness 166, 167
God:number one 78
Goodness, Law of 215
graciousness 89, 160
gratitude 6, 130, 134, 198-204,
   289
Gratitude, Law of
   198, 202, 203
gratitude, not greed, 202

greed 7, 129, 137, 199, 202
Greed, Law of 199
grief: when animals dies 310
grin 138
Grimshaw, Thomas 284
grounded: in self 117
growth: 2, 81, 91
grudge 179
guilt 230

H

Hall, Manly P. 113
happiness
    limited by judgment 62
harmony 249, 250
    between minds:
        to receive inspiration 20
Harmony, Law of 56
Harmony, Law of Health 287
hate 7
"have beens" 22, 146, 230, 237
healing power 146, 178
heart 92, 103, 243
    number 6, 78; soul 3, 8
heart seed atom 108, 109, 236
    memory par excellence 10
hell 230
    as a freeing process 143
hell fire 279
helping; how God helps 33
    questioning motive 112
Hodson, Geoffrey
    explains Matt. 11:27 271
    parable of prodigal son 270;
    meaning of John 3:17-21, 273
honesty 43, 94, 211, 224
humane societies 294
humility 115, 117, 124,
    146,149, 232, 225, 287
humor: to lift consciousness 64

I

I AM 3
Ideas, inspiration 289
identification 30, 192
    achieving balance 36
    becoming our belief 33
    being bound by limit 28
    controlling identities 30
    technique to identify
        with another being 37;
        with peace 38
    using in positive way 83
Identification, Law of
    Personal Responsibility 40
Identity, Law of 28
    changing 90
    directing energy to the
        positive 37
    enter illusion, delusion 28
    personal responsibility 31
    responsibility 30
    self or personality 29
    surrender 38
idols of "clay feet" 157
ignorance 137
ingratitude 198
illumination 3, 117, 119, 120,
    160, 226
illusion 18, 20, 55, 167
    as related to power 18
    belief: attachment 19
    freeing self 25
    how to counterbalance 26
    identification: judgment 28
    in creative process 136
imagination 44, 290
Imposition, Law of 217
incarnation
    created free and equal
        not born free and equal 9
    lessons from prior 239

inconsideration 126
Infinite Intelligence 3
inspiration 35, 288, 289, 291
  result of harmony
  conscious & subconscious 20
intellectualizing
  spiritual teachings 230, 231
Intention; see also motive 7
  setting law into motion 10
intimidation forces 217
intolerance 61, 95, 160, 231
  stems from judgment 60
intuition 208, 209
  spiritual psychology 212

J

jealousy 247, 260
Jesus 4, 234, 266, 270
  Avatar 3, 312
  casting pearls 50, 65
  explains salvation 278
  forgiveness 177, 178, 180
  how to pray 315
  "I speak not of myself" 104
  "If any man will come" 104
  Matt. 13:12 203
  proved continuity of life 276
  speaks on animals 299
  vicarious atonement 275
Jesus, the Avatar 312
John the Baptist
  "Repent ye" 85
joy 89, 129, 137, 204, 239, 249
judgment 17, 48, 57, 60, 62,
    101, 104, 124-135, 144,
    150, 151, 157, 160, 167,
    170-174; 190, 200, 210,
    215, 222, 223, 233, 239,
    286, 288; how affects
    hearing 57
  affects recall 56

nourishment of 58
basis of 60
binds illusion 28
breaking the back of 66
censoring how we feel 63
fear 70
giving to God 59
letting go of past 112
locked in subconscious 5
our uniqueness 63
over desires 122
positive use of 64
process at death 58
rejection 57
removing thru forgiveness 65
seat of conscience 208
understanding 58
judgment of others: causing
  experience to befall you 60
justice 180, 181
justification 41, 87, 111, 218

K

Karma 109; erasing bad
    strengthening good 10
  lessons 8
kindness 8, 160, 202, 226
kinship: of kingdoms 301
Krishna 266
Kubler-Ross, Elisabeth
  stages of grief 310

L

"later" entities 186, 188, 192
law 227, 243, 286,
  establishing:
    incurring responsibility 44
  ignorance no escape 48
  motive establishes 108
Law of Like Attracts Like 48
Laws 3; see also

Index

Abuse 168
Abundance 167, 204
Acceptance 101, 198
Appreciation 202
Asssociation 56
Attachment 40
Attraction 25
Balance 36
Cause and Effect 58
Change 35, 191
Consistency 258
Continuity 92, 248
Creation 29, 7
Denial 95, 101
Divine Flow 108
Divine Justice 181, 305
Duality 156
Evolution 66
Fear 129, 172
Fulfillment 289
Giving 166
Goodness 215
Gratitude, Law of Supply
198, 203
Greed 199
Harmony 56
Harmony, Law of Health 287
Identity 28, 29
Imposition 217
Judgment 54 ff, 101
John 10:34 3
lack of use 286
Light 7
Like Attracts Like 2, 14, 48
Limitation 118
Magnetism 2
Merit 48, 220
Non-interference 226
Obstruction 188, 196
Payment and Attainment 108
Personal Responsibility 10,
40

Personality 43
Procrastination 189
Progression 92
Promptness 187
Receiving 171
Rejection 95
Repetition 87, 193
Repetition, Law of Change
59, 193
Self 118
Self-preservation 29
Supply 198, 202, 289
Universe 40
laziness 283
Leadbeater, C. W. 15
Leeming, Joseph
explains John 5:34 276
meaning of salvation 270
salvation 282
lessons 97, 286
bless difficult ones 91
must be learned 42
failed previously 190
progressively difficult 240
return when pushed away 163
soul 8
get stronger as evolve 163
level of consciousness 25
ability to rise 240
moving through 59
when to work on 59
life eternal 264-267
light 214, 236, 240, 243
applied spiritual knowledge
16; service to Light 116
responsibility to 40
soul faculties 7
standing in own 96
value for 239
light, greater
light of eternal spirit 264
light of reason 88, 101, 124,

126, 127, 133, 138, 162,
211, 220, 240
Like Attracts Like 2, 170, 178,
198, 245
Law of 110, 132. 168
Limitation, Law of 118
listening
Rinpoche Sogal 248
living dead 171
loans 166, 172
lord 180
Lord's Prayer 315
love 7, 224, 226, 300, 301
Personal Responsibility
unconditional 42

M

"magic" 312
magnet 129
magnetism, law of 2
manifestation 168
in meditation 259
marriage 146, 147
meditation 248, 252-262
on peace 25
potential detriments 252
mediumistic ability 245
mediumship 117, 244, 245
memory: to educate desire 127
memory par excellence
108, 236
heart seed atom 10
permanently records 66
Merit, Law of 48, 220
merit system: discouragement 9
Militz, Annie Rix
on denial 104
mind: patterns: attitudes 95
playing on auto reverse 86
mirror:life reflects thoughts 40
misery: demands company 41

moderation of effort
in accomplishing desire 136
Mohammed 234
money
144, 147, 149, 150, 151, 152, 153
Morgan, James Coyle
salvation 277, Prayer 315
Mosaic law 279
Mother Earth 1
motivate 111
motive 108-114, 119, 207, 226,
231, 254, 261, 305;
creates reality 20;
desire 111
determines purity 108
euthanasia 308; explained in
Chinese poetry 113
for giving 167
for meditating 252
for serving 115
for sharing teachings235, 236
intention establishes law 108
lay foundation for pure 112
see also intention 7
setting law into motion 10
true or apparent 113
music
to lift consciousness 64
music and color 287

N

need 8, 56; denial 98
meditation 252
"negative signal"
counteracting 49
nervous breakdown 132
neutrality; peace 29
New Age of Aquarius 1, 74,
231, 313
New Dispensation 312
Non-interference, Law of 226
Numbers 5 & 9, meaning of 78

Index

O

observer: meaning 33
obsession 195
obstruction 101, 103
  facing 28; removal of 45
  law of 188, 196
odic power: balanced electromagnetic energy 14
only begotten son
  or daughter 4
opportunities 100, 172, 201
opportunity
  for service 116, 117
  to unfold soul 3
  when struggle is greatest 50
organization 193
Ouija boards 244
over-identification 191
  with physical form 23
overflowing cup 167

P

partiality 215
Patanjali:reality 30
path: of darkness 55
  of light 55
patience 8, 257, 135
  removing obstructions 45
  soul faculty 2
patterns of mind
  strengthen with use 142
pause: allows transmutation
  of form 55
  soul faculty: lion's strength
    22; strength of soul 162
  to control desire 135
payment 127
  for judgment desire 125
  freed from intimidation 217
  to move forward 103
Payment and Attainment.

Law 108
peace 8, 129, 216, 257, 258
  creates angelic forms 13
  harmonizes with all 25
  identifying with 38
  neutrality 29
  passeth understanding 2
  power in meditation 25
pearls, casting 50, 65
"people pleaser." 223
perception
  permits observing 33
  soul faculty
    cast light of reason 20
perfection 44, 143, 288
  personality need 84
persistant flow 128
Personal Responsibility 40, 45,
  51, 62,124,
  126, 135, 174, 184, 189, 199,
  203, 206, 216, 221. 232,
  283; accepting 23;
  brother's keeper 47, 48
  choosing identities 31, 41
  Law of Identity
    changing identities 31
  making changes inside 85
  spiritual law 10
  steps in accepting 43
  to Intelligent Energy 51
  weight of 44, 45
  delusion of blame 23
  facing to control desire 134
  how affected by refusing 42
  identifications 30
  judgment 58
  to accept life eternal 265
personality 105, 141. 142, 145,
  214, 215, 218, 220, 230,
  232, 241, 245
  align with soul 3
  as energy tool 5

blocks out God 74
conscious mind;:
    subconscious mind 19
cultivate strong one to serve
    143; denial of 105
educate 15;
light of reason 10
energy tool 140
examples of expressions 5
experiences 2
five-sensory personality 212
formidable force of 241
in dysfunction 6
influencing factors 9
key to money and sex 154
Latin per and sona 105
Law of Identity 29
low frequency vibrations 5
meditate for glorification 252
multisensory 212
opens door to delusion 19
purpose of 140
pursues power externally 5
selfish service 114
uneducated 225
weight of 44
Personality, Law of 43
Peter, Apostle
forgiveness 180
philosophy: guideline
    to awaken 164
Piscean Age 313
pity 41, 43, 161, 181, 226, 289
Poems: A Thread 292
    No one can carry your
        burden, 249
    When the lips 262
    There is a power greater 228
    "Forgive" 176
    "Giving" 169
    The Rime of the Ancient 303
    There is no death! 268

"Thoughts are Things" 12
poise
    reason reveals itself 143
possessions 173
possessiveness 225
potential
    for soul expression 4
power
    giving away control 26
    spiritual 4, 5
    weak search for 75
practice talents 290
prayer
    Lord's Prayer, New Age 315
praying 244
prejudices 54
pride 132, 206, 216, 288
    child of judgment 57
primitive mind 15
principle
    214, 216, 217, 220, 245
    of perceiving 215
priority for God 125
procrastination 35, 186-192,
    195, 208; leads to frustra-
    tion 46
Progression, Law of 92
promptness 192, 193
psychic abilities: dangers 244;
    misusing 245
    animals 306, 307
psychic centers 260
"puffivate" 219
punishment 61, 180

Q

quality 288, 289
quarrel 176
question
    doubt and fear 73
questioning

Index

existence of spirits 264
life eternal 264-267

R

Real Self: soul: spirit 3
reality: awareness of events
     motive 20
realms of deceit 254
reason 35, 55, 135, 218,
     222, 226, 238, 246
  freedom from illusion 25
  light of: educating
   personality 10
  poise 143
  servant of light 55
recall: affected by judgments 56
receiving 217
Receiving, Law of 171
redemption without effort 283
"re-do" vibration 288
reformers 231, 232
regret 123
reincarnation 2
rejection 95, 216
  caused by judgments 57
Rejection, Law of 95
reliance on God 134
religion 234; purpose of 233
remorsefulness 182, 279
repentance 279
Repetition, Law of Change 59,
     87, 195, 250
reprogramming
  how to make changes 21
  lessens emotions 24
  subconscious 20, 76
  to refine forms 62
"rescue work"
  by animals 309
resentment 178, 182
respect 163, 231

responsibility
  see Personal Responsibility
     45
  to animal path 297
  to refine form 62
responsible choice 24
  defined by Zukav 24
retaliation 218
retribution 180, 182
revelation 100, 168, 211, 242
rhythm 160, 250
ridicule 84
rise above, meaning of 60
rituals and dogma 230
robber, vibration of 137
root chakra 145

S

salvation 270, 277
  by character 283
  enter spiritual path now 282
saneness 7
satisfaction 124, 128, 137
saved, meaning of 274
self: gift of 35; law of 118
  thought of:Law of Identity 28
self will 96
self-awareness 30, 140
  changing identities 31
self-control 6, 15
  lessons get stronger 163
self-glorification 189
self-hypnotic trance 252
self-importance 104; danger of
  over-identification 33
Self-preservation, Law of 88
  identity: fear 29
selfless service 111, 114-117,
     226
  spiritual illumination 16
sell out

215, 216, 218, 219, 220
sense functions
  foundation is fear 75
  goal to spiritualize 5; Law of
    Creation 7;never annihi-
    late 15; tools to use 5
  transmuting into faculty 7
senses: five 5
Seven Rays 311, 312, 314
  Ceremonial Magic 312
sex 145, 146, 147
silence 258
Silver Birch
  compassion in animals 296
  euthanasia 307
  kindness to animals 304
  protective responsibility 303
sin: to be poor 149;
  original 140
Sixth Ray
  Devotion and Idealism 312
"slate" 181
Socrates: on judgments 64
soul 2, 118
  align with personality 3
  awakening 4:
  characterizing 3
  description 3; Divine Plan 1
  growth, expansion 5, 81
  potential for expression 4
  power from Christ Spirit 5
  selling out 215, 220
  soul faculties 2
  superconscious mind 19
  unfoldment 1, 3
soul faculties 4
  expressed by animals 294
  high vibrations 4; Law of
    Light 7; perception 20;
    revert to sense function 8,
    202
soul talent 286, 287; karma 10;

service to universe 286
soulless forms
  drain life force 25
souls of animals 294
source of supply 123, 128, 152
spirit: God: soul 3
spirit band 203
spirit body 15, 119
spirit communication 266
spirit guides 109, 194, 201,
    203, 245, 246, 253, 259,
    261
  teachers come to all 48
spirit healing
  of animals 307
spirit people 48
  Like Attracts Like 201
Spirit sayings see Index 336
spiritual commitment
  pride 57
spiritual conscience 208
spiritual discernment 65, 210
spiritual education
  purpose of 16
spiritual evolution:responsibility
    to all forms 294
spiritual growth
  measurement of 239
"spiritual high" 236
spiritual illumination
  path of selfless service 16
spiritual path 230, 245
  freedom from money
    temptations 152
spiritual philosophy 230, 233
spiritual psychology 1
  Gary Zukav 212
spiritual realms 245
spiritual responsibility 200
spiritual rewards 249
spiritual sensibility
  conscience 206

spiritual smorgasbord 230
Spiritualism 284
spiritualize: thinking 7,
    242, 243
spiritually evolvement
    requirements for 19
"spoiled brat level." 89
spoken word 82, 250
    life-giving energy
        building thought forms 11
spontaneity 290
St. Francis of Assisi 303
    on animals 301, 303
St. Paul: spiritual body 15
try spirit to see 131
    enter path now 282
stealing
    another's soul 225
strength 257
stubbornness
    defense mechanism 70
student-teacher relationship 246
subconscious 6; automatic
    negative thoughts 150
    magnetic 6; memory bank:
    controlling what is stored 6
    reprogramming 20, 24
    cleaning our garbage 237
        why necessary to clean out
        5
    serving by default 80
    talk to as to a child 76
superconscious mind
    communication w/soul 6
superstition
    fear 71
supply 202, 204
Supply, Law of 202, 203
suppressed desires 130-
    133, 138, 240
    rise in meditation 252
surrender 161, 255, 261

thoughts, emotions 7
symbology 254
sympathy 225, 226

T

tardiness 187, 188
teachings of Jesus 278
teacher-student relationship 246
teasing
    power trip 304
temptations
    on spiritual path 238
    freedom from money 152
testing 218
theft 123, 186
thought
    moving on vertical path 92
    stopping 176
thought forms 11, 55
    accepting as real you 19
    advice of Yogananda 21
    being master over 14
    consciously unaware of 163
    dealing with demands of 21
    demons: feed or starve 12
    factors of defense 13
    fighting 22
    form thought takes 15
    if no longer serving purpose
        62
    intelligence of 16
    pause in consciousness 22
    reacting to emotions 14
    responding to soul faculties
        88
thought of self 124, 129, 266
time 144
time pressure 56, 132,
    bombs 132
tolerance 61, 104, 200, 232
    for another's desire 133

opportunity to unfold 9
transgressions 225, 226; of law
265, 288
transitional period
between two ages 314
transmutation: of desire 136
of negative energy
exercising will power 24
trauma: judgment 57
trespasses 183
Trevelyan, George
describes five-sensory 5
Truth 43, 48, 122, 164, 218,
231,232, 233, 240, 262
separating from creation
18, 65, 158
Turner, Elizabeth Sand: explains
saved by belief alone 275

U

understanding 104, 178, 200
judgment 58
peace which passeth 2
uneducated personality 225
unfoldment 244, 283
affects everyone 164
soul 1, 2
unity 194
universal consciousness 29, 30
universal master teacher
student-teacher
relationship 246
universal motherhood
222, 224, 226, 227
dynamics of 223
Universe 203; as teacher 11
unsolicited help 65, 200

222, 224, 226, 227
dynamics of 223
Universe 203; as teacher 11
unsolicited help 65, 200

V

value 202
wanting to be liked 218
Van Dyke, Henry
"Thoughts are Things" 12
vengeance 180
vicarious atonement 276
victim 42, 217, 219, 226, 253
of desires 128
of mental game
confused about real you 19
of own intolerance 61
of own creations 23
of suppressed desires 130
visions 254
voices
hearing in meditation 253
volunteerism 116

W

want, need and desire 7
water center 244
weakness 44, 238, 239
preying on another 219
weight problems 22, 202
wisdom
220, 128, 135, 138, 243,
257
"withdrawal" from addiction
194; worry 8, 112
Y Yogananda 21

Z

zodiac 311
Zukav, Gary:explains thought
forms 11; personality
dysfunctions 6
describes personality 5
illusion holds power 18
no power in fear 71
responsible choice 24, 212

Index of Affirmations

Acceptance, something good is happening! 103

God is love. I am the child of love, and like my father, all loving . . . 185

God, help me to bow in humility that I may see the truth revealed in my thoughts and acts. Amen, Amen, Amen. 68

God, help me with personal responsibility and help me to see the childishness in my mind. 45

God, I declare the eternal truth. In this moment over which I have control, let me experience peace, joy, and freedom. 87

God, help me to do what is right. I must give up my need to control another soul and play God. 226

God, I'm grateful for what I have and when I've earned it, I know. . . 153

God is the true and only source of my supply. 149, 151, 153

God, I surrender my concern to you, and know that my weight . . .24

Help me, O God, to remember the motive I came for. 10

I have unshakable faith in the perfect outcome of every situation in my life, for I know that God is always at the helm. 100

I accept this feeling. I accept this is my thought that I have created . . . 44

I alone am personally responsible . . . 164

I am not the thought. I am the mover of the thought . . . 69

I bless you, and I bless you for the goodness of God within you. 179

I am not the illusion I am truth. 21

I speak my word forth knowing it will accomplish that which I send it 172

O God, help me through this crazy creation. I am not creation. I am the mover of creation. 66

O God, help me to see clearly in all your universes that there is nothing in form that is perfect, especially pride. 289

O God, I am grateful for all life's experiences, especially the difficult ones, for I know in truth they are my greatest blessings. 92

O, God, let me never forget that the degree of joy, goodness . . . 51

O God, help me to consider and accept the divine right of all your . . . 98

O God, help me to look in the mirror of life, which comprises all . . . 98

O God, I give to you this desire, which in my ignorance I have stolen, accepting with a humble heart the fullness of your divine will. 125

O God, that, too, for me is possible should I choose to make that 225

Thank you, God, I am at peace. 15

Thank you, God, I had forgotten for whom I was working. With your 58

Thank you, O God, for leading me through honesty in what I have trapped myself in. 212

Thank you, God, for granting me the opportunity to be your unobstructed vehicle for the divine flow. 155

Thank you, God, I have a right to the goodness of life, but I don't have the right to dictate what the goodness of life is, for the goodness of life

Thank you, God, for selling it. 158

Index of Spirit Sayings

A problem is nothing more than a lack of faith in the power 99

A thought strikes the mind and a fool reacts. A thought strikes 7

Abundance is the natural law; lack of using what you are 172

Acceptance is the miracle of transformation. 96

Adversity is caused by a dictate of superiority over that which 156

An apology is the acceptance and recognition that the vehicle 183

And so the Bible teaches us to judge not that we be not judged 49

Appearances are deceiving but truth is revealing. 240

Artist, paint your scene in part, knowing I AM all of art. 291

As freedom is in the moment of our acceptance, bondage is in 97

As freely as I give, so shall I receive. 168

As the spokes of the wheel are indispensable to the hub, so the 15

Attachment is the weakness of familiarity and the strength of 164

Awareness is the soul of action. 110

Be ever ready and willing to change. 82, 160

Be ever ready and willing to give that which you hold most 169

Be it in Divine Order, I will be on time. 192

Be not concerned with what you do and you will be free from 167

Be not concerned with the fruits of action. Take all of the joy 129

Be still, my child, and view and you shall know beyond the 1

Believe and receive. Doubt and do without. 73

Compassion has the light of reason; sympathy has no 226

Compassion is the key which locks the door of pride and frees 227

Conscience is a spiritual sensibility with a dual capacity, 206

Courage is the unwavering commitment of the soul to 220

Did you ever find a thought as good as an idea of God? 287

Discouragement is a fool's paradise. 87, 289

Discouragement is the path to hell. Encouragement is the path 41

Distortion is the direct effect of an obstruction to a persistant 128

Dreamer, dream a life of beauty before your dream starts 14, 20

Duty becomes direction when you use wisdom. 200

Emotions, like ceaseless waves, eternally wash the thirsty shore.127

Experience is not life. Experience is the effect of one's view of 10

Faith gives poise to keep the personality still to express 96, 154

Faith is an absolute conviction in our own mind that we already 130

Faith is the path that leads to God, fear the trap to hell. 77

Fear born of emotion compromises 218

Fear is a total denial of God. Fear is a total denial of faith. 99

Fear is the brain's control of the soul; faith is the beauty of the 70

Fear is the instrument of self-preservation, but an open heart 75

Fear is the revelation of faith in the judgment of the human ego.70

Fear protects but faith sustains. 70

Index of Spirit Sayings

Fools are the fathers of fear and courage the mother of 75
Forgiveness is a true feeling and an inner humble request of 179
God does not cease to forgive; it is wayward man that ceases 179
God is the epitome of quality and without quality there is no 289
God smiles through the angel's efforts. 291
God works through man and not to man. You must ask the 171
God's hand is the poet's pen. 114
Goodness shines in the smile of man. A smile is not a grin. 138
Gratitude, not greed, is the path of joy. 202
Griping, bitching, complaining, and blaming are the pillars 202
Growth of the soul is revelation, not change, in truth. 81
Half a soul with God is better than no soul at all. 238
He who accepts with a joyous hear the lessons that life has to 94
He who choses God, finds God . . . 242
He who does not accept the Law of Personal Responsibility 50
He who fascinates procrastinates and goes from temptation to 189
He who hurts another shall live to see the day when all his 108
He who sees the obstruction never finds the way.37
He who understands the thing controls the thing. 58
Hold not to form, for form will pass. 61
I am spirit, formless and free. Whatever I think, that will I 16, 262
If man is a law unto himself, then what are you doing with the 59
If the light is too bright, 'tis best we not see it now. 240
If the motive is pure, the method is legal. 112
If you aspire to function in a universal body, you must think 239
If your priority for desire is never higher than your priority for 71
Illusion melts like snow at high noon, for joy and the fullness 240
I'm only a witness of time passing on. A witness of things that 54
In all disasters, God's little light shines humbly, but bright, to 49
In all your getting, get understanding, and in all your giving 59
Inspiration is not limited to a few souls. All are inspired, for 291
Inspiration is the smile of God traveling faster than the speed 291
It is human to forgive; divine to forget. 67
It is our attachment to the decisions we have made in our life 159
It is through the sharing of truth with another soul that one 235
Keep faith with reason for the light of reason will transfigure thee.
    50, 55, 135, 138
Life is eternal and wise ones act accordingly. 267
Life shall ever be the way you take it, for life is always the way 90
Make friends with your adversities. They are in truth your own 156
Man insists on questioning God, yet God in humility never 264

Index of Spirit Sayings

Man takes pride in viewing what he has decided is weakness 60
Man's judgments are denials of God's rights. 94
Man's loss of God is dependent upon his purity of motive. 111
No one can carry your burden, no one can lift your load 249
Not only do the workers win, but the wise workers live the 288
O God, I am grateful for all life's experiences, especially 91, 201
Oft times no is God's direction. 135
One is freed in hell and saved in heaven. 143
One should never grant the difference at the sacrifice of 214
One who accepts the impossibility of change is governed and 92
One who cannot forgive oneself is not capable of forgiving 178
One who cares for others, in truth, cares for oneself. 226
One who chooses anything and respects with equal respect that 60
One who loses what one values and suffers is a fool. One who 172
One who loves God more than one loves creation does not deny 18
One who seeks that which is the right of another denies that 104
One who sees personality never finds principle. 215
One who serves another in truth serves oneself. 120
One who thinks one's gain is much and forgets the source 153
One who views for a truth what one cannot stop, stops making 96
Our adversities become our attachments. 162
Our judgment is just, and the false is uncovered but for the sole 64
Outward manifestations are revelations of inner attitudes 110, 187
Pause is the lion's strength. 22, 55
Pearls of wisdom are the tears of conscience. 211
Procrastination is the theft of all time, but it is greater than a 186
Put God in it, or forget it. 67, 179
Recognition of God is acceptance of God; acceptance of God 100
Remember that he who loves himself more than he loves Me 266
Reverence is engaging in a form and a depth of contact with all 305
Rewards tempts the personality while the soul waits to serve. 154
Ridicule is an uncontrollable expression of the human mind 84
See the good in all things by choosing to identify with the good 31
Service is the path to freedom when selfless is the goal. 119
Silence is the savior of the soul and peace the expression of 257
Silence on crime is endorsement. 218
Some errors seem so deeply rooted that it requires angelic 181
Stand guardian at the portal of your thought that you may 204
That that is mine knows my face and is already on its way to 125
That that is yours only your fear will take away. And that that 77
That that we have no value for, we guarantee to lose 202
That which begins in fear, dies in fear. 77

Index of Spirit Sayings

The ability to make change in consciousness is dependent 83

The act reveals the thought. 142

The business of common sense is the lack of self-concern. 173

The demonstration is the revelation, 100

The degree of resentment to the Law of Change is equal to the 93

The degree of suffering reveals the degree of attachment. 162

The desire to be liked is stronger than the desire for reason. 219

The ears of the personality hear not because the door is locked 70

The greater the truth, the simpler its tenet. 283

The guest will never quest. 172

The joy of living is known as the Law of Giving. 166

The key of wisdom to the door of freedom is the ability, the23,90

The theft of desire is the birth of attachment and the 124 157

The thought of self is the throne of judgment that stands 28

The uneducated ego hears only the echoes of its own 127

The weight of responsibility must never exceed the love of God 44

The world is what we make it. We take out of the world what 10

There is no more finely polished mirror for parents than their 225

Time pressure is a hailstone of petty desires demanding their 132

To be master is the desire of the senses. To be a servant is the 120

To forgive is human and to forget is divine. 177

To pause is lion's strength. 55

Today I reap the harvest of yesterday and plant the seeds of 196

Truth deceives the wisest minds of men, however, it does not 231

Truth is for honest seekers, not for those of idle curiosity. 230

Truth is like a river, it continuously flows. 26

Truth is simple that it may confound the seeming wise. 240

Truth is taught through indirection, demonstration, and 240

Truth is the awareness of the divinity within that we express at 314

Unsolicited help is ever to no avail. 65

We cannot receive anything in life that we do not first give. 129

We enter hell on the steps of judgment, holding on to the 57

We have eyes to see and see not, ears to hear and hear not. 102

We sit to meditate; we stand to agitate. 256

What of thy heart freely gives in God's love forever lives. 166

What today I criticize, tomorrow I shall idolize. 98

Whatever I give thought to, I give power to. 72

When desire becomes your servant, you are freed from being 137

When disrespect manifests, wisdom demands change and 163.304

When man is chained to dogma and creed, the soul of reason 230

When man serves man, he is in personality 215

When motherhood becomes brotherhood, the children will 227

Index of Spirit Sayings

When of my God I seek to know the purpose of my life 236,
When of thy mind thou seekest the truth, on the wheels of 74
When of thyself thou thinkest most, thine heart 101
When one smiles, the angels sing. When one grins, deception 24
When our cry for God is as great as our cry for money, we 154
When our desire to possess is greater than our reason to be free174
When our fear of man is greater than our love of God, 219
When our love of God exceeds our love of self, we are freed 159
When our love of God is greater than the love of our judgments, 68
When the dream of life becomes the nightmare of life, we change
When the fear of attachment melts away in the light of reason161
When the lips are sealed in silence . . . 262
When the mind is still , the light doth dawn within, because 262
When the motive is pure, the manifestation is pleasant. 114
When the tools no longer serve the worker, the worker 14, 80
When we feel the joy of attachment, in that feeling is the fear 156
When you accept from God, you are freed from paying creation171
When you are in need, you are the victim of the feeling. 98
When you educate the desires of your senses, you will find your 128
When you love your losses as you love your gains, you will 169
When you stop blaming outside, you will start growing inside. 42
While strength is control, weakness seeks control because it 75
Wisdom is total spiritual awareness 243
Wise ones live to serve. Fools serve to live. 120
With the blessings which come from on high, come also its 51
You can exist but you never truly live life until you have 26